ESSAYS (

ESSAYS ON BENTHAM

Studies in Jurisprudence and Political Theory

by
H. L. A. HART

CLARENDON PRESS · OXFORD
1982

Oxford University Press, Walton Street, Oxford OX2 6DP

London Glasgow New York Toronto
Delhi Bombay Calcutta Madras Karachi
Kuala Lumpur Singapore Hong Kong Tokyo
Nairobi Dar es Salaam Cape Town
Melbourne Auckland
and associates in
Beirut Berlin Ibadan Mexico City Nicosia

Published in the United States by
Oxford University Press, New York

British Library Cataloguing in Publication Data
Hart, H.L.A.
Essays on Bentham.
1. Bentham, Jeremy — Criticism and interpretation
I. Title
192   B1574.B34
ISBN 0-19-825348-6
ISBN 0-19-825468-7 Pbk

Library of Congress Cataloging in Publication Data
Hart, H.L.A. (Herbert Lionel Adolphus), 1907-
Essays on Bentham.
Includes bibliographical references and index.
1. Bentham, Jeremy, 1748-1832 — Addresses,
essays, lectures.   2. Jurisprudence — Addresses,
essays, lectures.   3. Political science — Addresses,
essays, lectures.   I. Title.
K334.H37   340'.1   82-3601
ISBN 0-19-825348-6 (Oxford University Press) AACR2
ISBN 0-19-825468-7 (Oxford University Press: pbk.)

Set by Hope Services, Abingdon
Printed in Great Britain
at the University Press, Oxford
by Eric Buckley,
Printer to the University

ACKNOWLEDGEMENTS

Five of the chapters of this book are corrected but substantially unchanged versions of previously published works, omitting matter dealt with elsewhere in this volume. These are Chapter I from the *Modern Law Review* (1973), Chapter II from *Atti del Convegno Internazionale su Cesare Beccaria* (Turin 1964), Chapter III from the *Journal of Law and Economics* xix (3) (1976), Chapter VII from *Oxford Essays in Jurisprudence*, 2nd series, ed. Simpson (Oxford 1973), Chapter VIII from the *Yale Law Journal* lxxx (1972). Parts of the Introduction and of four other chapters have been previously published as follows: Introduction in *Proceedings of the British Academy* xlviii (1962) and *American Law: The Third Century*, ed. Schwartz (New York School of Law 1976); Chapter IV in the *New York Review of Books* xxvii (8) (1980); Chapter V in *Rechtstheorie* ii (1) (1971); Chapter VI (in Italian) in *Rivista di Filosofia* (1966); Chapter IX in the *Irish Jurist* NS ii (1967).

CONTENTS

ABBREVIATIONS

Works   *The Works of Jeremy Bentham* published under the superintendence of John Bowring (11 vols., Edinburgh 1838–43). Roman numerals refer to volumes and Arabic numerals to pages.

CW   *The Collected Works of Jeremy Bentham*, London 1968–.

UC   Bentham's papers in the Library of University College London. Roman numerals refer to boxes and Arabic numerals to leaves.

OLG   *Of Laws in General* by Jeremy Bentham (ed. Hart in *CW*, London 1970).

PML   *An Introduction to the Principles of Morals and Legislation*, by Jeremy Bentham (ed. Burns and Hart in *CW*, London 1970).

Comment   *A Comment on the Commentaries* by Jeremy Bentham, in *A Comment on the Commentaries and a Fragment on Government* (ed. Burns and Hart in *CW*, London 1977).

Fragment   *A Fragment of Government*, in *A Comment on the Commentaries and a Fragment on Government* (ed. Burns and Hart in *CW*, London 1977).

Note. References are given by page to *OLG* in *CW*, but by chapter and paragraphs, as well as by pages, to *PML, Comment*, and *Fragment* in *CW*.

INTRODUCTION

I

Sydney Smith, in his brilliant review of Bentham's *Book of Fallacies*, said that Bentham needed a middle-man:

Neither gods, men nor booksellers can doubt the necessity of a middle-man between Mr. Bentham and the public. Mr. Bentham is long: Mr. Bentham is occasionally involved and obscure; Mr. Bentham invents new and alarming expressions; Mr. Bentham loves division and sub-division, and he loves method itself more than its consequences. Those only therefore who know his originality, his knowledge, his vigour and his boldness, will recur to the works themselves. The great mass of readers will not purchase improvement at so dear a rate but will choose rather to become acquainted with Mr. Bentham through the medium of the reviews — after that eminent philosopher has been washed, trimmed, shaved and forced into clean linen.[1]

In this collection of essays on various aspects of Bentham's political thought and jurisprudence I offer myself as a middle-man only for a small, though important, segment of Bentham's works. For the volume and range of these works are of course enormous. Those that are published run to many millions of words and there is still more to come. He wrote on almost every conceivable subject to which the application of utilitarian principles can make a difference and on many subjects to which those principles might at first seem totally irrelevant. Most of this work consists of the detailed working out of the Greatest Happiness Principle in relation to law and legal institutions, but Bentham's range also includes topics as diverse as poor relief, Christianity and the Church of England, model prisons, birth control, grammar, logic, usury, and much of economics. On nearly all of these subjects he offered both searching, detailed analysis and constructive criticism, and so played the dual role of what he himself termed Expositor and Censor. For, as I attempt to show in Chapter I of this book, Bentham believed that all laws and all social institutions had been protected and their life unduly prolonged,

---

[1] 'Bentham's Book of Fallacies' in *Edinburgh Review*, xlii (84) (1825) 367.

with evil consequences for humanity, by myths, misunder-
standings, and fictions which it is necessary for the Expositor
to identify and clear away before the Censor can get to work.
So he thought it important to pursue studies in logic and
linguistic theory in their abstract form, and then to apply
their results directly to political argument as he does in his
diverting and instructive *Book of Fallacies*, or to the law, as
he does in his vivid discussions of lawyers' 'jargon and jargon-
isation' which he thought of as a superior form of thieves'
cant hiding the defects of the law. Such studies were important because language had so often been used as an instrument of mystification and oppression to deceive men as to
the true character of their social life and institutions, including
above all, their laws, and to conceal from men the possibilities
of reform.

Bentham had as vivid an appreciation as Karl Marx (who
described him as the 'pedantic, leather-tongued oracle of the
ordinary bourgeois intelligence') of the ways in which mysteries and illusions, often profitable to interested parties,
have clustered round social institutions, concealing the fact
that they with their defects are human artefacts, and encouraging the belief that the injustices and exploitation
which they permit must be ascribed to nature and are beyond
the power of men to change. 'Law' says Bentham 'shows itself in a mask', and much that he wrote was designed to
remove it.

Bentham's detailed concern with language and his sense of
it as a source of mystification, and the need for what has
been called the 'nettoyage de la situation verbale' as the
essential accompaniment of any serious study, is one of the
features of Bentham's thought which distinguish him from
thinkers of the European Enlightenment from whom he drew
much inspiration. I attempt in Chapter II to assess Bentham's
debt to one such European thinker, Beccaria, whom Bentham
admired as the first to distinguish clearly between the functions of Expositor and Censor. From this chapter it is, I
hope, evident how great a break Bentham made with his pre-
decessors' habit of thought in insisting as he does on an
exhaustive study and mastery of the concrete detail that lies
hidden behind unanalysed general terms and concepts used in
many fields of study. It is true that the conception of an

'exhaustive analytic method' classifying the phenonema to be studied by a 'dichotomous' or 'bipartite' division of generic terms, which Bentham favoured, and as he knew, was known to D'Alembert and other eighteenth-century thinkers, can be traced through Porphyry to Aristotle.[2] But Bentham was unique in his time in undertaking what he himself acknowledged as the fatiguing and sometimes arid labours of 'the exhaustive method', involved in the construction of vast classifications of the detail which he thought essential for the discovery 'of the truths that form the basis of political and moral science'.[3] It is easy to imagine how shocked he must have been to find in Beccaria the acknowledgement that the logic of his enquiries required an examination and classification of the various kinds of crime, blandly coupled with the statement that it was enough to indicate only the most general principles because the result of such a classification would be a mass of 'enormous and boring detail' ('un dettaglio immense e noiso'). When Bentham himself came, in the *Introduction to the Principles of Morals and Legislation*, to consider this topic, he devoted to it a chapter entitled 'The Division of Offences', occupying almost a third of the book, identifying and classifying hundreds of individual offences according to the human interests which they adversely affected. Bentham put this forward as a universal 'natural' arrangement of those forms of conduct which a code constructed on utilitarian principles would require to be treated as offences, and it was designed to serve both as a critique of existing legal systems and as the basis for the construction of new rational codes of law. So too, since a proper understanding of the Greatest Happiness Principle required a grasp of the full extension of the concepts of pleasure and pain, Bentham thought it an indispensable preliminary to construct under the guidance of the exhaustive method lists of fourteen simple pleasures and twelve simple pains and then to proceed to their subdivisions.

Sydney Smith was therefore right in thinking that the love of division and subdivision was one of the distinctive features

---

[2] *Chrestomathia*, Appendix IV (*Essay on Nomenclature and Classification*), *Works* VIII 63 ff.; *Essay on Logic, Works* VIII 266-70.

[3] *PML* Preface in *CW* 9.

of Bentham's mind but it is important to see that this, in spite of occasional excesses, was not mere, obsessive pedantry. Perhaps John Stuart Mill's essay on Bentham[4] may have done something to convey the misleading impression that this was so. For in his assessment of Bentham's qualities Mill asserts that the novelty and value of what he did 'lay not in his opinions but in his method' which Mill described as the 'method of detail'. My own view which I shall shortly attempt to substantiate is that this is a misleading dichotomy between opinions and methods. Methods sufficiently novel, as some of Bentham's were, cannot be mere innovations of method. They presuppose too fundamental a reorientation of the direction of enquiry, and too radical a shift in the conception of what is to be considered an acceptable answer. Bentham's marshalling and discussion of concrete detail too often forces upon our attention new questions rather than new answers to old questions for its innovations to be considered as matters of method alone.

In any case Mill does not, I think, do justice to Bentham's extraordinary combination of a fly's eye for detail, with an eagle's eye for illuminating generalizations applicable across wide areas of social life. He says that Bentham's novelty of method lay in his remorseless insistence on the criticism of existing law and institutions, and in his schemes of reform on 'treating wholes by breaking them down into parts, abstraction by resolving them into things and generalisations by distinguishing them into the individuals of which they are made up'. These are of course among the habits of thought and the modes of investigation of the scientist, and it may well be thought that when they are used in the application of the principles of utility to such subjects as the Panopticon prison, or the reform of the Poor Law or the Court of Chancery, nothing of lasting speculative importance is likely to emerge. Haphazard experimentation with what I shall call (of course inaccurately) the unread Bentham, is apt to confirm this impression. A *sors Benthamiana* made with the finger at random is likely to bring to light a passage prescribing, perhaps, the precise shape and size of the beds or the form of central heating to be used in prisons, or the clothes or even

---

[4] *10 Collected Works of John Stuart Mill*, ed. Robson (1969) 75.

the bedding to be used in workhouses. The following passage on the paupers' bedding perhaps conveys the flavour sufficiently well:

> Beds stuffed with straw: one side covered with the cheapest linen or hempen cloth for summer; the other with coarse woollen cloth for winter. Stretching the under sheet on hooks pins or buttons will save the quantity usually added for tucking in. In cold weather that the woollen may be in contact with the body the sheet might be omitted. A rug and two blankets and an upper sheet to be of no greater width than the cell and to be tacked on to one of the blankets. . . . Straw, the more frequently changed the better particularly in warm months. To the extent of the quantity wanted for littering cattle, the change will cost nothing, and beyond that quantity the expense will only be the difference between the value of the straw as straw and the value of it as manure.[5]

It is perhaps difficult when immersed in this—or indeed sunk in it—to remember that this is a philosopher writing; but two things should prevent our forgetting it. The first is that embedded even in this kind of detail there are bold and provocative reaffirmations of the general principles which gain in clarity and in a sense reveal more of their meaning when applied to small things. Thus only eight pages before this disquisition on bedding there is a discussion of 'the only shape which genuine and *efficient* humanity [in dealing with the indigent poor] can take'.[6] As in the State so in the poorhouse 'the duty-and-interest-juncture-principle' is to be applied so that throughout it shall be in the interests of the managers to look after those in their care. The salary of the governor is to be reduced for every woman who dies in childbirth and to vary with the number of juvenile inmates who survive from year to year. Extra premiums and bounties are to be awarded for less than average mortality. Why so? Because, says Bentham,

> every system of management which has disinterestedness pretended or real for its foundation is rotten at the root, susceptible of a momentary prosperity at the outset but sure to perish in the long run. That principle

---

[5] *Outline of Pauper Management Improved* (*Works* VIII 389) first published in Young's *Annals of Agriculture* (1797). Cf. Bentham's elaborate provision for a Night Duty Chamber in which a judge on night duty might hear urgent cases from his bed (*Works* IX 540).

[6] *Works* VIII 381.

of action is most to be depended upon whose influence is most powerful, most constant, most uniform, most lasting and most general among
mankind. Personal interest is that principle and a system of economy
built on any other foundation is built upon a quicksand.[7]

But the same 'duty-and-interest-juncture-principle' thus
applied to the microcosm of the poorhouse became for
Bentham also the utilitarian foundation of the case for representative democracy as an alternative to the detested theory
of natural rights. I trace in Chapter III Bentham's double
transition from the conservatism and anti-Americanism of his
youth to passionate support for representative democracy
(with the full radical programme of manhood suffrage, secret
ballots, and annual parliaments) and to extravagant admiration of the United States of America 'that newly created
nation, one of the most enlightened if not the most enlightened in the globe'. Slow and tortuous as Bentham's conversion to democracy was, he early perceived that its merits
as a system of government lay in its conformity to the duty-
and-interest-juncture principle, since placing the appointment
and dismissal of 'the ruling few' in the hands of the majority
afforted the best hope of making their interest coincide with
their duties to the masses they governed. This remained
throughout Bentham's life, after he had shaken off the panic
engendered by the excesses of the French Revolution, his
utilitarian case for democracy. It enabled him to give his full
allegiance to the cause of Parliamentary Reform without
accepting any of the wild and half intelligible assertions, as
he thought then, of natural rights which he found in the
French Declaration of the Rights of Man and the Citizen.
So, too, his discovery of a utilitarian argument for American
Independence made it possible for him to welcome its success
while maintaining his contempt for the philosophy of natural
rights expounded in the American Declaration of Independence which he had first attacked and ridiculed in 1776.

Yet the extraordinary combination in Bentham of a fly's-
eye view of practical detail with boldness or even rashness in
generalization, especially about human nature, is of more
than psychological interest. It was part of the intellectual
tactics if not the strategy of the campaign for reform. It was

7 Ibid.

said by Bentham's critics that he believed mistakenly that if he could articulate to the last detail the application of a general theory, he believed that this showed the theory to be sound.[8] This interesting criticism is, I think, false; what is, however, true is that he thought the criticism of existing institutions unaccompanied by demonstrably practical alternatives was worthless; and he believed this not only because criticism, like everything else, was to be judged by its utility, but because hatred of anarchy and disorder was as strong a passion with him as hatred of blind custom and conservatism. For all his vehemence against the oppressors of his day and their abettors the judges and lawyers, his advice was 'To obey punctually; to censure freely'[9] until a sober calculation in terms of utility showed a clear profit in disobedience. But to criticize and destroy *without* a clear conception of what was to follow was, for Bentham, the mark of the anarchical spirit, and the now tiresome blueprints with their forests of detail did more than manifest Bentham's strange temperament. They were intended to be a demonstration that a middle path between conservatism and anarchy was possible, and this was itself to destroy what he termed 'the hydrophobia of innovation'[10] which was one of the major obstacles to reform.

II

I have already said that Bentham was as much inspired by hatred of anarchy and revolution as he was by hatred of the apologist for the established order and the worship, as he called it, of 'dead men's bones'. Now Bentham thought in a wholly original way of these two sets of adversaries blocking the path of rational criticism and reform. This is hardly represented in the few texts of his which are regularly discussed. For he thought of them as both equipped with poisoned weapons[11] for blinding men to their real interests and making them, on the one hand, submissive to tyranny and the oppression of the many by the few and, on the other, prone to insurrection and violence. These poisoned weapons were, in a

---

[8] Leslie Stephen, *The English Utilitarians*, I 283.
[9] *Fragment*, Preface in *CW* 399.   [10] *Comment* in *CW* 346.
[11] *The Book of Fallacies, Works* II 486.

sense, intellectual ones and are vastly heterogeneous. Some of them were old and false saws or fallacious maxims repeated so often and handed down so long that they have acquired a spurious patina of sanctity. Bentham thought that they stood in the path of the rational criticism of law and social institutions, just as the maxims of scholastic philosophy, wrongly held to be both universally applicable and self-evidently true, stood in the way of progress in the natural sciences,[12] as if, to take a modern example, Darwin's evolutionary theory with its supporting evidence had been met with some hoary causal maxim of the Middle Ages such as 'The less cannot produce the greater' ('Minus nequit gignere plus').

A great many of these stale shibboleths of reaction are collected, criticized, and exploded in Bentham's vastly entertaining *Book of Fallacies* which was conceived by him mainly as an assault on the rhetoric of despotism. The general neglect of this work in the teaching of political theory seems to me strange[13] for it is as readable and entertaining as it is instructive and it is full of contemporary relevance. Here are dissected The Chinese Argument or the argument from the Wisdom of Our Ancestors; The Hobgoblin Argument or 'No Innovation'; the argument called the Official Malefactors Screen with its slogan, still used, 'Attack us and you Attack all Government'. Here, too, is 'Non Causa pro Causa', by which the cause of progress and obstacles to it are confounded: as when the influence of the Crown and the presence of bishops in the House of Lords are represented as the cause of good government, or the education provided at Oxford and Cambridge as the causes of the spread of useful national learning. Yet for all their importance fallacies of this sort were not the most dangerous poisoned weapons in the armoury of reaction nor did their identification and exposure call for the most original of Bentham's talents. For these fallacies, however beguiling, were largely of the nature of false statements of fact. Many of them are indeed pseudo-truisms and their exposure consisted very largely in rubbing people's noses in the earth of plain fact and plain language about plain fact. Why speak of learning from the wisdom of

---

[12] *Fragment* Preface in *CW* 403, n. g.
[13] It was published as a paperback in 1962 (Harper Torch-books, New York).

our ancestors rather than their folly? 'It is from the folly not the wisdom of our ancestors that we have so much to learn.'[14] After all, the best-informed class of our wise ancestors were grossly ignorant on many subjects compared with the lowest literate class of the people in modern times.[15] How many of the laity in the House of Lords in the time of Henry VIII could even read? 'But even supposing them all in the fullest possession of that useful art, political science being the science in question, what instruction on the subject could they meet with at that time of day?'[16] So Bentham urges what are called old times—the wisdom of old times—ought to be called 'young' or 'early' times; for to give the name old to earlier and less-experienced generations is not less foolish than to give the name of old man to an infant in his cradle.[17] So in the very name 'old times', says Bentham, 'there is virtually involved a false and deceptious proposition'.[18] As the last point shows, Bentham passes easily from a criticism of fact to a critique of language, and the *Book of Fallacies* has much to say under the headings of 'question-begging appellatives',[19] 'passion-kindling appellatives',[20] and 'imposter terms'[21] concerning the use, in political and moral argument, of what is now called emotive language and persuasive definition.

But behind these sources of deception Bentham saw others more insidious and less easy to identify which arose quite naturally from the very forms of human communication and reasoning. Language was, he thought, an ambiguous instrument in the sense that though possession of it raised men above the beasts (for not only communication but thought itself depended on it), yet its complex forms contained possibilities of both confusion and deception which had been exploited consciously or unconsciously by reactionary and revolutionary alike. Bentham's writings on language and on logic are among the most unsatisfactory of the Bowring texts, and a recension of them by an understanding editor is certainly overdue. Yet the main lines of his doctrines are clear. In the first place he insists on the practical utility of

---

[14] *Book of Fallacies, Works* II 401.
[15] Op. cit. 400.   [16] Ibid.   [17] Op. cit. 398-9.
[18] Op. cit. 398.   [19] Op. cit. 436.   [20] Op. cit. 438.
[21] Ibid.

these studies and says they are subordinate branches of the study of human happiness.[22] Logic had not come to an end with Aristotle and the scholastics are blamed by Bentham both for conceiving of the subject in too narrow[23] a way and for failing to make clear what was the utility which they claimed for it.[24] In insisting on its utility, Bentham was not making an automatic gesture to his own principles. He really did think that the possibility of sane judgement in politics, and indeed in the conduct of life, depended on an awareness of the snares latent in the very texture of human discourse, the clarification of which was the province of logic.

I do not mean that Bentham's logical writings are only of value as so many blows against reaction and revolution. There are indeed many things of great speculative importance in them. Among these I should count his insistence on the pregnant truth 'that nothing less than the import of an entire proposition is sufficient for the giving full expression to any the most simple thought'[25] with its important corollary that the meaning of single words are the result of 'abstraction and analysis' from sentential or propositional forms. This idea—that sentences not words are the unit of meaning—was not to appear again in philosophy for fifty years. It was then asserted by Frege[26] and stressed in Wittgenstein's *Tractatus Logico-Philosophicus.*[27] Bentham's main innovations as a philosopher are based on this insight; for he believed that the relation of language and so of thought to the world is radically misunderstood if we conceive of sentences as compounded out of words which simply name or stand for elements of reality and thus as having meaning independently of sentential forms. Philosophy—and not only philosophy—has been perennially beset by the false idea that whenever a word has a meaning there must be some existent thing related to it in some simple uniform way appropriate to simple atoms of language. Unfortunately Bentham makes this seminal point in the context of a characteristically sketchy genetic theory.

---

[22] *Essay on Logic, Works* VIII 221-2, 240-1.
[23] Op. cit. 220, 232.   [24] Op. cit. 232-4.
[25] *Essay on Language, Works* VIII 322.
[26] 'Nur im Zusammenhange eines Satzes bedeuten die Wörter etwas', *Die Grundlagen der Arithmetik* (Breslau 1884), 73.
[27] London 1933. Propositions 3.3 and 3.3:4.

He rightly contrasts his own doctrine with the Aristotelian doctrine of terms and ridicules the idea which he thinks is implicit in it: the idea that at some stage in the history of mankind 'some ingenious persons, finding these terms endowed each of them somehow or other with a signification of its own, at a subsequent time took them in hand and formed them into propositions'.[28]

Bentham's best-known contribution to logic and linguistic theory is his doctrine of Logical Fictions which anticipated the early writings of Bertrand Russell on logical constructions and incomplete symbols. I give a compressed account of Bentham's doctrine in Chapter VI in a discussion of his theories of legal duty and obligation which he frequently takes as an example of a logical fiction and as a paradigm to exhibit his special method of analysis. Bentham used this doctrine of logical fictions to dissipate the idea that words like 'duty', 'obligation', and 'right' were names of mysterious entities awaiting men's discovery and incorporation of them in man-made laws or social rules. Because names of logical fictions had been confused with names of real entities and had been thought to have the same simple relation with reality 'they have raised', says Bentham, 'those thick vapours which have intercepted the light. Their origin has been unknown; they have been lost in abstractions. These words have been the foundation of reasoning as if they had been external entities which did not derive their birth from the law but which on the contrary had given birth to it.'[29] Words like 'duty', 'obligation', 'right' did indeed, according to Bentham, require special methods of analysis which he invented for logical fictions as a substitute for the straightforward form of definition by genus and species which he held inapplicable to them. Yet, though complex in this way, statements about men's rights or duties were reducible by proper methods to statements of plain unmysterious fact. We cannot say what the words 'obligation' or 'right' name or stand for because, says Bentham, they name nothing; but we can say what statements employing these words mean.

However, the most original of Bentham's contributions to logic is his form of imperative or deontic logic which he calls

---

[28] *Works* VIII 322.   [29] *Works* III 160.

The Logic of the Will. Here Bentham is conscious of entering on a particular branch of logic 'untouched by Aristotle'[30] exhibiting the relationships of "opposition and concomitance" between commands, prohibitions, and permissions which he terms 'forms of imperation' or 'sentences expressive of volition'. This is, Bentham says, 'a leaf which seems to be yet wanting in the book of science'[31] and it seems quite clear that Bentham was justified in his claim to originality. In discussing in Chapter V Bentham's Logic of the Will I attempt to supply a theoretical basis for the logical relationships which he identifies here, while avoiding what I take to be Bentham's erroneous belief examined in Chapter X that commands and prohibitions and permissions are statements which may be true or false.

Sometimes Bentham writes about logic in his very wide sense with an eye very closely on political argument and on the strategy for educating men into a proper awareness of its snares and pitfalls. Thus he believed that, in general, tyranny and oppression in politics were possible only where claims to infallibility of judgement were presumptuously made and stupidly conceded. It was necessary to oppose to these arrogant claims the truth that all human judgement, 'opinion', or 'persuasion' is fallible. This truth, says Bentham, 'whether for the exclusion of obstinate error, or for the exclusion of arrogance, overbearingness, obstinacy and violence [to which he added in a later passage 'bigotry'[32]] ought never to be out of mind.'[33] John Stuart Mill rightly identified this as a very important element in Bentham's teaching, and his own vindication of freedom of thought and opinion in his essay *On Liberty* is an elaboration of this same theme; for his central argument is that just because individual human judgements are fallible, freedom of thought and discussion are indispensable. But Mill does not attempt to explain why the claim to infallibility, so often made in defence of authority or the *status quo*, is false. Bentham did attempt to do this but I think failed. He thought that the falsity of all such claims to infallibility was a consequence of some simple truths about the character of human judgements;

---

[30] *PML* Chap. XVII, para. 29, n. b2, in *CW* 299.
[31] Ibid.   [32] *Works* VIII 321 n.   [33] Ibid. 300 n.

but here I think his limitations as a philosopher begin to appear. For his doctrine is the surely false one which also infects his conception of commands, prohibitions, and permissions, that 'of no matter of fact external to, of no matter other than that which passes in a man's own mind can any immediate communication be made by language'. He adds (using a dangerously ambiguous phrase) 'That to which expression is given, that of which communication is made is always the man's opinion nor anything more.'[34] So, according to Bentham most of our ordinary statements of fact are elliptical and even the simplest is complex in a way not suspected by Aristotle. If, to take Bentham's example, I say that Eurybiades struck Themistocles, all I really assert and all I can assert is: '*It is my opinion* that Eurybiades struck Themistocles. This is what I can be sure of and it is all that, in relation to the supposed matter of fact, it is in my power to be assured of.'[35]

This way of disposing of claims to infallibility must be mistaken. No doubt there is an intimate and important connection between the statement (call it *p*) made by a speaker (call him *X*) on a given occasion, and the statement that *X* believed *p*. The natural way of expressing this connection is that *in* saying *p*, *X implied* that he believed it. Of course the sense of a *person* implying something by stating something needs to be clarified and distinguished from the logical relation between two statements where one entails the other. That is, we must distinguish what is implied by *what* a man says from what is implied by *his saying* it. This is perhaps not easy to do; though it is a distinction as important in the law of evidence as it is in philosophy and logic. The analysis of this relationship shows it to be of a general kind in which Bentham himself in his writings on logic and language was much interested. For it seems clear that the intimate connection between *X* saying *p* and his believing it, and the strangeness of saying '*p* but I do not believe *p*', depend on the fact that one of the purposes for which human beings make statements is to invite or induce others to believe them by showing that the speaker believes them too. It may even be true that human discourse could not

---

[34] *Works* VIII 321.   [35] Ibid.

function as it does unless there is a generally, though not universally, respected convention that we do not say what we do not believe. But none of this supports the theory that the simplest statement is logically complex, so that in asserting p we are asserting that we believe p. Well-known paradoxes follow from such a theory.[36]

III

When Bentham turned from the logical and linguistic defences of blind custom and oppressive authority to his other adversaries—the forces of revolution and anarchy—he thought their principal appeal lay in their exploitation of the idea of an individual right. Here was the centre of the fallacies of Anarchy which tempted men to insurrection and violence by playing upon the very terminology of the law. But it seems to me that Bentham really was afraid not merely of intemperate invocations of natural rights in opposition to established laws but he sensed that the idea of such rights would always excite a peculiarly strong suspicion that the doctrine of utility could not provide an adequate account of all men's moral ideas and political ideals. There is I think something strident or even feverish in Bentham's treatment of rights which betrays this nervousness.

None the less, even in his early brief attack on the American Declaration of Independence and amid the panic-stricken rhetoric of his elaborate polemical criticism in his *Anarchical Fallacies* of the French Declaration of the Rights of Man and the Citizen there are some simple but powerful criticisms which became for decades the standard objections to doctrines of fixed inalienable rights. Not only are inalienable rights construed as guarantees of specific liberties doomed to constant conflict with each other, but, Bentham also urged, there is an absurdity in combining the assertion that there are inalienable rights with the assertion that government was necessary to protect them and legitimate only if it does so. This is absurd because the exercise of the necessary powers of

---

[36] It would follow that two speakers would not be contradicting each other if one of them said 'This is red' and the other 'No; it is not'; they would simply be comparing autobiographical notes about their beliefs. Also if the theory were correct the truth of the statement 'I do not believe this is red' would entail 'this is not red'.

any government must necessarily restrict the exercise by the individual of the alleged inalienable rights. Taken strictly as offering unqualified guarantees of certain liberties the doctrine is essentially anarchical and anarchists have not been slow to invoke it in support of their claim that the state is morally speaking illegitimate. Bentham insisted that no political principles with the rigidity of the doctrine of inalienable specific rights could have any application in the real world in which men have to live their lives. Such principles belong to Utopia: that is, nowhere or an imaginary world. Accordingly Bentham stigmatizes the doctrine as a product not of reason but of imagination and complained that its advocates would look at no calculations which 'if, instead of imagination reason were consulted, would be seen to be necessary'.

The continued vitality of such criticisms is paradoxically confirmed by a prominent modern writer's defence of a right-based political theory. For Robert Nozick confronts in his well-known *Anarchy, State and Utopia* the same issues as those raised by Bentham's criticism when, at the outset of his book, he asks 'how much room do individual rights leave for Government?'. What is astonishing is that Nozick in effect gives Bentham's answer: 'no room except in an imaginary world'. For that is the message of this ingenious modern work. Thus Nozick argues that granted a set of moral rights, such as not to be killed, assaulted, coerced, and not to have property taken or destroyed and not to be limited in its use, only a minimal form of State, the so-called nightwatchman state whose functions are limited to the functions of punishment of violations of such rights, can be legitimate. Moreover, given these natural rights, even this minimal form of State could be justified only under conditions of which Bentham never thought, and might be forgiven for failing to do so; for they are conditions produced out of Nozick's lively imagination which are highly unlikely to be satisfied except in an imaginary world. The conditions in question are that the State should have arisen by individuals voluntarily joining a private protection association which might eventually achieve without infringing any natural rights, dominance in a limited territory even if not everyone joins it. But all this seems indeed 'imaginary' and to have little relevance to a world where states do not arise in this way.

So this modern right-based theory seems just tailor-made for Bentham's accusation that talk of unalienable rights taken strictly belongs only to the world of the imagination. Bentham of course realized that defenders of the doctrine would disclaim such rigid unqualified interpretations of it, and while continuing to speak of rights as inalienable would admit limitations of scope, qualifications and exceptions, and balancing, both of right against right and right against general welfare, or might even be content to view them merely as ideal directions to governments to do the best they can for certain individual interests. To support this point he could have cited some famous examples from America where express declarations of natural rights to liberty incorporated into state constitutions were held not to affect the slaveowners' rights to property in his slaves. So Bentham depicted advocates of natural rights as on the horns of a dilemma between the impossible and the nugatory.

In Chapter IV I turn aside from this part of Bentham's attack on natural rights and his detailed criticism of the French Declaration of the Rights of Man and the Citizen in order to examine in detail his theoretical objection to a moral or non-legal right as self-contradictory and the more formidable charge which he makes that it is an indeterminate or, as I call it, a criterionless notion and so, 'a mere sound to dispute about'. But one of my principal concerns in this chapter is to make clear the surprising and instructive similarities and differences between Bentham and John Stuart Mill in their treatment of non-legal moral rights. Far from sharing Bentham's criticism of the notion as nonsensical or indeterminate, Mill thought it impossible to give an account of justice as a distinct segment of morality without recognizing that men have moral as well as legal rights including certain basic rights to liberty and security from harm. Yet in spite of this difference when Mill attempts, as he does, in my view unsuccessfully, to reconcile the recognition of certain universal moral rights with utilitarianism, he takes seriously as a definition of moral right a half-mocking suggestion, made by Bentham, as to what those who talk loosely about natural or non-legal rights might conceivably mean by asserting their existence. I argue that Mill's attempt to provide an indirect utilitarian foundation for such rights fails, and that the charge

of indeterminacy or criterionlessness which Bentham made
against the notion of basic moral rights, still awaits a satisfactory answer from those modern writers who have put forward various forms of right-based political theory.

IV

Chapters VI, VII, and VIII of this book on Legal Duty
and Obligation, Legal Rights, and Legal Powers, are concerned
with the merits and defects as I see them of Bentham's
analysis of the basic organizing concepts in terms of which
the contents of the law especially at its point of impact on
individuals are customarily described by lawyers, whether
practitioners, judges, or jurists, and, with less uniformity, by
theorists of other disciplines interested in the law, and by
ordinary citizens. Statements of legal obligation, rights, and
powers state respectively what individuals legally must do or
must refrain from doing, what legally they may do or are
entitled to have others do or abstain from doing, and the
ways in which they may with the assistance of the law change
their own or other persons' legal positions in these respects.
Since these are the basic ways in which the law in its distinctive way restricts human freedom of action or leaves it free,
protects it from interference, or facilitates its exercise, legal
obligation, rights, and power are focal points of legal thought
to the clarification of which any serious philosophy of law
must address itself.

Bentham's analysis of these basic concepts, though simple
in structure, is rich in detail, most of which is untidily
scattered through his vast works. I have assembled and
attempt to assess critically what I take to be the essentials of
his views, without the over-simplification the risk of which is
the occupational hazard run by any interpreter of Bentham's
thought not inspired by a passion for detail comparable to
his. It is clear that the form of his analysis of these basic concepts is largely dictated by two features of his thought which
have led to his being regarded in contemporary works of
jurisprudence as a prime exponent or even the founding
father of legal positivism. The first of these features is his imperative theory of law according to which laws are the explicit
or tacit commands and prohibitions, standardly supported by

coercive sanctions, issued by a sovereign legislator or legislative body or their subordinates, and the permissions to act or refrain from acting issuing from these same sources. The second of these two main features of Bentham's thought is his view that law has no necessary or conceptual connection with morality, although, as he clearly saw, there are many important and often complex contingent connections between them. He recognized that laws may and often do mirror or incorporate the requirements of morality and that legal systems may not only be morally admirable when this is so, but also most stable, yet these connections between law and morality were none the less contingent.

At various points in these chapters and in the two that succeed them I argue that the first of these two features, Bentham's imperative theory of law, is a great weakness in his jurisprudence, leading him to present in spite of great ingenuity, a distorted account of aspects of law which he himself sees to be important though they cannot be fitted into the cramping framework dictated by his imperative theory. What he is thus forced to distort includes among other things the fact that legal obligation may arise from many different legal sources and not only from legislative commands; that the power of a supreme legislature may be both conferred by law and limited by it; that what is done by way of the purported exercise of legal powers, public or private, may be assessed as valid or invalid, and not merely, in the terms of the imperative theory, as permitted or prohibited. The conceptual resources which Bentham draws from his imperative theory are too meagre to accommodate these notions which are of crucial importance for the description and understanding of any modern legal system. I argue both in Chapter V and Chapter X that to accommodate these features of law it is necessary to bring into the analysis the idea of an authoritative legal reason, that is a consideration (which in simple systems of law may include the giving of a command) which is recognized at least in the practice of the Courts, in what I term their rule or rules of recognition, as constituting a reason for action and decision of a special kind. Reasons of this kind I term 'peremptory' and 'content-independent' and they constitute legal guides to action and legal standards of evaluation.

Though I think Bentham's imperative theory of law must be discarded his conceptual separation of law and morality, sensitive as it is to many important empirical connections between them, seems to me a permanently valuable feature of his thought which can and should be retained when his imperative theory is discarded. It is valuable, I think, not only because it reproduces the way in which law in modern societies appears to many of its subjects but also because it permits the construction of a general theory of law applicable to legal systems whatever their moral quality, justice or injustice, or the moral belief of its subjects or officials. I am however vividly aware of the fact that such a view of the merits of this view of legal positivism is much disputed at the present time, and that there are distinguished contemporary philosophers of law on both sides of the Atlantic who would claim that it is impossible to find a substitute for Bentham's imperative theory which does not involve the recognition of important conceptual connections between law and morality. I attempt in Chapter V to show how in the case of two modern thinkers opposition to this aspect of legal positivism takes the form of an insistence that the expressions 'obligation', 'duty', or 'right' have the same meaning in legal and moral contexts, so that a legal obligation, for example, is simply a moral obligation differing from others only because men have it in virtue of the existence of law, and that there are no obligations which are legal but not also moral. Of the two variants of this view hostile to Bentham's conceptual separation of law and morality, the first seems to me to fail, in spite of its sophisticated character, in reconciling its account of legal obligations or rights with the recognition that legal systems may contain laws of great moral iniquity. The second, more moderate version of this view seems to me to fail because it imputes unrealistically at least to the judges of the legal system either moral beliefs which they may not hold, or a willingness publicly to pretend that they do. I recognize, however, that the issues opened up by such modern critics of legal positivism are large ones not to be disposed of finally in a book of essays devoted to Bentham's thought.

In the last two chapters I attempt to probe more deeply than I have done before into the twin foundations of his jurisprudence: the idea of a sovereign legislator and the idea of a command. In Chapter IX I discuss the hints which Bentham throws out as to the way in which the phenomenon of a legally limited supreme legislature might find a place within the framework of his general theory. But my conclusion is that however generously the elements of that theory are interpreted the task that Bentham here sets himself cannot be completed, and that again the notion of an authoritative legal reason recognized by the Courts of a legal system must be brought into the analysis. In Chapter X I consider in detail Bentham's account of the central idea of a command. This account is, as I have already said, vitiated by the misconception that commands and the other expressions of legislative will which Bentham treats as laws are forms of indicative statements about the state or contents of that will. Yet it is I think something of a paradox that though there is much to dissent from in Bentham's account of command, it is yet true that correctly analysed commands can be seen to contain elements out of which the important idea of an authoritative legal reason may be constructed. It is as if buried in the notion of a command there are elements which are crucial for the understanding not only of many different forms of law but also, as I argue in Chapter X, the general phenomenon of authority. So I would say of Bentham's mistake in focusing on the idea of a command what the late Professor Austin said in general terms: 'In philosophy there are many mistakes that it is no disgrace to have made: to make a first water, ground floor mistake so far from being easy takes one form of philosophical genius.'[37]

---

[37] Austin, *Ifs and Cans in Philosophical Papers* (Oxford 1961) 153.

I

THE DEMYSTIFICATION OF THE LAW

I

The words 'mystification' and 'demystification' have appeared fairly recently among us in the literature of the radical New Left. The central idea that these words are used to express is that unjust, anachronistic, inefficient or otherwise harmful social institutions, including laws, are frequently protected from criticism by a veil of mystery thrown over them. This conceals their true nature and effects, perplexes and intimidates the would-be reformer, and so prolongs the life of bad institutions. The forms of mystery thus used in defence of established abuses are, according to these radical critics, various. They include not only glorification by open eulogy and pomp and ceremony; not only the use of archaic dress and diction unintelligible to the layman, but also, and more importantly, mystification consists in the propagation of a *belief*: the belief that legal and other institutions of society are infinitely complex and difficult to understand, and that this is an invincible fact of nature, so that long-standing institutions cannot be changed without risk of the collapse of society. The attitude appropriate to this belief is one of humble deference to tradition: 'we ought to understand it according to our measure and venerate where we are not able presently to comprehend.'[1]

'Demystification,' as used in the vocabulary of radical politics, is simply the tearing aside of the veil of mystery so as to exhibit these claims about the nature of social institutions as an illusion, if not a fraud; and such 'demystification' is, according to radical thought, a necessary step for any serious critic of society and an indispensable preliminary to reform. Of course these ideas of mystification and demystification are not new, they have indeed what to my mind is a quite respectable ancestry, most notably in the works of

---

[1] Burke, 'An Appeal from the New to the Old Whigs' in *Works of Edmund Burke*, ed. Bohn, III 114. Burke's reference is to the British constitution.

Marx and Engels, and even beyond them in the literature of the eighteenth-century Enlightenment.

In this chapter I shall attempt to show how these ideas permeate the work of Bentham, himself a child of the Enlightenment, and in fact unify what he has to say not only about the many different legal institutions which he set out to reform, but also his general legal theory or philosophy of law. But I should be disappointed and Bentham would certainly be furious if his ideas were thought to be of interest only to the historian of ideas. He himself was prepared to wait a long time for the law to learn the lessons of utility and to submit to reform on Benthamite lines. Indeed in his great work on the law of evidence[2] which is itself largely a sustained protest against what he considered a special form of mystification, Bentham picked out the year AD 2440[3] —but, as he says, 'only in the way of reverie'—as the date when things might start to get better. This was too pessimistic; for certainly some of the most important Benthamite reforms have long been conceded. But the rate of progress has not been great and we might do well to look about us to see whether or not there are forms of mystification still to be dispelled. Certainly some sober contemporary critics, by no means all representatives of the New Left, have found some areas of our contemporary law and legal practice where mystery, complexity, artificiality, and superstitious belief in the impossibility of change are still producing harmful social effects.[4] At the end of this chapter I shall consider some examples which Bentham might fasten on were he with us now. But my main concern is with the place in Bentham's jurisprudence of the theme of mystification.

It is, I think, quite characteristic of Bentham, who commanded both a fly's-eye view and an eagle's-eye view of the law, that variations of this theme are to be found at all the different levels of his critical thought about law. It is present alike in his general theory of the nature of law and the sciences of law, in his fierce criticism of the law of evidence

---

[2] *An Introductory View of the Rationale of Judicial Evidence, Works* VI, and *The Rationale of Judicial Evidence, Works* VI, VII.

[3] *Works* VII 320.

[4] e.g. Abel-Smith and Stevens, *In Search of Justice, Society and the Legal System* (London 1968), 360.

and procedure and of the customs and traditions and again the language of English lawyers. Throughout all these, as he tells us, he is concerned 'to draw aside that curtain of mystery which fiction and formality have spread so extensively over the Law' and not 'to embroider it with flowers' as he accused Blackstone of doing. 'Law', says Bentham in the same passage, 'shews itself in a mask and this mask our Author instead of putting off has varnished.'[5]

Let us consider first how what I shall call the demystification motif colours his general theory of law. This is the theory, in which indeed most of us have been brought up, that laws are simply expressions of the will of a human lawgiver,[6] they are essentially of the nature of commands or prohibitions or permissions to act or to forbear to act. But this fundamentally imperative character of law is, according to Bentham, 'clouded and concealed from ordinary apprehension'[7] not only obviously by the doctrine of natural law but more insidiously by the fact that in statutes, codes, and treatises and in the language of the courts and of lawyers the law is very rarely formulated in imperative language.[8] Hence the illusion arises that there are laws which are not imperative at all: among these, for example, are property laws; some of these appear to tell us things, to say what constitutes a good title or a valid conveyance, others confer legal powers such as the various powers of alienation.[9] Laws conferring powers do not appear on their face to be concerned with the business of issuing commands or prohibitions, so the conventional formulation of such laws conceals their imperative character. Frequently they appear to be describing something already existing, not prescribing something to be done.[10]

This, then, is one form of mystification which Bentham thought it important to dispel by preaching (some may think *ad nauseam*) the doctrine that laws are at bottom nothing but commands, prohibitions or permissions, artefacts of the human will. But though for Bentham laws are but artefacts

---

[5] *Comment* Chap. II, s.1, in *CW* 124.

[6] See Chaps. IX and X *infra*.

[7] *PML* Concluding Note, para. 14, in *CW* 305; cf. *OLG* 302 ('imperative matter may be masked under the assertive form').

[8] *OLG* 105-6, 178-9, 180-1, 302-3.

[9] *OLG* 178-81.   [10] *OLG* 26.

and there are no natural laws, there are indeed natural and
rational principles for the guidance of legislators and the
criticism of law. These are the principles of utility which tell
us what is a good reason for a law, but a reason for a law,
even a good reason—so Bentham warns us—is not itself a
law.[11] If we ask why Bentham regarded the articulation of
this imperative theory as so important and devoted so much
energy and passion to the demonstration that beneath the
surface of conventional formulation of any law, there is always a basic imperative structure, the answer suggests a
rather surprising affinity between Bentham and Karl Marx, in
whose works the ideas of mystification and demystification
play so large a part. I say this affinity is surprising for two
reasons. The first is that we know what Marx thought of
Bentham and how indignant he would be at the suggestion of
any affinity with him. 'The arch philistine Jeremy Bentham,'
Marx wrote, 'that insipid, pedantic, leather-tongued oracle
of the ordinary bourgeois intelligence of the nineteenth
century.' Bentham—so Marx goes on—'is a purely English
phenomenon' who 'with the dryest naïveté takes the modern
shopkeeper, especially the modern English shopkeeper, as the
normal man. . . . Had I the courage of my friend Heinrich
Heine I should call Mr. Jeremy a genius in the way of bourgeois stupidity.'[12]

Bentham himself was no mean hand at invective and though
we have not, unfortunately, the benefit of Bentham's observations on Marx it would not be difficult to concoct a
Benthamite reply. But we are concerned here with the similarities and differences between these two great social thinkers.
Of course they *were* very different. Bentham was a sober
reformer who examined society with the eye of a business
efficiency or cost-benefit expert on the grand scale, and condemned the society of his day for its inefficient failure to
satisfy, in an economic or optimal way, the desires that
characterize human beings as they are. He contemplated no
radical change or development in human nature and, though
he thought things would be immensely better, if laws were
reformed on Benthamite lines, he envisaged no millennium

---

[11] *Works* II 501; III 221.
[12] *Capital*, I (3rd edn. transl. Moore and Aveling, corrected reprint 1970),
609-10.

and no utopia. There would always, he thought, be 'oppo-
sitions of interest' and 'painful labour, daily subjection, and
a condition nearly allied to indigence will always be the lot
of numbers.'[13] So there would always be need for the coercive authority of law to protect property and society. 'Perfect
happiness,' Bentham said, 'belongs to the imaginary regions
of philosophy and must be classed with the universal elixir
and the philosopher's stone.'[14] So he relied mainly on the
increase in numbers of a prosperous middle class and its progressive enlightenment, to reform the law in accordance with
utility and to secure a gradual and gentle progress towards
equality in property. This was to happen, he said, 'without
revolution, without shock,' and equality was always to be
subordinate to security.[15] This bourgeois gradualism, for
such it is, was of course anathema to Marx, who was both
much more pessimistic in the short run than Bentham and
wildly more optimistic in the long run. Marx condemned the
existing forms of society not for mere inefficiency, but because its economic system stunted and distorted human
beings and prevented the exploited masses, and indeed also
their exploiters, from developing their distinctively human
powers. This could be rectified, not by the mere spread of
ideas or enlightened education or piecemeal reform, but only
by a radical and, if necessary, violent transformation of the
economic and social structure of society. But with that
transformation complete there would be conditions under
which all men could achieve their full development in a form
of society where men were humanly related to each other.
Such optimism about the aftermath of revolution contrasts
with Bentham's sober warning that 'it may be possible to
diminish the influence of but not to destroy the sad and
mischievous passions.'[16]

Notwithstanding these great differences of both temperament and political thought, Bentham and Marx agreed on
two fundamental points which are relevant to my present
theme: first, that their tasks as social thinkers were to clear
men's minds as to the true character of human society, and,
secondly, that human society and its legal structure which

---

[13] *Works* I 194.   [14] Ibid.
[15] *Theory of Legislation*, transl. Hildreth (2nd edn. London 1874), 123.
[16] *Works* I 194.

had worked so much human misery, had been protected from criticism by myths, mysteries, and illusions, not all of them intentionally generated, yet all of them profitable to interested parties. Bentham found the law obscured by mysteries and so spoke of it as wearing a mask; Marx spoke of the 'mystical veil' of the life-process[17] of society, though unlike Bentham he thought this could be removed only by radical social change in the course of a long and painful historical development. For both of them such mystery was made possible by the failure on the part of ordinary men to realize that the forms of law and human society were at bottom merely human artefacts, not natural necessities but things actually made by men, and hence things which could be unmade and remade. Marx thought that just as man has made a god in his own image and succumbed to the illusion that God has made man,[18] so man under certain social conditions, 'alienated' man, has come to think of the structure of society, legal and economic, not as a human creation but as an external object having power over man. 'His own creation [appears as] a force alien to him . . . his power over the object as the power of the object over him, the master of his creation appears as its slave.'[19]

Bentham contemplated and elaborately documented the abuses of the English law of his day, the fantastic prolixity and obscurity of its statutes, the complexity and expense of its court procedure, the artificiality and irrationality of its modes of proof. He was horrified by these things, but even more horrified by the ease with which English lawyers swallowed and propagated the enervating superstition that these abuses were natural and inevitable, so that only a visionary would dream of their radical reform. He believed that only those who had been blinded to the truth that laws were human artefacts could acquiesce in these absurdities and injustices as things to be ascribed to nature; and one way of opening men's eyes was to preach to them the simple but important doctrine that laws were but expressions of the human will. Law is something men add to the world, not find within it.

[17] *Capital* I 80.
[18] 'Towards the Critique of Hegel's Philosophy of Law' in *Writings of the Young Marx on Philosophy and Society*, ed. Easton and Guddat, 249-51.
[19] 'Excerpt Notes from 1884' in op. cit. 272.

Another very distinctive part of Bentham's general theory of law can be presented illuminatingly as another step towards demystification. He found embedded in the language which men use to speak of the law, certain recurrent expressions which he calls in his instructive *Book of Fallacies* 'passion-kindling appellatives' and 'imposter terms'.[20] These are words which, while appearing to be merely descriptive and so neutral as to the merits of what they describe, in fact have a disguised eulogistic or dyslogistic force. They have indeed what later philosophers of language have called emotive meaning.[21] Bentham was sure that such 'imposter terms' with a hidden conservative ideology were frequently used as a cloak for misgovernment. One most conspicuous example of these is still with us in the use of the expression 'the maintenance of law and order'[22] or 'the maintenance of order' instead of neutral expressions such as the 'enforcement of law' and 'obedience to government.' Bentham pointed out that 'the maintenance of order,' with its implicit and favourable value judgement, had been applied to a state of affairs where the most iniquitous laws existed and were enforced, such as ob-tained under Nero and Caligula. The word 'order' with its eulogistic ring glossed over the horrors of such regimes just as it would if used of law enforcement in Nazi Germany or contemporary South Africa. So Bentham begs us not to slide into the easy use of expressions of a 'eulogistic cast'[23] to describe the law, when neutral terms are at hand. To use them is to mystify, and to mystify may be to cloak tyranny.

Bentham was, of course, constantly preoccupied with the abuse of language to cloud the issues in controversy, especially political controversy. But the point which he made about the mystifying force of imposter terms such as 'the main-tenance of order', is really part of something much wider. For it is just a particular manifestation of a very fundamental and original feature in Bentham's whole austere approach to the philosophy of law and politics. Bentham was certainly not the first to define law as a command: Hobbes, for ex-ample, had anticipated him in that, and even the despised

[20] *Works* II 438.
[21] Stevenson, *Ethics and Language*, Chap. 3.
[22] *Works* II 441.   [23] Ibid.

Blackstone's definition of municipal law was in terms of command. But Bentham differed from Hobbes and, as far as I know, from all previous social theorists in insisting that we must not so define our terms in legal or political theory as to make the practical conclusions which we favour follow from them. Such definitions have been aptly called 'persuasive definitions'[24] and among Bentham's many claims to be an innovator none is better founded nor, I think, more important than his insistence on a precise and so far as possible a morally neutral vocabulary for use in the discussion of law and politics. This insistence, though it may seem a merely linguistic matter, was the very centre, and I would say the sane and healthy centre, of the legal positivism of which Bentham may be regarded as the founder. It accounts for many important themes in his general theory including the form of his own definition of law. The terms that Bentham uses to define law are all flatly descriptive and normatively neutral: so whereas Hobbes had treated the commands of the Sovereign that make law as issued to those who are under an obligation to obey him, Bentham will have nothing of this antecedent obligation or the social contract alleged to generate it, and defines the Sovereign merely in the flat terms of habits of obedience. Hence nothing in his definition is owed to morality, and therefore nothing follows from the statement that laws so defined exist as to any moral reason for obedience: that vital issue, Bentham thought, must await the judgement of utility on the content of the laws. This calculatedly neutral approach to definition of legal and social phenomena is now familiar to us, but when Bentham applied it to the law it was new, shocking and a tonic for reformers. Of course, Bentham's steady refusal to recognize that the morality of law is relevant to the validity of law, his insistence that the existence of law is one thing and its merit or demerit another, has never lacked its critics, especially in America; and indeed a new and sophisticated attack upon this central tenet of positivism has been presented, at least in outline, by my distinguished American successor in the Oxford Chair of Jurisprudence.[25]

[24] Stevenson, op. cit., Chap. 7.
[25] See Ronald Dworkin, *Taking Rights Seriously* (2nd impression, London 1978), *passim*.

II

But let us now leave the arid heights of legal theory and hurry on down to the humbler spheres of legal practice. Bentham often referred to this as 'lawyer craft',[26] and continually returns to a comparison between the mysteries of the law and lawyer craft and those of religion and priest craft.[27] He bewailed the fact that though religion had at least had the benefit of the Reformation, the legal reformation had not yet arrived. 'In pointing out the artifices of priest craft', he said, 'what multitudes have already exercised themselves! The artifices of lawyer craft have been not less numerous, not less successful, not less wicked. Yet scarce has any hand lifted up so much as a corner of the veil that covers them. Near three hundred years has religion had her Luther. No Luther of Jurisprudence has yet come; no penetrating eye and dauntless heart have as yet searched into the cells and conclaves of the law.'[28]

Bentham surely recognized in himself the Luther of Jurisprudence, and he thought that two principal instruments of mystification were wielded by the lawyer. First there was lawyer's language: jargon and jargonization. Bentham's examination of jargon[29] and its different effects on legislators and lawyers, on ordinary citizens and would-be reformers, are a sort of anatomy of the topic which I cannot reproduce here. He claimed that the employment of lawyers in their formal documents, in contracts or conveyances, in indictments, pleadings, and judgements, of a language so prolix and different from what men naturally use, served a triple sinister purpose. First, like thieves' cant, or the language of the sham sciences of alchemy, palmistry, magic, and astrology, the cant or 'flash language' of lawyers forms a bond of union among them, setting them apart from society and reinforcing their complacency and resistance to reform. Secondly, it was also an instrument of depredation, since its complexities enormously multiplied lawyers' business and lawyers' fees. Thirdly, it created an atmosphere of awe around the lawyer, which intimidated the critic and fostered

[26] *Works* VII 270 n, 451, 453.
[27] *Works* VI 11; VII 210.   [28] *Works* VII 270 n.
[29] *Works* III 209, 270; VII 3, 236, 390; VII 210, 280-2.

the impression that human faculties are not really equal to the task of law reform.

The effect of all this was to hide the defects of the law where ordinary language would make them obvious. So Bentham wrote:

Seated in a chair in the character of a justice of the peace with common language in his mouth, a common coat upon his back, and no hair upon his head but his own, Solomon himself would not gain the praise of wisdom. Seated on a woolsack, Bartholon would pass muster while talking about entering appearances or filing common bail, clothed in purple and fine linen, artificial hair and ermine.[30]

In this passage we find the second set of lawyers' instruments of mystification. These are devices used to make the lawyer and the judge appear more than life-size. So under the general heading of 'delusion'[31] Bentham attacked the use of titles or 'factitious dignity', elaborate ceremonial robes and forms of address and indeed all the traditional apparatus lending to persons in authority what he calls 'splendour' and 'lustre' and obscuring the fact that they are merely human beings. Even the use of the word 'court'[32] for the judge he held objectionable as tending to depersonalize the judge and because of its suggestion of royalty which imparted to the law's working a spurious and unhealthy aura.

Bentham did not think that a legal profession was actually dispensable, though he flirted with the idea of 'everyman his own lawyer';[33] but he did think that the need for and the cost of lawyers' services could be very much reduced if the artificial encrustations of the law and its procedure were cut away. Real substantial progress, he thought, ultimately depended on the radical recasting of the form of the law and the adoption of codes, framed in a language freed from the lawyer's triple mystifying blight of 'ambiguity, obscurity and over-bulkiness'.[34] Pending that vast reform, however, Bentham thought that there was a most pressing evil which should be separately tackled: this was the complexity and irrationality of a trial in an English lawcourt. Here he found long established

---

[30] *Works* VII 282.
[31] *Works* IV 437-9; IX 76-7, 540-1.
[32] *Works* IX 76.
[33] *Works* III 209; V 236.
[34] *Works* III 239-47.

what he called the 'technical system'[35] bristling with irrational exclusionary rules of evidence, requirements of corroboration, and privileges against disclosure.

When Bentham began his onslaught on the technical system neither the parties to a civil trial at common law nor their spouses could give evidence, nor could any person pecuniarily interested in its outcome; and neither a person accused of a crime nor his spouse could give evidence at his trial. Yet these excluded witnesses were the very persons likely to know most about the facts in issue. In attacking these and other evils of the technical system, Bentham found again that it was necessary to combat the old mystifying claim that these evils were not man-made but to be ascribed to nature and could not be reformed. 'The cause to which they were imputed was the invincible and irremediable nature of things and not the factitious and therefore remediable imperfections of the law.'[36] Bentham's attack inspired the great statutory reforms of the law of evidence of 1843, 1851, and 1898, which, as the lawyers who lived through these changes said, amounted almost to a juridical revolution.[37] But as well as its great practical importance, Bentham's attack on the old technical system is very relevant to the theme of demystification because, in the course of it, he was led to develop his own conception of what is 'natural', to oppose to the conception, to which conservative lawyers were wedded, that the true natural order is to be found in traditional legal forms and institutions which have slowly evolved in a people's history. So, in his critique of the rules of procedure and evidence which Bentham thought disgraced the law courts of his day, he took as a paradigm what he terms 'the domestic or natural system' of settling disputes: commonsense rules such as the head of a household might use.[38] There, no sensible man would refuse to hear and question the parties interested or the persons under suspicion or refuse to draw obvious conclusions from their silence. This at any rate should be our starting-point or

---

[35] Summaries of the vices of the technical system and the virtues of the natural system are in *Works* II 169-78; V 7-16; VII 197-9, 222-6, 321-5.

[36] *Works* VI 206. Cf. VII 330.

[37] *Life of Lord Campbell*, ed. Hardcastle, II 292, 328.

[38] *Works* V 7; VII 197, 598.

regulative ideal for the law of evidence, and he considered it a damaging criticism of the technical system that, as he said, 'no private family composed of half a dozen members could subsist a twelvemonth under the governance of such rules.'[39] The natural system needed only common sense for its discovery 'because in principle there is but one mode of searching out the truth': it is, Bentham says, 'all the same, in all times and in all places—in all cottages, in all palaces—in every family and every court of justice.'[40] Its principal injunction is to be summed up thus: 'Hear everybody who is likely to know anything about the matter, hear everybody but most attentively of all, and first of all those who are most likely to know most about it—that is the parties.'[41]

III

Bentham's preoccupation with the evils of mystification and with innumerable remedies for demystification extended over the whole field of law. Law was to be made simpler, more like common sense, better expressed, better known, and better understood. I have merely illustrated Bentham's gigantic exposition of this theme from the two extremes of the general theory of law and the detail of lawcourt practice. But, it may well be asked, why bother about all this now? What sort of relevance has it to our contemporary affairs? There are indeed some *prima facie* reasons for thinking that it may have very little. Some may believe that whatever was sound and realistic in Bentham's criticism has now been absorbed into the main body of our law by our properly slow and gradual reforms. On this view, the force of Bentham's furious criticism is now spent and his further proposals for more radical change are the dreams of a wild ideologue untouched by any sense of history. In any case it may be quite plausibly urged that our society has grown so much more complex since Bentham's day that it is absurd now to call for radical simplifications of our law and legal proceedings, or to hold out even as an ideal the natural simplicities of the cottage and of family life.

So these are reasons for thinking that though there was

---

[39] *Works* VI 205.   [40] *Works* VII 599.   [41] Ibid.

once 'gold in them thar hills' the Benthamite vein has now
been worked out. But this I think would be a great mistake
and I shall end this chapter by indulging a fantasy which may
show it to be so. Let us suppose that that old mummy which
is kept at University College—Bentham's auto-eikon—is
galvanized into life and that Bentham after his long sleep of
140 years is among us, surveying our contemporary law and
legal practice. Would he still find mystification to demystify
and the need to press upon us the adoption of more natural
and simpler forms instead of complex and artificial ones
masquerading as inevitable? I am sure he would find it in
many places and I choose two examples. They are very different in character and, perhaps, in importance, and I am sure
that many who would follow Bentham eagerly in one case
would turn away in anger or even horror in the other.

Consider first Bentham's condemnation as an instrument
of 'delusion', of the fancy dress of authority, or as he calls it
disparagingly, its factitious 'lustre and splendour': its apparatus of pomp, pageantry, and ceremony, wigs and gowns and
antique formal modes of address. Of course, there are old
arguments for traditional rituals: it is often urged that society
needs ceremonials to bind it together and that their emphasis
on a nation's past is among the unifying forces of society,
giving it not only colour but also solidity. Of course it may
well be that our traditional legal forms have hitherto maintained respect for the law or at least instilled fear, perhaps
healthy fear. But surely, in the light of a changed general
attitude, not only to ceremonies and forms but to authority
of all kinds, we should reconsider the question whether our
legal rituals help us now or obstruct us. Do not our inherited
forms instead of inspiring irrational or undeserved respect
(as Bentham chiefly feared[42]) make the law appear anachronistic, out of touch because out of date, or, as one critic
has illuminatingly put it,[43] do they not make the law and
lawyers appear like 'some contemporary remnants of a society
dominated by the upper classes', marked off from the rest by
a special style of dress and diction? Would not dropping these
forms, dimming the lustre and the splendour, do something

---

[42] 'Traps to catch respect', *Works* IX 540.
[43] Watson, 'Could the Legal System be more humane?' in *What's Wrong with
the Law?*, ed. Zander (London 1970), 65.

to lessen the risks of dissociation between law and the rest of the community, which is surely among the great dangers of our time? Would it not be better to let judge and lawyer appear, as Bentham wished, merely as life-sized contemporary figures, so that in entering a lawcourt the plain man would no longer feel that he is entering a strange world of half-intimidating and half-comic historical pantomime? We do not when we go to a doctor find ourselves confronted with someone in the guise of a seventeenth-century apothecary, complete with ruff and doublet and sword, and if we did we might feel even more uncomfortable than we do about swallowing his, that is, our, medicine. At a time when authority of all kinds is under the most irrational forms of attack why make authority more difficult to accept by dressing it up as a ghost from the past?

Now for my second, perhaps more important and contentious example. Bentham, were he among us now, would I am sure most anxiously inquire about the progress of his other great work of demystification: the substitution of a natural and rational law of evidence for the technical artificial system of his day. He might well, after inspecting the record, think that the rate of progress had slowed down after the first great dawn of reform of the 1840s and 1850s; he might, for example, share the astonishment which all laymen still feel when they are told that with certain minor exceptions it was not until 1898 that the accused could give sworn evidence on his own behalf. But he would be delighted to know that in recent years the pace of reform had quickened. He might think from the advance news of the recommendations of the Criminal Law Revision Committee strikingly confirmed by the publication of its Eleventh Report,[44] that the goal for which he had long striven was at last in sight, and that there would soon be established in our courts that natural system in which all logically relevant evidence would be admitted at trials and its weight there assessed.

The recommendations of the Criminal Law Reform Committee are indeed Benthamite in substance and in spirit. It will be found that nearly all the substance of the many changes now recommended to us had been argued for by

---

[44] Cmnd. 4991 (June 1972).

Bentham in 1828. The Committee's recommendations in relation to hearsay, privileged communications between spouses, corroboration, and the privilege against self-incrimination or the so-called right to silence, all these would gladden Bentham's heart, and all of them reduce in some measure, as Bentham would have wished, the protection afforded by the existing rules or practice to the accused at his trial. Undoubtedly the most contentious of these changes is the double inroad on the right to silence which the Committee recommends.[45] The first and most drastic of these is in the form of a provision that the judge, in deciding whether there is a case for the accused to answer, and the jury in considering its verdict may draw, where appropriate, adverse inferences from the silence of a suspect when interrogated or charged by the police about any matters which he seeks to rely on at his trial. The second, lesser, inroad is the provision that the jury, once it has been found that there is a case for the accused to answer, may draw such inferences from his refusal to give evidence at his trial.

Since 1898, when for the first time it became the general rule that the accused could, if he wished, give evidence at his trial, the interpretation which our law has given to the right to silence has ruled out all comment by the Prosecution on his failure to give evidence at his trial, and it has been difficult in view of the caution at present given by the police for the Prosecution to comment effectively on the accused's failure to tell to the police, when interrogated or charged by them, the story which he puts forward in his defence at the trial. Though the judge may comment on the accused's silence or refusal to give evidence at the trial, he must stop short of suggesting to the jury that the failure to give evidence or his silence under interrogation may in the circumstances constitute evidence of guilt.

Bentham would regard these restrictions, which will be abolished if the Committee's recommendations are accepted, as a kind of embargo on rationality, blinding the court to

---

[45] The text above gives only a simplified version of the Committee's recommendations in relation to trials on indictment. For the full detail and application of the proposed reforms to committal proceedings, summary trials and trials on indictment, see clauses 1 and 5 of the draft Bill annexed to the Report (p. 169), and paras. 1–52 and 109–13, and notes thereon at pp. 211–12 and 216.

what he thought was one of the plainest deliverances of the natural system, which he phrased thus: 'between delinquency on the one hand and silence under inquiry on the other, there is a manifest connection: a connection too natural not to be constant and inseparable.'[46] So he would certainly endorse these recommendations of the Criminal Law Reform Committee. For Bentham, as for the Committee, a suspect's silence under interrogation or the accused's refusal to give evidence at his trial is not to be regarded as an offence or contempt, but unless substantially explained may count as affirmative evidence against him.[47]

It is at this point that many who would follow Bentham with enthusiasm in his other criticisms of the mystery and complexities of English law and legal practice might begin to feel doubts, and perhaps to sense that in an exclusively utilitarian philosophy there is something very dangerous to contemporary as well as to older conceptions of civil liberties. Undoubtedly utilitarianism in Bentham and his followers' hands was a fountain of splendid reforms. It has had a noble history, ridding the law of much irrational and oppressive rubbish; but this same philosophy put forward as a sole criterion of the morality of legal institutions has a darker side. This shows itself in its willingness to make negotiable, for the sake of general social security, protections which many would consider to be the fundamental rights of all individuals against the State, including the citizen's right to remain silent when suspected or accused of crime and not to have his silence used as evidence against him.

So the present proposals to remove these protections from accused persons have stirred much controversy, and it may well clear our minds to know how Bentham saw the issues. He thought that this protection given to the accused rested on no rational principle at all, but partly on irrelevant memories of the Star Chamber,[48] and chiefly on two non-reasons. These were sentimentality which he called disparagingly 'the old woman's reason'[49] and a mistaken conception of fairness which he called 'the foxhunter's reason.'[50] The 'old woman's reason' insisted that it was bad and inhuman that any pressure

[46] *Works* VII 446. [47] *Works* VII 445.
[48] *Works* VII 455-6. [49] *Works* VII 452. [50] *Works* VII 454.

should be brought to bear upon a guilty person to contribute to his own conviction. The 'foxhunter's reason' was that the accused, innocent or guilty, must, like the fox when it is hunted by gentlemen, be given a fair chance to escape. This meant that we should make the contest between prosecutor and accused more nearly equal by making it as difficult as possible for the jury to learn of the naturally most cogent evidence of the accused's guilt. Lord Denman in his review of the French version of Bentham's work on evidence took the foxhunter's reason seriously and, as Bentham would think, irrationally. 'Human beings are never to be run down like beasts of prey, without respect of the laws of the chase. If society must make a sacrifice of one of its members, let us carve him as a feast fit for the gods, not a carcase for the hounds.'[51] Bentham did not overlook the danger that innocent persons exposed to questioning might be confused or trapped. But he thought that this danger arose mainly from hectoring or bullying methods of interrogation or cross-examination, or from the intimidating formalities and strange atmosphere of a criminal trial, which a decent legal system, following a natural procedure, would eliminate.[52] But he also thought that the common slogan that 'it is better that ten guilty men should be acquitted than one innocent man be convicted' diverted attention from the real utilitarian issue. Of course, if the acquittal of the guilty meant only that a criminal did not get his 'deserts' in the form of retribution, no innocent person should be jeopardized merely to stop that, because 'desert' and 'retribution' were, to Bentham, themselves mere mystifying superstitions: not reasons for

---

[51] *Edinburgh Review* 40 (1824) 186.

[52] *Works* VII 451. Bentham nonetheless thought that by the right to silence 'only are the guilty served' since the innocent would rarely avail themselves of such 'subterfuges' (*Works* VII 454). Hence there is nothing to support the suggestion that Bentham intended the right to silence to be maintained until the legal system had been reformed and the 'natural' procedure introduced. This suggestion is made tentatively by Professor Twining in his article questioning the description of the Committee's Report as 'Benthamite' ('The Way of the Baffled Medic: Prescribe First; Diagnose Later If At All', *Journal of the Society of Public Teachers of Law*, NS xii (1972) 348). Throughout Bentham considers the right to silence in unreformed systems where there are bad laws as well as good, and concludes that its weakening effect on good laws is a greater evil than the conviction of greater numbers of offenders against bad laws or of innocent persons to which its abolition might lead (*Works* VII 454, 457, 522, and see p. 38, n. 53 *infra*).

punishment but emotional reactions posing as reasons. The appropriate contrast, Bentham would insist, was not between the one innocent and the many guilty but between two sets of innocents:[53] those who might be wrongly convicted if the right to silence is withdrawn and those too often overlooked who become directly or indirectly the innocent victims of those criminals whom the law, because it concedes the right to silence, fails to incapacitate or fails to deter.

Bentham included among the criminals' innocent victims not only those directly injured but the vastly greater number of citizens to whom alarm and apprehension are caused by the thought of criminals at large. He thought that a rational calculation of the sufferings of innocent persons made a plain case for the abolition of the right to silence. Some of those who disagree accept that the issue is in principle to be settled by such a calculus of sufferings caused to the innocent, but simply dispute the facts, adding in, on the other side of the account, various indirect sufferings or evils besides those of innocent persons who are actually wrongly convicted.

It is, however, clear that the most ardent supporters of the right to silence do not talk this language of utility with its calculus of sufferings, but instead invoke a doctrine of individual moral rights against the State: moral rights which define those relationships between government and citizen which are worthy of free men. They urge that there is something profoundly wrong with a legal system which imposes on citizens, guilty of no crime, duties sanctioned by the risk of conviction to give an account of themselves to the police; and that a society where this was accepted with docility, even if it meant that the guilty never escaped conviction, would be a worse society than one where there was a right to silence even though some criminals escaped. No doubt there would be a limit: such rights might have to be suspended as in wartime if the scale of escape of the guilty threatened the fabric of society in which alone rights can be enjoyed. But the

---

[53] *Works* VII 522. In discussing the claim that innocent accused persons are protected by rules requiring corroboration Bentham contrasts the two sets: 'the innocents who scarce present themselves as by so much as scores or dozens engross the whole attention and pass for the whole world' and 'the innocents who ought to have presented themselves by millions, are overlooked and left out of account.'

analogy of war—war against crime—is not lightly to be invoked for the general ordering of our affairs.

For Bentham such talk of rights lessening the security of the majority which law affords, was not only like the pomps and ceremonies of the law, mere mystifying nonsense; it was also cruel because it jeopardized the majority, and he brought these two objections together when he said that such talk of rights overriding the dictates of 'reason and utility' was but 'the effusion of a hard heart on a cloudy mind'.[54]

So in conclusion I would say this. Bentham's utilitarianism has so long been a source of progressive social policy and the main intellectual support of the criticism of our law that we have not yet developed a theory of individual rights, comparable with utilitarian theory in clarity, in detailed articulation and in appeal to practical men. At present although we can point to institutions—like the presumption of innocence—which seem to embody such rights we have only the fragments of a theory. So it is true that on this subject as on others, that where Bentham fails to persuade, he still forces us to think.

[54] Bentham, 'Supply without Burthen' in *Economic Writings*, ed. Stark (London 1952), I 335.

II

BENTHAM AND BECCARIA

Bentham's debt to Beccaria[1] was great and is well known. Indeed, Bentham himself took the greatest pains to secure that all his readers should realize how greatly Beccaria had contributed to his own thought. Many of the phrases in which Bentham acknowledges his debt are eloquent and striking. It is true that in his old age Bentham professed himself uncertain whether he had first learnt from Priestley or from Beccaria, 'the sacred truth that the greatest happiness of the greatest number is the foundation of morals and legislation',[2] but he never had any doubt that it was Beccaria who had suggested to him the ways in which this general principle might be made precise and used in framing good laws. 'It was from Beccaria's little treatise on crimes and punishments that I drew as I well remember the first hint of the principle by which the precision and clearness and incontestableness of mathematical calculations are introduced for the first time into the field of morals.'[3] Here Bentham is referring to Beccaria's stress on the importance for any rational system of penal legislation of the distinctions between such properties of punishment as its intensity, duration, certainty, and proximity. Bentham took this idea—'this hint' as he calls it— and generalized it into a theory of the 'dimensions' not only of punishment but of all pleasures and pains. It thus became the source of Bentham's famous conception of a 'moral arithmetic'. On some matters, for example on the use of the

---

[1] Beccaria's *Dei delitti e delle pene* was first published in 1764. All references here to this work (hereafter *Crimes and Punishments*) are to the English translation, *On Crimes and Punishments* translated with introduction by H. Paolucci (The Library of Liberal Arts, Indianapolis 1963).

[2] *Works* X 142. Beccaria's phrase is 'La massima felicità divisa nel maggior numero' translated in the first English version of his work (1767) as 'the greatest happiness of the greatest number'. For the history of this phrase and Bentham's use of it see R. Shackleton, 'The greatest happiness of the greatest number' in *Studies in Voltaire and the Eighteenth Century*: xc (The Voltaire Foundation 1972) 1461.

[3] *Works* III 286-7.

death penalty, Bentham thought that Beccaria had said all that needed to be said: 'the more attention one gives to the punishment of death the more he will be inclined to adopt the opinion of Beccaria—that it ought to be disused. This subject is so ably discussed in his book that to treat it after him is a work that may well be dispensed with'.[4]

But Bentham admired Beccaria not only because he agreed with his ideas and was stimulated by them but also because of Beccaria's clear-headed conception of the *kind* of task on which he was engaged. According to Bentham, Beccaria was the first to embark on the criticism of law and the advocacy of reform without confusing this task with the description of the law that actually existed. He never pretended that the reforms which he advocated were already, in some transcendental sense, law or 'really' law; and so he made the distinction that Bentham himself continually stresses between what the law is and what it ought to be, or, as Bentham often describes it, between 'expository jurisprudence' and 'censorial jurisprudence'. 'Beccaria was the first writer whose work is "uniformly censorial."'[5] According to Bentham, previous writers such as Grotius, Puffendorf, and Vattel had, under the baneful influence of the doctrine of Natural Law, confused expository with censorial jurisprudence—the law that is with the law that ought to be. For this and other reasons Bentham spoke of Beccaria as being received by the intelligent as an angel from heaven would be by the faithful.[6]

However, these well-known passages in which Bentham acknowledges his debt to Beccaria do not by themselves give an adequate picture of the relationship between these two thinkers, and I propose to present in some detail the more important similarities and differences between them. But I must confess that I found the task more difficult than I anticipated and my account may very well be both too speculative and incomplete. The reasons for this are two fold. The volume of Bentham's work is enormous: his published work amounts to very nearly 6,000,000 words of which I myself can claim to have read no more than half; though that, I am sure, is a good deal more than most of my

---

[4] Bentham, *Theory of Legislation*, op. cit. (p. 25 n. 15 *supra*), pp. 353–4.
[5] *Works* I 150.   [6] Ibid. I 231 n. g.

English colleagues have read. There is of course a general index to the edition of Bentham's collected works published by Bowring in 1838-43 where there are listed a dozen or so references to Beccaria which are certainly very helpful. But this is an incomplete guide for various reasons. There are some important works of Bentham's which were not included in the Bowring edition and indeed there are manuscripts of importance which still await publication. But a more important difficulty is this: it is clear to any one well acquainted with Bentham's thought that Beccaria's influence on him was much deeper and more pervasive than could be disclosed by any list of passages however complete in which Bentham acknowledges Beccaria's influence by name. There are many ideas, I think, which Beccaria throws out, often in a rough and general form, which struck Bentham forcibly and which he elaborated with his characteristic passion for detailed analysis, classification, and minute subdivision. This of course he did in the case I have already mentioned of the various dimensions of pains and pleasures; but unless I am mistaken there are many other cases where he does the same without mentioning Beccaria's name. Let me give two examples of what may be unconscious borrowing. In a footnote to Chapter 4 of *Crimes and Punishments* Beccaria says:

The word 'obligation' is one of those that occur much more frequently in ethics than in any other science, and which are the abbreviated symbol (*segno abbreviativo*) of a rational argument and not of an idea. Seek an adequate idea of the word 'obligation' and you will fail to find it; reason about it and you will both understand yourself and be understood by others.[7]

Anyone who has studied closely Bentham's remarkable theory of logical fictions, which till recently was buried away in the less frequently read volumes of the Bowring edition, cannot fail to see that here Beccaria presents, no doubt in general and rough terms, the central part of a logical doctrine to which Bentham came to attach great importance. For in the analysis of law and morals Bentham frequently insisted that many of the most problematic concepts are expressed in words such as 'right', 'duty', and 'obligation' which cannot be defined by ordinary methods as

[7] Op. cit. 15, n. 20.

if they were like the names of concrete material things. It is a mistake to suppose that the same simple relationship exists between such words and reality as exists between a proper name and the bearer of the name. The reason for this is, as Beccaria says, because such words as obligation are 'abbreviated symbols'. This doctrine Bentham expands and explains as follows: instead of looking for a definition of such words taken alone Bentham says we must examine complete sentences in which they are used; so we must ask for the meaning not of the *word* 'obligation' but of the *statement* that a man has obligation, and search for a translation or synonym of such statements; for it is these translations or synonyms that the word obligation 'abbreviates'.[8] In this doctrine Bentham anticipated the ideas of Logical Constructions, Incomplete Symbols, and Definition in Use which are a marked feature of Bertrand Russell's philosophy and the forms of analytical philosophy which stem from it. Bentham thought that only in this way could the clouds of mystery and bad metaphysics which had surrounded the notions of rights and duties and obligations be dissipated. What to my mind makes it probable that this little footnote of Beccaria's in which he claims that obligation is an 'abbreviated symbol' stimulated Bentham's general doctrine is that when Bentham expounds his doctrine, as he does in many different places, he most frequently illustrates it with the example of obligation which he treats as an abbreviation for the statement that a man is likely to suffer a 'sanction' if he does not behave in some stipulated way.

Let me add another example, equally speculative, where Beccaria appears to me to have dropped hints which profoundly affected Bentham's thought. In the *Fragment on Government* and also in the *Theory of Legislation* Bentham ferociously attacks Blackstone and makes fun of various characteristic forms of argument used by conventional lawyers in defence of existing laws. Among these is the fallacy of drawing consequences from various legal fictions; 'a fiction' insists Bentham 'is not a reason for a law' and under this slogan he denounces the use of the fiction that a

---

[8] *Works* III 160, 180-1, 217; VIII 125-7, 206-7, 247-8, and *Fragment* Chap. V, para. 6 in *CW* 494, n.b. and *OLG* 294-5.

traitor's blood is corrupt to defend the rule that the property of a convicted traitor cannot be inherited by his descendants and must be forfeited to the state[9] and the similar use by Blackstone of the fiction that the whole people are present in the House of Commons to defend the rule that there is no need to promulgate or publish to the people the enactments of Parliament.[10] Readers of Beccaria will see that these are fallacies of the same form as that identified by him in Chapter 8 of his book where he criticizes the rule that the evidence of a condemned criminal is to be excluded. 'He is civilly dead', say the peripatetic jurists, and a dead man is incapable of any action.[11] Beccaria says that this is the use of 'an empty metaphor'[12] and to sustain it many men's lives have been sacrificed. In the same chapter Beccaria refers to many 'senseless maxims'[13] which have supported iniquities and absurdities of legal practice such as the maxim that 'in atrocissimis leviores conjecturae sufficiunt et licet judici jura transgredi'. Bentham, it will be remembered, compiled into a book called the *Book of Fallacies*, which is as instructive as it is entertaining, all the more important of such 'senseless maxims' which have been the support of bad laws and bad political arguments.

If I am wrong in tracing in these examples the actual influence of Beccaria on Bentham let them be taken merely of examples of similarity of their thoughts. But I myself in general am inclined to accept the hypothesis of actual influence because of the following facts. It is clear to me after examining the relevant dates that Bentham must have read Beccaria when he was both young and impressionable enough to be very open to influence and yet was already deeply engaged in thinking out his own vast and detailed theories of punishment. The first English translation of *Crimes and Punishments* was published in 1767 when Bentham was nineteen: now Bentham's first detailed survey of the subject of punishment touching on many of the same topics as Beccaria's book and mentioning Beccaria frequently and usually with praise is the *Rationale of Punishment*. It is true that

---

[9] Bentham, *Theory of Legislation*, 71.
[10] *Fragment*, Preface in *CW* 406, n. l.   [11] Beccaria, op. cit. 23.
[12] Loc. cit.   [13] Op. cit. 24 n.

this was not published in England until 1830[14] though it had appeared in French in Paris in 1811.[15] But as Bentham's translator Dumont tells us in his preface to the French version of this work the main manuscripts on which it was based were written by Bentham as early as 1775. Bentham was then only twenty-seven and Beccaria's book had been available in English for eight years. So it is clear that Bentham must have conceived and thought about his first considerable work on punishment while still very young and fresh from the study of Beccaria's already famous book. It is therefore likely that Beccaria's influence was present at many points in Bentham's work even where he was not mentioned.

I shall now leave these rather speculative themes to identify some of the major similarities and differences between these two writers. First and foremost I would put something which is distinctive of the Enlightenment in all countries: namely that such a topic as the forms and severity of punishment is a matter to be *thought* about, to be *reasoned* about, and *argued*, and not merely a matter to be left to feeling and sentiment. Both Bentham and Beccaria are plainly of the view that many of the useless barbarities which disgraced the penal systems of their time were maintained only because as Beccaria says 'reason has almost never been the legislator of nations'.[16] Men resorted to hideously severe punishments and especially to the death penalty, partly to relieve their feelings of hostility and hatred of the offender and partly to save themselves the labour of thinking out the effects of different forms of penalty. Bentham generalizes this point by inquiring 'What is it to offer a good reason with respect to a law?'[17] and among the several different answers which he rejects is that the legislator's hostile feeling or 'antipathy' may in itself be a reason. Antipathy, says Bentham, is not a reason and here he not only acknowledges his debt to Beccaria but the latter's courage. 'Reasoning by antipathy is most common upon subjects connected with the penal law: for we have antipathies against actions reputed to be crimes; antipathies against individuals reputed to be criminals . . . this

---

[14] Bowring republished it in *Works* I 388–532.
[15] Under the title of *Théorie des peines et des récompenses*.
[16] Beccaria, op. cit. 39.
[17] Bentham, *Theory of Legislation*, 66.

false principle has reigned like a tyrant throughout this vast province of law. Beccaria first dared openly to attack it.'[18]

So much for the great conviction which Bentham and Beccaria shared that punishment, like every other institution of social life, both could and should be subjected to rational criticism and not left to the untrustworthy guides of feelings of antipathy or of sympathy. If we now consider the general principles which according to these writers should determine the severity of punishment we find a striking measure of agreement. Here too Bentham seems to take Beccaria's loosely formulated principles and project them into his own precise, detailed and sometimes pedantic idiom. Both insist on the uselessness of the traditional savageries of penal law: both insist that the punishment to be used should be the least which is sufficient to counterbalance the advantage men hope to derive from their crimes and both draw the same convincing picture of the ways in which excessively severe punishment may actually increase crime. It may do so by hardening men to the spectacle of cruelty when they see it employed by the state; it may do so by making it impossible to arrange scales of proportionate penalties which will induce men to commit lesser rather than greater crimes and it may do so by providing men with an incentive to commit fresh crimes rather than be caught and tortured for those that they have committed. It is typical of Bentham that he presents these ideas in the form of a detailed economic model.[19] His counterpart to Beccaria's principle that we should use the least punishment sufficient to exceed the advantage of a crime is termed by Bentham the principle of 'frugality' or of economy: a balance sheet is to be constructed in which the pain of punishment is treated as an expense hazarded for the sake of an anticipated profit which is the prevention of harmful crime; and the expense to be hazarded is the least which is likely to bring in the anticipated gain. In these economic terms Bentham develops a number of rules for the 'measure' of punishment many of which are implicit in Beccaria's book.

When Bentham deals as he does at great length with the *quality* as distinguished from the severity or quantity of punishment much that he says is again a detailed extension

---

[18] Ibid. 76.   [19] *Works* I 398–9.

of some of Beccaria's ideas. He endorses Beccaria's principle
that punishment should be both speedy and certain,[20] not
only for reasons of humanity but because speed and certainty are required to fortify the association of ideas between
punishment and crime. Both writers considered this associa-
tive link[21] a vital part of what was for them the main mech-
anism of punishment, namely, deterrence by example, and
consequently both insisted on the importance of an analogy
between a crime and its punishment. To this topic Beccaria
devoted half a page;[22] Bentham in his earliest work on
punishment devotes to it and to the related topic of retalia-
tion two chapters carefully distinguishing the different
possible sources of analogy and suggesting forms of punishment often repellent to modern taste. The same instrument
may be used in punishment as was used in committing the
crime; the same injury may be inflicted on the criminal as he
inflicted on his victim; the punishment may be applied to the
same bodily member as was used by the criminal in his crime;
if the criminal used a disguise in order to commit his crime
a picture of this disguise might be imprinted on the criminal's
body and the fabricator of base coin might have an impression of the coin made on some conspicuous part of his
face.[23] In considering these grim and sometimes grotesque
analogies proposed by Bentham it must be remembered that
when he wrote the crimes for which he proposed them were
punishable with death.

Apart from their striking measure of agreement concerning the principles determining the severity and manner of
punishment and many other aspects of penal law, Beccaria
and Bentham agree in their general views concerning the
nature of the rule of law and the proper function of legislator and judge. These views are not characteristic of English
or American legal thinking and for this reason Bentham and
his illustrious pupil Austin have often seemed to English
lawyers un-English in their general approach. I refer of course
to the constant insistence of both Beccaria and Bentham that
the law should consist of general enactments of the legislature
and that these should be both as comprehensive and as clear

[20] Beccaria, op. cit. Chaps XIX, XX; Bentham, *Works* I 401-2, 558-9.
[21] Beccaria, op. cit. Chap. XIX; Bentham, *Works* I 403-11.
[22] Beccaria, op. cit. Chap. XIX.   [23] Bentham, *Works* I 407-11.

as possible and that judicial law-making and discretion even under the name of interpretation should be reduced to the minimum.[24] In their view the function of the judge is to decide whether or not laws have been broken and not to make laws; he should, as Montesquieu thought, be the faithful mouth-piece of the legislator. Both writers hated *ex post facto* judicial legislation and thought it vital that men should be able to know beforehand what the laws required of them and what the costs of disobedience were likely to be.[25] Both denounced various frauds used to conceal the fact that where the laws are obscure a decision is often an act of retrospective judicial legislation. Thus Beccaria criticizes the invocation of 'the spirit of the law', which he says might be the product of a judge's good or bad logic or his good or bad digestion,[26] and Bentham compares punishing a man for disobedience to a law the meaning of which is only determined when the judge decides his case to punishing a dog.[27] Of course Bentham's hatred of judge-made law and his passion for clear and detailed legislative codes was in part the product of his experience of the Common Law system of case law; whereas Beccaria was appalled by the looseness and vagueness of codes and statutes. But none the less their views on this subject and sometimes their words are very similar; both contrast the spirit of tyranny with the spirit of literacy or of clear comprehensive legislative enactments and think the latter necessary for the government of a society of free men.

Though many other important similarities exist between Bentham and Beccaria I must now turn to the other side of the picture. Not everything that Bentham said of Beccaria consisted of praise. He frequently criticizes not only specific ideas and propositions of Beccaria such as that the duration of a punishment is a more effective deterrent than its intensity[28] or that criminals should not be encouraged to betray each other[29] but he also attacks the very style of Beccaria's thought and the philosophical assumptions which he finds in it. Two sorts of criticism may be distinguished. It

[24] Beccaria, op. cit. Chaps. IV, V; Bentham, *Works* I 323, VII 311–15.
[25] Beccaria, op. cit. Chap. XXV; Bentham, *Works* I 326, V 442.
[26] Beccaria, op. cit. Chap. IV.
[27] Bentham, *Works* V 235, 519–20.
[28] Ibid. I 441–5.   [29] Ibid. II 224.

is plain that Bentham thought Beccaria was rather a lazy man: that he shrank from those laborious and infinitely detailed tasks in which he himself delighted. Bentham always thought it necessary to accompany his criticism of the law with detailed plans for reform in order to demonstrate that reform was both possible and quite different from the merely destructive activity of the anarchist or revolutionary. So he complains that though Beccaria used against the existing abuses of the law 'arms which were of celestial temper'[30] and had done much to destroy bad laws he had done little towards the establishment of a new and more equitable rule. So too, though he welcomed Beccaria's insistence on the need for a proper *proportion* between crime and punishment, he reproached him for not explaining and analysing this idea. Beccaria's statement on this point in the absence of a detailed account of what 'proportion' means was, says Bentham, 'more oracular than instructure'.[31] It is easy indeed to imagine how shocked Bentham must have been to find Beccaria giving as a reason for not examining and distinguishing the various kinds of crime and modes of punishment the fact that the result would be a catalogue of enormous and boring detail—*un dettaglio immenso e noioso*.[32] No doubt these words—'un dettaglio immenso e noioso'—aptly describe many pages of Bentham's writings, but Bentham would not have thought them for that reason unnecessary in the great campaign for reform.

More important is the fact that Bentham found in Beccaria a terminology and certain specific forms of argument which to him seemed laden with confusion and bad metaphysics. Not only does Beccaria set his own utilitarian doctrines of punishment within the framework of a theory of social contract but he speaks freely of men's natural rights and of the 'nature of things'. Bentham refers to Beccaria's 'false sources'[33] of reasoning and gives as an example his use of the 'obscure notion' of relations. Beccaria objected to the interrogation of an accused person on the ground that to interrogate a man in order to find out whether he is innocent

---

[30] Bentham, *Theory of Legislation*, 76.
[31] Bentham, *Works*, I 399.
[32] Beccaria, op. cit. Chap. I.
[33] Bentham, *Theory of Legislation*, 67.

or guilty is to force him to accuse himself and this, says Beccaria, is 'to confound all relations'.[34] Bentham complains that these abstract terms excite no ideas in his mind and they cannot be translated into the language of Utility. 'I am absolutely indifferent about relations,' says Bentham, 'pleasures and pains are what interest me'.[35] Again it will be remembered that Beccaria urged that society has no right to impose the death penalty because he thinks that men could not have surrendered the right to live when entering into that social contract from which sovereignty and the laws derive. Bentham in his own purely utilitarian criticism of the death penalty which shows he had closely studied Beccaria's chapter on the same subject does not even mention the question of society's right to inflict it[36] because for him the whole notion of a natural or non-legal right limiting the scope or range of positive law was an absurdity. In Bentham's view the only questions which could be meaningfully asked about rights were first, whether they were actually conferred by positive law and secondly, whether reasons of utility required that the law should confer such rights. Perhaps it is not fanciful to believe that Bentham had Beccaria's arguments against the death penalty in mind when he wrote the following passage which is to be found amongst Bentham's still unpublished manuscripts:

It is a situation full of unhappiness when poeple are agitated by doubts which are of such a nature as to admit of no solution . . . as when the terms in which they conceive them have in reality no meaning. The word 'right' when disjoined from positive law and expediency is of that sort: he who persists in seeking a third sense for it must expect only to plunge himself more and more into darkness and distraction.[37]

It is plain from these and many other examples that if Beccaria was a utilitarian his utilitarianism was qualified in ways which Bentham thought absurd. Quite apart from the doctrine of social contract and of the rights created by it there is in Beccaria a respect for the dignity and value of the individual person which is absent in Bentham. This absence indeed at times gives to some of Bentham's speculations an

---

[34] Beccaria, op. cit. Chap. XII, 31.
[35] Bentham, *Theory of Legislation*, 69.
[36] Beccaria, op. cit. Chap. XVI; Bentham, *Works*, I 525-32.
[37] UC. XCVI, and see Chap. IV. *infra*.

almost inhuman flavour; as if he was concerned with mani-
pulable and predictable animals or machines—pleasure and
pain machines—rather than men. Indeed one can find con-
trasting texts on this very point, though too much importance
should not be attached to them as they relate to very different matters. Beccaria says 'there is no liberty when the laws
permit that in some circumstances a man can cease to be a
person and become a thing.'[38] Bentham never appealed to
any such considerations. His attack on slavery for example
was conducted entirely in terms of utility and was based
mainly on the fact that mass slave labour in the end would
be found to be unprofitable to society.[39] On the other hand,
when various objections were made to his own schemes
especially for the education of the young that under them
men were regarded as things rather than as persons, he
replied: 'Call them soldiers, call them monks, call them
machines; so they were but happy ones I should not care.'[40]
I think that very often where Bentham and Beccaria differ
in detail this is traceable to Beccaria's conviction that what
may be done in the name of utility should be limited by consideration of what befits the dignity of a man. Certainly
Bentham's indifference to this kind of consideration is pal-
pable at many points: it is to be seen not only in the lengths
that he was prepared to go to make punishments analogous
with their crimes or to encourage treachery among criminals.
One could never imagine Beccaria, had he considered the
topic, arguing as Bentham did that a wife's right to the con-
tinuance of a marriage 'when time had effaced the attractions
which were its first motive' was based simply on the principle
that unless a wife's past services to her husband were rewarded in this way it would be impossible or léss easy to
obtain such services.[41]

The difference between Beccaria and Bentham on these
matters concerns some very fundamental philosophical
issues; at the root of their divergencies lie very different conceptions of the idea of justice which Bentham considered to
be merely a subordinate aspect of utility (whereas Beccaria
contrasted it with utility) and very different estimates of the

[38] Beccaria, op. cit., Chap. XXVII, 69.
[39] Bentham, *Works* I 343–7.
[40] Ibid. IV 64.   [41] Bentham, *Theory of Legislation*, 192.

intelligibility of the idea of individual rights not created by positive law or social convention.[42] Divergence on these issues is a feature of contemporary discussions both in England and the United States of the ability of utilitarianism to accommodate the moral importance of the fact that humanity is divided into separate individual persons and of the need for a doctrine of 'natural' human rights as a constraint on the pursuit of aggregate utility at the cost of individuals.

[42] See Chap. IV *infra*.

III

THE UNITED STATES OF AMERICA[1]

I

In 1776, the year of the American Declaration of Independence, and an *annus mirabilis* in English letters, Jeremy Bentham opened an epoch in political and legal theory; for not only did he announce in *A Fragment on Government*, published anonymously in that year, his first formulation of the principle of utility, according to which, 'It is the greatest happiness of the greatest number that is the measure of right and wrong,'[2] but in the same year, 1776, he fired the first shot, in Lind's *Answer to the Declaration of the American Congress*,[3] of a long sceptical campaign conducted against the doctrine of natural and unalienable rights of man. In legal theory Bentham's sharp severance in the *Fragment* between law as it is and law as it ought to be and his insistence that the foundations of a legal system are properly described in the morally neutral terms of a general habit of obedience opened the long positivist tradition in English jurisprudence.

It may be that the epoch which Bentham thus opened is now closing: certainly among American political and legal philosophers utilitarianism is on the defensive, if not on the run, in the face of theories of justice which[4] in many ways resemble the doctrine of the unalienable rights of man; and there are now new forms of old theories holding that there are important conceptual connections between law and morality obscured by the positivist tradition.[5]

---

[1] I am deeply indebted to Professor J.H. Burns for many constructive criticisms and for placing at my disposal his unrivalled knowledge of the Bentham MSS.

[2] *Fragment*, Preface to the First Edition in *CW* 393.

[3] [John Lind], *An Answer to the Declaration of the American Congress* (1776). See p. 63 *infra*.

[4] See Robert Nozick, *Anarchy, State and Utopia* (1974); and John Rawls, *A Theory of Justice* (1971).

[5] See, e.g. Dworkin, *Taking Rights Seriously*, op. cit. (p. 28 n. 25 *supra*) viii, 46 ff., 105 ff., 338–45.

In the *Fragment*, Bentham makes no explicit reference to America but in fact we know, from a source about which I shall have more to say later, that all the rights and wrongs, legal and moral, of the American colonists' case against the British government and their claims to independence, had engaged Bentham's closest attention during much of the time when he was writing the *Fragment*.

The story of Bentham's concern with America is in fact a complex and, in the end, a rather sad one. In it there are two distinct phases: the first was one of antipathy and rejection, both of the legal arguments of the Americans' case before the break with Britain and of the philosophy of the Declaration of Independence which made the break; the second was a phase of enthusiasm and, in many ways, indiscriminate admiration of America after the Union and of its developing democracy. From 1817 when he first publicly took up the cause of reform of the British constitution, the injunction 'Look to America' became Bentham's favourite slogan[6] in urging his own countrymen towards democracy and the full radical programme of manhood suffrage, secret ballots, short parliaments, and equal electoral districts.[7]

II

The first phase of this story, the phase of Bentham's hostility to the American cause, has some curious features; not the least curious of them is the fact that though arguments from Bentham's pen against the American colonists' case were actually published, they were published not under his own name but as part of the work of another remarkable man whose name is rarely mentioned in the history of this period. This was John Lind, the son of an impoverished Anglican clergyman whose affairs had been looked after by Bentham's father, the attorney Jeremiah Bentham. As some very vivid and moving letters testify, Bentham formed with Lind a

[6] For examples see *Plan of Parliamentary Reform* (1817), in *Works* III 433, 447, 472, 494; *The King against Edmonds and Others: Set Down for Trial at Warwick on the 29th of March 1820* (1822), in *Works* II 239, 246; and the earlier *Draught of a Code for the Organization of the Judicial Establishment in France* (1790), in *Works* IV 287, 363.

[7] Plan of Parliamentary Reform, in *Works* III 435 *passim*.

most intimate friendship. Indeed, on Bentham's side it was a passionate one, so that when the friendship cooled after a quarrel, Bentham could write sadly to Lind, 'There was a time when I doubted whether, so long as you were alive, I could live without you. It became necessary for me to try: I have tried and I have succeeded.'[8] Lind was an interesting and attractive figure, energetic and intelligent with a taste and gift for polemics. He was very much a man of the world and indeed of fashion, generous and high-spirited, somewhat slap-dash by Bentham's standards; his attraction for Bentham had certainly something of the attraction of opposites. His qualities emerge plainly enough from the barest description of his career. He was born in 1737 and was thus eleven years older than Bentham. When Bentham came to Queen's College Oxford as a precocious child of twelve, Lind then at Balliol aged twenty-three called on him and reported to Bentham's father that the minute figure at which the whole university was staring had in him, as Lind put it, *multum in parvo* and all was well with him.[9] After taking his degree, Lind took holy orders and in 1761 went out to Constantinople as chaplain to the Levant Company. Here he lived for six years and was dismissed from his post for 'being too agreeable', as Bentham said, to the British ambassador's mistress.[10] He then abandoned holy orders, leaving his clergyman's habit to be sold in the bazaar, and went to Poland, first as tutor to the king's nephew Prince Stanislaus Poniatowski, but his energy and intelligence attracted the attention of the king who made him the governor of his Military Cadet School. After serving very successfully for six years, Lind returned with a pension to England in 1772 and acted as agent and, in all but name, as minister for Poland. In 1773 he renewed his friendship with Bentham and was called to the English Bar in 1776. The two became fast friends and collaborators, and it was Lind who first suggested the project of an attack on Blackstone and a detailed critical examination of the famous

---

[8] Letter from Jeremy Bentham to John Lind, 9 Dec. 1775, in *The Correspondence of Jeremy Bentham*, ed. Timothy L.S. Sprigge (1968) in *CW* I 289 (hereinafter cited as *Bentham Correspondence*).

[9] Letter from John Lind to Jeremiah Bentham, 17 Nov. 1760, in *Betham Correspondence* I 22.

[10] *Fragment* in *CW* 519, Historical Preface Intended for the Second Edition.

Commentaries and who wrote the first draft of the opening chapter of what eventually became Bentham's *Comment on the Commentaries*,[11] of which the *Fragment on Government* was itself an offshoot.

Though they were occupied with these hostilities against Blackstone, the two friends were also participants in the great dispute of the day with the American colonies. In 1775 and 1776, Lind published three works in defence of the British government's policy and for these won the favour of Lord North and Lord Mansfield. To each of these works Bentham contributed anonymously in different ways. The first of them, published in May 1775, under the title of *Remarks on the Principal Acts of the Thirteenth Parliament of Great Britain*,[12] was designed to show, by an exhaustive review both of the charters granted to the colonies and the history of British legislation as well as by examination of constitutional principles, that Parliament had had full power to enact the so-called 'Intolerable Acts' of 1774—including the act shutting the port of Boston—which had aroused such great indignation in America.[13] Bentham not only spent months, during which time he lived in Lind's house, helping him to revise his first drafts for publication of this work, but contributed two pages setting the structure of the book and defining with great precision the issues to be discussed in it, distinguishing between points of law, points of historical fact, and the merits of the legislation in question. But apart from the contribution of specific passages, the whole work is full of Bentham's thought and may be regarded as the first published version of many of his leading ideas.

The main theoretical argument of the book concerns the legislative powers of Parliament and attempts to show that, contrary to the cry of 'no taxation without representation', there was in fact no reason for insisting that representation

[11] The edition of the *Comment on the Commentaries* in *Comment* in *CW* includes Lind's drafts and an account of their collaboration.

[12] [John Lind], *Remarks on the Principal Acts of the Thirteenth Parliament of Great Britain by the Author of Letters concerning the Present State of Poland* (1775). For Bentham's description of his part in this work see *Works* X 62–4 and *Fragment* (Preface for Second Edition) in *CW* 520.

[13] Lind's book dealt with four acts of 1774: The Boston Port Act; the Massachusetts Bay Regulation Act; the Impartial Administration of Justice Act; and the Quebec Act.

and taxation were inseparable. The idea that they were so arose, according to Lind,[14] from a misconception of the nature of property as something that belonged to individuals independently of the law. On the basis of this misconception there had developed the further erroneous idea that when the subject pays taxes he is making a gift of what is his and which, since it is a gift, requires his consent. This is a misconception since there is no natural property; 'that *only* is my property', Lind explained, 'which the legislature declares to be so.' 'Take away the fence which the law has set around this thing . . . and where would your right or property be then?'[15] So when taxes are imposed the law is simply drawing a line, assigning part of the available common stock of the community to the support of government and the general needs of the community, and part to individuals. How much should be allowed to the community by way of taxes and how much to individuals as private property, and what the scope of property rights should be, all this is a matter for argument and for the law to settle. These ideas are of course now familiar to us from Bentham's later published work elaborating the idea that there was no 'natural' property[16] and developing utilitarian principles of taxation policy.[17] But the idea that all property rights are the creation of the law, which here was used against the claim that taxation and representation were inseparable, was, for Lind, borrowing (as he acknowledged) from Bentham, only a part of a wider general theme about the nature of rights. This general theme was that the whole conception of a right which is not a legal right or of rights which are antecedent to the law and limits what the law may properly do either by way of taxation or otherwise was nonsense; indeed it was a contradiction which Bentham later compared to the idea of a 'species of cold heat, a sort of dry moisture, a kind of resplendent darkness' and said that men resort to talk of non-legal or natural rights when they wish to get their own way without arguing for it. Such language, Bentham said, is the 'effusion of a hard heart

---

[14] John Lind, *supra* n. 12, at 54–6.
[15] Ibid. 71, 56.
[16] See, e.g., *Principles of the Civil Code*, in *Works* I 297, 308; and *OLG* 255.
[17] See, e.g., *Manual of Political Economy*, in *Works* III 31, 75–80.

operating upon a cloudy mind.'[18] So here in this early work
Lind voices Bentham's doctrine by saying, 'I know of *no*
other rights in a state of civil society,' save those that are
created by the law. 'The terms of *natural* and *inherent* rights,
when applied to men in such a state, are to my understanding,
perfectly unintelligible. . . . I think the *Citizen* is to look for
his *rights* in the laws of his country.'[19]

Apart from this, what is most important for the student of
Bentham's thought in this work is that though it is impregnated with Bentham's ideas, there is no assertion or discussion
of the idea that a sovereign legislature could not be in principle subject to legal limitations.[20] So in this work there is
no invocation of the famous passage from Blackstone's *Commentaries* so often thundered forth against the recalcitrant
Americans. 'There is and must be in all [governments] a
supreme, irresistible, absolute, uncontrolled authority, in
which the *jura summi imperii*, or the rights of sovereignty,
reside.'[21]

These words of Blackstone were published in 1765, and
by the time the spate of pamphlets on the American question
had become a flood on both sides of the Atlantic, defenders
of the British government's policy had come to think not
merely that Parliament had unlimited legislative powers as a
matter of English constitutional law but that it was a general
necessary and indeed self-evident truth that government by
law could not be limited by law. To this flood Dr Johnson
in 1775 contributed a sonorous but somewhat ill-tempered
pamphlet, *Taxation no Tyranny*, written to confute those
whom he termed the American 'zealots of anarchy' and their
English supporters whose pro-American 'antipatriotick prejudices,' he declared, were 'the abortions of folly impregnated
by faction' and 'produced against the standing order of

[18] *Supply without Burthen*, in Bentham's *Economic Writings*, ed. Stark, I
283, 335. See Chap. IV *infra* for Bentham's critique of the concept of non-legal
and natural rights.
[19] John Lind, *supra*, n. 12, 191.
[20] There is, on the contrary, the admission that the terms of charters granted
to the original colonists, though granted by the King alone, are binding on the
whole legislature since such grants are made by the King in his 'procuratorial
capacity' as Parliament's agent: ibid. 30–8, 79–81.
[21] William Blackstone, *Commentaries on the Laws of England* I (1765) 49.
See also, 'that absolute despotic power, which must in all governments reside
somewhere': ibid. 156.

nature.' Here Johnson in effect produced a layman's version of Blackstone's principle: 'all government is ultimately and essentially absolute . . . in sovereignty there are no gradations. . . . there can be no limited government. There must, in every society, be some power or other, which . . . enacts laws or repeals them, erects or annuls judicatures, extends or contracts privileges, exempt itself from question or control, and bounded only by physical necessity.'[22]

More than fifty years later these assertions were to find an echo in John Austin's claim that legally limited government was a contradiction in terms.[23] But Bentham's thoughts on this matter as they first appeared in the *Fragment on Government* were in fact much more complex than Blackstone's or Austin's. They were subtle, hesitant, and at times obscure. He was convinced that the conception of the impossibility of legal limitation on supreme legislative power was mistaken since he thought it could not be reconciled with the patent facts of history, ancient and modern, which presented many examples of federal states where no legally unlimited legislature was to be found, among which he noted the Dutch provinces, the German empire, the Swiss cantons, as well as the Achaean League of ancient Greece.[24] So the unqualified statements of Blackstone and Dr. Johnson were wrong. None the less, Bentham had shifting views on this matter and found great difficulty in reconciling with his own general imperative theory of law the idea of constitutionally limited government and the possibility that an enactment of a supreme legislature might be outside its powers and held legally void. For according

---

[22] Samuel Johnson, *Taxation no Tyranny: An Answer to the Resolution and Address of the American Congress* (1775) in *The Works of Samuel Johnson, LL.D.*, 225, 234 (Oxford edn. 1825). The same principles were expressed in many pamphlets of the period: e.g. 'In all forms of government, so long as the powers exist, the degree of power is the same; in all, alike absolute', *Experience Preferable to Theory: An Answer to Dr. Price's Observations on the Nature of Civil Liberty, the Principles of Government and the Justice and Policy of the War with America*, (1770), 10. 'No maxim in policy is more universally admitted, than that a supreme and uncontroulable power must exist somewhere in every State.— This ultimate power, though justly dreaded and reprobated in the person of *one man*, is the first spring in every Political Society', [James Macpherson], *The Rights of Great Britain Asserted Against the Claims of America: Being an Answer to the Declaration of the American Congress*, (1776), 3.

[23] John Austin, *The Province of Jurisprudence Determined and the Uses of the Study of Jurisprudence*, ed. Hart (1954), 254.

[24] *Fragment* Chap. IV, para. 34, in *CW* 489; cf. *OLG* 70-1.

to Bentham's imperative theory, all law is the expression, direct or indirect, of the will of the sovereign legislator whose powers are not conferred by any law, as those of his subordinates are, and so cannot be limited by any law as the powers of his subordinates can. Bentham wrestled with great honesty and tenacity with this conflict between his general theory of law and the facts. He does so first in the *Fragment*, and then in his masterpiece of analytical jurisprudence *Of Laws in General*, and later in the incomplete *Constitutional Code*.[25] He resorted to a variety of very different ideas (which I examine elsewhere)[26] to explain the possibility of legally limited government, but all his attempts at solutions of the problem run into great difficulties and fail to account for the phenomenon that laws issued by a supreme legislature might be held by courts to be ultra vires and void: a possibility which Bentham envisaged in the *Fragment*[27] twenty-seven years before *Marbury* v. *Madison* was decided by the United States Supreme Court. In fact a far more fundamental transformation of Bentham's imperative theory of all law as an expression of the legislative will is required for the explanation of constitutionally limited government than is afforded by the various patchwork additions to the imperative theory which he made to cope with the problem. The minimum required must be the admission that the notion of law be extended to include those principles according to which the courts treat the satisfaction of certain conditions, substantive as well as procedural, as criteria of the validity of a legislature's enactments, even though these principles are not themselves the product of the sovereign legislator's will and so are not law according to a strictly imperative theory.

So much for Lind's first book written with Bentham's aid. In the next year, 1776, Lind followed up his defence of the British government's American policy with an attack on a prominent advocate of the American cause, Richard Price, the non-conformist minister, economist, and philosopher. Price had supported the colonists' case with his *Observations on the Nature of Civil Liberty, The Principles of Government, and the Justice and Policy of the War with America*,

---

[25] *Fragment* Chap. IV, paras. 31-3, in *CW* 487-8; *OLG* 18 notes a, b.; *Works* IX 119-24.
[26] See Chap. IX *infra*.   [27] *Fragment* Chap. IV, para. 31, in *CW* 487.

published early in 1776.[28] This was an attempt to demonstrate, on the basis of a theory of a natural right to liberty, that democracy, direct or indirect, was the only legitimate form of government. Price defined liberty as 'self-government' and for him laws made without the participation of those governed reduced subjects to the condition of slavery. So the maxim by which sound political thought should be guided was 'every man his own legislator'. On Bentham, Price had a profoundly irritating effect. Price's slogan 'every man his own legislator' seemed to him the height of absurdity and years later, in explaining why he had taken the government's side against the Americans who had so reasonable a cause, Bentham said, 'Dr. Price with his self-government made me an anti-American.'[29]

The looseness of Price's arguments made his book an excellent target for Lind's polemical talents, and in 1776 he published a detailed attack, first in the form of letters to a newspaper and then in book form.[30] Though Bentham did not make written contributions to this work, it is full of his doctrines and references to the *Fragment* published three months earlier, and it resounds with many of Bentham's most famous phrases including 'the greatest happiness of the greatest number.'[31] Lind's book confronted Price with the argument, admittedly borrowed from Bentham,[32] that 'liberty is the name of nothing positive' but is merely the absence of coercion, and it contains such leading Benthamite ideas as that the authority of government depends on a habit; that duty is created by punishment; and the expression 'a right' is a purely legal term so that where there is law there is no

---

[28] Price's work was published in Philadelphia as well as in England and enjoyed a success comparable to Thomas Paine's *Common Sense*. For Price's conception of liberty and democracy see Morton White, *The Philosophy of the American Revolution* (Oxford 1978), 262 ff.

[29] UC CLXX 175 (1793).

[30] The *Gazetteer and New Daily Advertiser*, 2, 21, 25, 27, 29 Mar.; 1, 4, 9, Apr., 1776. The letters are signed 'Attilius'. Lind's book appeared anonymously as *Three Letters to Dr. Price Containing Remarks on His Observations on the Nature of Civil Liberty* . . . , by a *Member* of Lincoln's Inn (1776).

[31] Bentham himself used this phrase for the first time in his Preface to the *Fragment* in *CW* 393. For his subsequent use of it see Chap. II *supra*, p. 40 n. 2.

[32] This acknowledgement is made in the letter to the *Gazetteer* of 29 Mar. (where it includes also the borrowing of the analysis of the nature of a right) and in the later book, [John Lind], *supra* (n. 30), 16 n. See *OLG* 253, for Bentham's identification of liberty with absence of coercion.

right.[33] There is even an anticipation here of Bentham's suggestion that in some contexts the statement that a man had a natural moral or nonlegal right might have a meaning and where this was so it was a misleading way of stating that it was fit and expedient that a certain legal right should be established.[34]

The most important ideas which emerge from Lind's exchange with Price concern the notion of a free government.[35] For Price, arguing the American case, a government is a mere despotism and its subjects are in a condition of slavery unless two conditions are satisfied. First the powers of the government must be recognized as limited, and secondly the legislators must be the whole male adult population or their democratically chosen representatives. For Price the merely negative liberty granted by the law to the citizen when it prohibits coercion is not enough for real freedom. If the law allows and protects such liberties, this is not free government but merely government under which liberty happens to be enjoyed, as a slave might enjoy a precarious liberty under an indulgent master. Civil liberty must be enjoyed as a right secured by the limitations of the legislature's powers and by a fully democratic constitution. In reply to this, Lind used[36] ideas which appear in an expanded form in the *Fragment on Government*[37] and urges that there is no absurdity at all in saying that the legislature of a free country is omnipotent. The distinction between free and despotic government is not to be sought in any limitation of governmental power, but in the manner in which the whole power is distributed amongst those who must combine to exercise it, and in other political arrangements to secure that the exercise of govern-

---

[33] [John Lind], *supra* (n. 30), 105, 'in the habit of acknowledging our authority'. See also ibid. 21, 141 citing the *Fragment*.

[34] See Chap. IV *infra*, p. 88, for details of this suggestion and the echo of it in John Stuart Mill's account of moral rights.

[35] [John Lind], *supra* (n. 30), 71–4, dealt briefly with Price's claim that Parliament's legislative powers were limited and quotes from Bentham's *Fragment* (Chap. IV, para. 26 in *CW* 485–6) the statement that to speak of legal limits on the supreme government of a state was an 'abuse of language'. Lind does not reproduce Bentham's qualifications or hesitations nor his own earlier admission in the Remarks on the Principal Acts of the Thirteenth Parliament, *supra* (n. 12), that Parliament might be bound by charters granted to the colonies.

[36] [John Lind], *supra* (n. 30), 71–2.

[37] *Fragment* Chap. IV, paras. 23–5, in *CW* 484–5.

mental power will aim at the greatest happiness of the greatest number. The most important requirement is that there should be frequent changes of condition between some of the governors and governed so that the interests of the governors should be more or less identified with those of the governed. Lind thought, and at this stage Bentham did also, that a mixed constitution containing an elected element, such as the British Constitution of Crown Peers and Commoners at that time, was enough to secure the required identity of interest. But as we shall see, Bentham, while maintaining his hostility to the doctrine of natural rights, later came to think that only a full democracy could secure this condition and could be accounted free.

The third and last contribution made by this remarkable pair to the great debate with America was a response to the Declaration of Independence itself. Three months after its publication on 4 July, Lind published an *Answer to the Declaration of Independence of the American Congress.* This is, for the most part, concerned with the detailed examination of the specific charges in the Declaration of Independence made against George III, charging him with injuries and usurpations. At the end of the pamphlet, however, there is a short 'Review of the Declaration', including some pages[38] devoted to fiercely critical observations of the philosophical passages in the second paragraph of the preamble. Here Bentham anticipated some of the elaborate scrutiny of the doctrine of natural rights which he made years later after the outbreak of the French Revolution when he characterized the doctrine as so much '*bawling* upon paper'.[39]

In this *Answer* of 1776, Bentham's main attack consists of

---

[38] [John Lind], *An Answer to the Declaration of the American Congress* (1776), 120-32. It is established that most of this part of Lind's pamphlet was written by Bentham since he communicated his draft by letter to Lind though, since not all the letter survives, Bentham's authorship of the whole remains only a highly probable conjecture. See letter from Bentham to John Lind, 2 Sept. 1776, in *Bentham Correspondence* I 341-4. As noted there, at 342 n., previous extracts in Mary P. Mack, *Jeremy Bentham: An Odyssey of Ideas 1756-1792* (1963), 168, are apparently not connected by Mack with Lind's *Answer* but with his earlier *Remarks on the Principal Acts of the Thirteenth Parliament, supra* n. 12.

[39] *Anarchical Fallacies*, in *Works* II 494, and see Chap. IV *infra*.

a claim that there is an unexplained and indefensible inconsistency in both asserting that men have inalienable rights to enjoy life and liberty and to pursue happiness and also accepting the necessity of government, since the exercise of the powers which every government must have and use will at times involve the taking of life, the limitation of liberty, and the interference with the ways in which men choose to pursue their happiness. 'If the right of pursuit of happiness is a right unalienable why (how) are thieves restrained from pursuing it by theft, murderers by murder, and rebels by rebellion?'[40]

This challenge to the authors of the Declaration of Independence to show how rights described as unalienable could be reconciled with the necessary powers of government, and indeed with each other, may seem now very simple, indeed very crude. Yet the point was not only the heart of Bentham's more sophisticated formulation of his objections to the later French Declaration of the Rights of Man, but dictated the form of much subsequent criticism by other writers of the doctrines of natural or human rights from Bentham's time until our own day. Only comparatively recently have new sophisticated versions of the doctrine been produced which attempt to demonstrate that the spirit at least of the doctrine can be reconciled with the necessary qualifications and exceptions and weighing or balancing of right against right, or even of right against general welfare, which is required if the doctrine is to have any concrete application in the criticism of law and political arrangements. In this modern version, in spite of the necessary compromise involved in resolving conflicts between rights, rights are thought of as having a property at least analogous to 'unalienability' since a weight, independent of and additional to utility, is attributed to them even when overriden by other rights or considerations of general welfare; and this independent weight reflects the moral significance of relationships of respect between separate individuals which utilitarianism is said to disregard. It was because no such malleable conception

[40] The words quoted here are from Bentham's own draft in his letter to Lind (*Bentham Correspondence* I 343). The text actually published by Lind differs in certain points of detail but reproduces their substance and adds '*here* then they have put the axe to the root of all Government.' [John Lind], *supra* (n. 38), 122.

of unalienable rights was forthcoming that Bentham stigmatized the doctrine of natural rights as the product not of reason but of mere imagination—'*imagination*, with its favourite instrument, the word *right*'[41] —and complained that such principles were 'deaf, unyielding, and inflexible:—a principle which will hear of no *modification*—will look at no *calculation*' which, if 'instead of *imagination, reason* be consulted', would be seen to be necessary.[42]

III

I turn now to consider the second phase of Bentham's thoughts on America. Bentham never abandoned his antipathy to the doctrine of natural rights. But he was early reconciled to the *fact* as distinct from the philosophy of American independence and in his old age explained that his opposition in 1776 was the result of the bad arguments used to support it and the neglect of 'the only good one, viz. the impossibility of good government at such a distance, and the advantage of separation to the interest and happiness of both parties.'[43]

Early in his development as a social thinker, Bentham had formed the views that, except in rare circumstances, the possession of colonies was a benefit neither to the mother country nor the colony and there was a standing utilitarian argument in favour of emancipation of colonies.[44] He had noted that the prophecies that the separation of the American colonies from Great Britain would be disastrous for both had been falsified.[45] By 1789 when Bentham came to publish his famous *Introduction to the Principles of Morals*

[41] *Plan of Parliamentary Reform,* in *Works* III 515.

[42] Ibid. 467 n.

[43] John Bowring, *Memoirs of Jeremy Bentham,* in *Works* X 63. In spite of his admiration for Jefferson, Bentham continued in his old age to speak disrespectfully of the Declaration of Independence as a 'hodge-podge of confusion and absurdity, in which the thing to be proved is all along taken for granted.' Ibid.

[44] Bentham's most explicit formulation of these views was made in 1793 in his *Emancipate Your Colonies! Shewing the Uselessness and Mischievousness of Distant Dependencies,* in *Works* IV 408-18. He argued his case against the retention of colonies on more technical economic grounds in his *Manual óf Political Economy,* in *Works* III 52-7, written about the same time. But the same thoughts had occurred to him earlier still when considering between 1788-90 a postscript to a second edition of his *Defence of Usury,* in *Economic Writings* I 124, 191-4, 202-4.

[45] Ibid. 194. See also the fragment *Colonies and Navy* ibid. 211.

and Legislation, he had become an enthusiast and spoke of the United States as 'that newly created nation, one of the most enlightened, if not the most enlightened, at this day on the globe',[46] adding only:

Who can help lamenting, that so rational a cause should be rested upon reasons, so much fitter to beget objections, than to remove them? But with men who are unanimous and hearty about *measures*, nothing so weak but may pass in the character of a *reason*: nor is this the first instance in the world, where the conclusion has supported the premises, instead of the premises the conclusion.[47]

What then about American democracy as distinct from American independence? Here the development of Bentham's thought is more tortuous and less easy to trace with confidence. For more than a decade before 1776, agitation for reform of the franchise had burst out in England, especially London, into frequent demonstrations, demands, and petitions. There is no echo of this in the *Fragment* though much of it is dedicated to exhibiting the confusions, the fiction, and the empty rhetoric in Blackstone's demonstration of the glories of the 'matchless' British Constitution. In fact Bentham himself at this period, while repudiating Blackstone's arguments, was in fact content with the old constitution. In his reminiscences of the period, Bentham—speaking of John Wilkes who in 1776 had made a famous speech in Parliament demanding the just representation of the people —said:

I was a determined aristocrat in [Wilkes's] time—a prodigious admirer of Lord Mansfield and of the King. . .
I was, however, a great reformist; but never suspected that the people in power were against reform. I supposed they only wanted to know what was good in order to embrace it.[48]

So as late as 1782, Bentham wrote of the unreformed Constitution, 'The constitutional branch of the law of England, taking it in its leading principles, would probably be found the best beyond comparison that has hitherto made its appearance in the world; resting at no very great distance, perhaps, from the summit of perfection.' How conservative

---

[46] *PML.* Concluding Note in *CW* 309.
[47] Ibid. 311.
[48] *Works* X 66.

Bentham was at this period appears in the almost Burkean remark, which he added to this reflection, on the near perfection of the British constitution, that it was the happiness of the British 'to have stumbled upon so invaluable a possession.'[49]

In 1788 Bentham turned his attention to events in France. His first thoughts were expressed in an open letter written in French to Mirabeau.[50] In this letter, Bentham made it clear that as far as Britain was concerned he was still content with the unreformed constitution. While he was certain that the state of France called for radical reform and that only with equal representation could France hope to secure the freedom of the press, the control of executive powers of arrest, a fair system of taxation, and a proper subordination of the armed forces to the civil authorities, he was equally convinced at this time that in England all these elements of good government were firmly established and secured. So he wrote, 'I have not yet found any sufficient reason for wishing for the introduction of a system of equal representation in my country.' 'Not yet found' (*Je n'ai pas encore trouvé*)—there is here perhaps a tentative note. At any rate, in the next year while still concerned with French affairs, he composed, but never completed or published, what he himself called an *Essay on Representation*, making a case for representative democracy and again intended for the French.[51] It may well be, as some scholars have urged, that at this time Bentham never intended his arguments to be used in British politics, and certainly if he did, his views were to change violently when the character of the French Revolution became apparent. But in the following year, 1790, Bentham composed in English an essay *On the Efficient Cause and Measure of Constitutional Liberty*.[52] Here for the first time Bentham

[49] *Of the Influence of Time and Place in Matters of Legislation*, in *Works* I 171, 185 and footnote 'written in 1782'.

[50] UC CLXX 3 (1788).

[51] UC CLXX 87–121 (1788–9). Extracts from it are printed in Mary P. Mack (*supra* n. 38), 424–39.

[52] UC CXXVI 8 (*c.* 1790); printed with omissions in Mary P. Mack, *supra* (n. 38), 453. This essay, which is continued in UC CXXVII 4 (*c.* 1790), was an attack on the theory (which Bentham terms 'the current theory of government' and criticizes as 'hollow and delusive') that good government and constitutional liberty is best secured by the distribution of political power among different bodies or its division into different branches.

identified the precise form of the utilitarian principle which, instead of a doctrine of natural rights, was to serve as his leading argument for democracy when twenty-seven years later he had publicly shaken off his doubts and become an active advocate of radical reform.

This utilitarian argument for democracy was an application in the sphere of constitutional law of the same principle which in the criminal law secured an artificial harmony between the interests of the individual and the general welfare by the use of sanctions and so maximized the general happiness. Criminal punishment for Bentham was simply an artificial expedient designed to *make* it in the interest of the individual who is tempted to break the law and act against the public interest to conform his conduct to the public interest. Bentham came indeed to view governments, 'the ruling few', as potential criminals perennially tempted to pursue their personal interests at the expense of the public. This was the standing conflict between the sinister interest of the ruling few and the interest of the subject many. Rulers therefore were to be regarded like potential robbers whom it was necessary always to suspect and always to subject to the control of the public. So he fashioned the slogans 'minimise confidence' and 'maximise control', and claimed that the appropriate form of control in constitutional law was to place the power of appointment and dismissal of government in the hands of the people. Many different formulations and applications of this principle securing the artificial harmony of interests are to be found throughout Bentham's works. But the first formulation of it in the constitutional sphere was in this short unpublished essay of 1790:

... the propositions I lay down are these:
(1) That the efficient cause of constitutional liberty or of good government which is but another name for the same thing is not the division of power among the different classes of men entrusted with it but the dependence immediate or mediate of all of them on the body of the people.
(2) That the whole sovereign power ought to rest in the hands of persons placed and displaceable by the body of the people.[53]

This simple formulation which was elaborated at very great length in the pleas for parliamentary reform which Bentham

---

[53] UC CXXVII 5 (*c.* 1790).

published only after the lapse of twenty-eight years, was followed by an argument designed I think to quiet Bentham's own qualms about committing himself thus far to representative democracy. For in a note apparently written in the same year,[54] he emphasized that plans to give men equal votes in the election of their government were quite distinct from levelling doctrines of equality of property—which Bentham feared as much as Blackstone or Burke ever did. This too was an early forerunner of his later more elaborate arguments in *Radicalism not Dangerous*.[55]

Within three years when the French Revolution entered its violent phase, Bentham's fears which he had earlier dismissed were realized, and it is not too much to say that he was frightened out of his wits. Like Burke and Wordsworth, he came, as Leslie Stephen said, to see the glare of hell in the light which others (Richard Price and Tom Paine among them) took to herald the dawn of the millennium. So he turned his back on democracy and occupied himself in writing papers (also never published), attacking projects of parliamentary reform, under such reactionary titles as *Reform No Improvement*[56] and *Rottenness No Corruption, or a Defence of Rotten Boroughs by the author of The Defence of Usury*.[57] In another such paper[58] he explained his position by saying 'No man has a fuller comprehension of the imperfections of the law, no man a more painful and indignant sense of them, no man has been more assiduous in investigating them nor more successful in discovering them . . . it is with this body of grievances before my eyes, that I say notwithstanding, no change in the Constitution nor in the form of Parliament.' In the earlier essay of 1790 which expounded the utilitarian case for popular government, Bentham did not mention America, but in the later pamphlet, *Reform No Improvement*, America is indeed mentioned, but only to explain why progress towards democracy in America had not been accompanied by the anarchy and disorder which Bentham, in this phase of panic, feared must accompany it in

---

[54] UC CXXVII 19 (*c.* 1790).

[55] *Radicalism Not Dangerous* (1819–20), in *Works* III 599–622; note Part III, 'Defence from Experience in the Case of the United States', at 612–13.

[56] UC XLIV 2 (1794).

[57] UC XLIV 3–5 (1795).   [58] UC CLXX 173 (1793).

Europe. So he raises the question about America 'Why so quiet?' and attributes the peace 'of the American republics' to a variety of factors: the absence of large towns and urban mobs, the great proportion of population occupied as husbandmen, the general belief that domestic concerns were more important than public ones, and the fact that there were in America no swarms of mischief-making unemployed lawyers, players, news vendors and artists. 'The business of government with them is not an end but a means to security and repose.'[59]

When did Bentham's panic fear of representative democracy subside and what caused it to do so? It is not possible on the evidence to answer these questions with any precision or certainty, but it seems clear that America had much to do with it.[60] By 1809 when he wrote the Parliamentary Reform Catechism,[61] he was certainly fully convinced of the need in England for the full radical programme of universal suffrage, secret ballots, annual parliaments, and equal electoral districts; and when in 1817 he published the *Catechism on Reform* together with the immensely long and, it must be confessed, tedious introduction full of injunctions to 'look to America', he spoke of himself as having been convinced for a long time[62] before the writing of the *Catechism* in 1809 of the necessity for reform.

Most authorities have attributed what they call Bentham's conversion to democracy to the influence of James Mill, John Stuart Mill's father, whom he met first in 1807, and that influence together with what Bentham saw as the iniquities of governmental repression in England permitted by the unreformed constitution were no doubt very powerful influences on him. But it seems to be impossible to doubt that the spectacle of peace, prosperity, freedom, and the safety of property in America, in spite of the growing approximation there to manhood suffrage, played a great part in

[59] *Reform No Improvement* (*supra* n. 55), 2-3.

[60] See the lucid and careful discussion of this subject by J. R. Dinwiddy, 'Bentham's Transition to Radicalism', *J. Hist. Ideas* xxxvi (1975) 683. I differ only from the views expressed there in emphasizing the importance of Bentham's early formulation in his unpublished essay of 1790 (*supra* n. 51) of a utilitarian defence of democracy.

[61] *Plan of Parliamentary Reform*, in *Works* III 468.

[62] *Works* III 435.

dissipating Bentham's earlier fears.[63] What is clear is that Bentham never forgot his panic of the 1790s, and when later he appealed to the example of America to calm or to ridicule the fears of democracy, he spoke in terms obviously inspired by his past experience. '*Anarchy* is one bugbear; *Democracy* another. Separately, or like dogs coupled, they are sent forth by periodicals—ministerial and absolutist—to strike terror into weak minds . . . to frighten men out of their wits and prevent them from forming any sound judgment . . . *Fear* is a *passion* by which judgment is laid prostrate and carried away captive.'[64] There is here, surely, a note of self-castigation.

In the end, praise of American democracy as a kind of Utopia of utilitarianism—'the best government that is or ever has been'[65]—dedicated to the pursuit of the greatest happiness of the greatest number came to figure in almost all of Bentham's later writings and not merely those arguing the case of parliamentary reform. He conceded that in this 'matchlessly felicitous system' there were 'imperfections of detail'[66] but the virtues far outweighed them.

First then the virtues: as Bentham saw them, they were the polar opposites of the evil features of governmental repression in England during the Napoleonic wars and the period of hunger and unrest that succeeded them. 'No dungeoning acts, no gagging acts, no riot acts',[67] such as disgraced England still in 1817. Instead America enjoyed great freedom of an untaxed press and of speech;[68] and there was no standing army, no established church, no hereditary

[63] As early as March 1790, Bentham in discussing French plans for the popular election of judges wrote 'I have not that horror of the people. I do not see in them that savage monster which their detractors dream of . . . Much sooner would I look to America, where the people bear undisputed sway, and ask, in so many years of popular government, what violences or injustice to the prejudice of their servants have ever yet been presented by the history of thirteen commonwealths?' *A Draught for a Code for the Organization of the Judicial Establishment in France*, in *Works* IV 363.

[64] *Jeremy Bentham to His Fellow-Citizens of France on Houses of Peers and Senates*, in *Works* IV 419, 448.

[65] *Plan of Parliamentary Reform*, in *Works* III 472.

[66] *Constitutional Code*, in *Works* IX 63.

[67] *Radical Reform Bill*, in *Works* III 558, 562.

[68] *Plan of Parliamentary Reform*, in *Works* III 473; *The King Against Edmonds and Others* (1820), in *Works* V 246; *Constitutional Code*, in *Works* IX 38; and *Letters to Count Toreno* (1822), in *Works* VIII 510.

honours but great simplicity and economy. About each of these Bentham had much to say. He had valued freedom of speech even in his Tory days no less than his famous disciple John Stuart Mill. He valued simplicity greatly as a most important feature of good government and some of Bentham's most effective rhetoric applauded the absence of the dazzling show which surrounded the monarchies and aristocracies of Europe, or as Bentham termed them the instruments of 'delusion' or 'factitious dignity', 'lustre' and 'splendour' designed to mystify and hide the defects of the ruling few from the subject many.[69] He was delighted also that in America public services were rewarded only by personal and not hereditary honours. So the Americans were right not to have a hereditary peerage or honours nobility: 'bestow rewards, erect statues, confer even titles so that they be personal alone but never bind the crown of merit upon the brow of sloth.'[70] Further, though Bentham conceded among the few vices which he saw in the system the growth of a vast 'tribe' of lawyers, he could at least congratulate America on the relative cheapness of justice and the small salary of $4,000 'not so much as pounds 1,000' paid to the Chief Justice compared with the enormous annual fees of £23,000 extracted by Lord Eldon.[71]

Most serious of the vices in Bentham's eyes of the American system was its disfigurement by the institution of slavery. This indeed Lind had fastened upon, in the work containing so many of Bentham's ideas which he wrote in 1776 criticizing Price. There he had attacked the Americans for speaking as if their professions of faith that men were created equal meant that America 'where *men* and *cattle* are offered for *sale* in the same advertisement'[72] was in fact to be the home of equal liberty. Bentham condemned the system of slavery as a monstrosity, but he thought that the Americans were by 1821 employed in combating it[73] and seems to have thought that it would soon disappear without friction when

[69] *Jeremy Bentham to His Fellow-Citizens of France* (1830), in *Works* IV 437-9; and *Constitutional Code*, in *Works* IX 76-7, 540-1.

[70] *The Rationale of Reward*, in *Works* II 189, 201.

[71] *Observations on Mr. Secretary Peel's House of Commons Speech 21st March 1825*, in *Works* V 344.

[72] [John Lind], *supra* (n. 30), 46.

[73] *Jeremy Bentham to the Spanish People*, in *Works* II 277, 294.

its disutility in terms of the general welfare became, as he thought it would, increasingly apparent.[74] But though less reprehensible than slavery, Bentham blamed America for its failure to throw off what he somewhat absurdly described as 'the yoke'[75] of the formless and obscure English common law, and for their neglect of the great opportunity afforded by the break with England to introduce clear comprehensive rational codes instead of the 'non-cognoscible' and trackless wilds of case law which, for Bentham, was no law at all, though so profitable to lawyers. Lastly, he thought the institution of a second Chamber in the form of the Senate was both an absurd expense and an obstruction to the popular will. He wrote much specifically designed to persuade Americans of this mistake, which he thought a weak-minded imitation of the House of Lords.[76]

Amid these glowing tributes to American government, there are some staggering misjudgments to be found. Perhaps the most startling among them is Bentham's reiterated conviction that the Americans were wise not only in abjuring the delusive splendours of a palace and the society of an aristocratic court in which to house their President but were wise too in providing him with no special protection such as surrounds an English king.

> In the Anglo-American United States, [he wrote] no such extra protection is afforded them: and in the Anglo-American United States, instead of being the less secure, they are the more perfectly secure. No King of England—no other man whose seat is called a throne, is so secure against hostile attacks by individuals, as the President of the Anglo-American United States is.[77]

Indeed on this point Bentham seems to have developed almost a genius for false prediction. He asks concerning the President, '. . . is he the less safe? Not to speak of Asia exists

[74] *Constitutional Code*, in *Works* IX 63.

[75] *Letter to the Citizens of the Several American States, July 1817*, in *Works* IV 478, 482 n., 483-91.

[76] *Anti-Senatica: An Attack on the U.S. Senate, Sent by Jeremy Bentham to Andrew Jackson. President of the United States*, 209-67 (Smith Coll. Stud. in History, XI, ed. Charles Warren Everett, 1926). Bentham preached the same lesson to the French and to the Spanish, arguing the general disutility of a second legislative Chamber. See *Jeremy Bentham to His Fellow-Citizens of France* in *Works* IV 420 and *Three Tracts on Spanish and Portuguese Affairs*, in *Works* VIII 465, 468-70.

[77] *Principles of Judicial Procedure*, in *Works* II 121.

there in all Europe a monarch by whom anything like equal
security is enjoyed? Oh, no: nor ever will nor can there be.
The monarch is a mark for every madman to shoot at.'[78]
Perhaps more excusably in discussing the President's patronage of the army, Bentham made the confident statement
that under a really existing constitution 'which has for its
end in view the greatest happiness of the community' the
vast powers of the President as commander-in-chief of the
armed forces could never be a menace to security at home
since 'to power in every situation, checks so efficient and
adequate are applied.'[79]

The great system of patronage, placemen, and sinecures,
through which the administration of George III had been
able to manipulate Parliament, came to figure in Bentham's
later views as one of the greatest vices of the unreformed
British constitution. He seemed to have thought that for
this, as for everything else, democracy on American lines
would be a panacea and that no parallel to the vices of royal
patronage were to be found in the States. 'Look now to the
United States!—look to the General Congress! See whether,
in that head seat of democratic government, corruption in
any such shape is in any instance to be found.'[80] It was a
government 'without so much as a single *useless place, need-
less place, overpaid place, unmerited pension*—not to speak
of *sinecures*—no not so much as a *peerage*, to settle or a
borough to buy off a country gentleman.'[81] In short, Bentham had come to the conclusion that the only vices with
which democracy in America could be charged were those
like its retention of a second Chamber and the uncodified
common law, things inherited from Britain.[82] There is no
hint to be found in Bentham of the possibilities of the
tyranny of the majority over standards of conduct or taste
to which three years after his death Tocqueville would draw
attention and inspire cooler assessments of America.

So Bentham's enthusiasm for American democracy never

---

[78] *Letters to Count Toreno on the Proposed Penal Code*, in *Works* VIII 487,
523.
 [79] *Constitutional Code*, in *Works* IX 363–4 n.
 [80] *Plan of Parliamentary Reform*, in *Works* III 494.
 [81] Ibid., *Works* III 437.
 [82] '. . . thoughtless continuation of the usages of the corrupt monarchy out
of which it sprung.' *Constitutional Code*, in *Works* IX 346.

wavered. It was 'a never-to-be-expunged reproach to our Matchless Constitution—matchless in rotten boroughs and sinecures!'[83]

If much of this may seem now an uncritical and even silly enthusiasm, it is to be remembered how repressive of fundamental liberties widely enjoyed in America British government had become. Bentham's extravagance in his wild enthusiasm for the world's greatest experiment in democracy still developing before his eyes can easily be matched by pronouncements from the side of those who feared the American example. Even Sydney Smith could write, 'In the four quarters of the globe, who reads an American book? . . . what does the world yet owe to American physicians and surgeons? . . . what new constellations have been discovered by the telescopes of Americans? What have they done in mathematics? who drinks out of American glasses? or eats from American plates?'[84] as if these identified permanent failings of the American democratic system. Moreover there is this to be said. Bentham seems to have discerned that there were and would continue to develop in American life powerful trends corresponding to virtues which he possessed himself and valued most in others: a certain homespun simplicity; enlightened benevolence; youthful energy and inventiveness; a hard-headed self-reliance, a suspicion of pomp, pretence, snobbery, and social hierarchy, and a compassion for human suffering. In the most bitter of the passages in which he urges the opponents of reform to look once more at the American United States and to see how free from any sign of anarchy or danger to property was the country of 'the supposed destroyers of all property and all government,' he challenges them thus: '. . . has there at any time been that day, in which the door of that immense country has not stayed wide open to the *scum of the earth*, as you would call it? and amongst others, to your own wild Irish—to those wild Irish, who by your misrule, and by the fear of your *torture-mongers*, have been driven into banishment?'[85]

[83] *Plan of Parliamentary Reform*, in *Works* III 437.
[84] [Sydney Smith], Book Review in the *Edinburgh Review* 60 (1820) 79-80, as quoted by David Paul Crook, *American Democracy in English Politics 1815–1850* (1965), 72.
[85] *Plan of Parliamentary Reform*, in *Works* III 472 n.

The sad finale of Bentham's concern with the United States is soon told. For the second time in his life a great country's revolutionary break with the past seemed to him to offer a glorious opportunity for the use of that 'genius for legislation' which he believed himself to possess. At the beginning of the French Revolution he wrote much for the guidance of the new Constituent Assembly, and though he was made an honorary citizen of France and one of the best of his works for the guidance of the new French legislature on parliamentary tactics was translated into French, nothing came of his earlier high hopes of influencing the form and substance of the law in France. The full story of this first disappointment has been told in illuminating detail by Professor J.H. Burns, who opens the story with Bentham's cry of disappointment, 'God Almighty predestinated me to be the *âme damnée* of France.'[86]

America was perhaps a more bitter blow to Bentham and one to which age had perhaps made him more vulnerable. His enthusiasm for codification had become a passion and his hatred of the uncodified formless 'uncognoscible' common law had become very near a mania. Between 1815 and 1817, he wrote and published letters and circulars urging America, the country which he saw as the uncorruptible, 'every day more and more flourishing commonwealth' to complete its break with England, that 'seat of ill-disguised despotism and self-acknowledged corruption', and to shake off the inherited yoke of the common law, indeed to shut American ports to it and to accept from his hand the free gift of a complete code of law.[87]

There is indeed a tragicomedy in the papers, later published together as papers on codification, in which the sharpest acumen in detailed argument is displayed together with a naively optimistic belief in the power of such detailed argument to persuade. In 1811 Bentham wrote[88] offering his services as codifier to President Madison; Madison replied

---

[86] Letter from Jeremy Bentham to Etienne Dumont, in BPU (Bibliothèque Publique et Universitaire, Geneva), Dumont MSS XXXIII 56; and J.H. Burns, 'Bentham and the French Revolution', *Trans. Roy. Hist. Soc.* 16 (5th ser. 1966) 95.

[87] *Letter to the Citizens of the United States* in *Works* IV 479, 504; and letter from Jeremy Bentham to James Madison, Oct. 1811, in *Works* IV 453, 460-2.

[88] *Works* IV 463.

in 1816,[89] after an interval of five years, courteously refusing the offer and understandably softening the blow with a number of vague phrases. To this reply Bentham replied,[90] subjecting to microscopic examination every evasive word used by Madison. In 1817 he published a circular[91] to all the governors of all the states in the Union and finally a vast collection of eight letters addressed to the citizens of the American United States. In these, at enormous length and with remorseless detail, he defined and expounded the cardinal virtues of a properly drafted code of law. These were: 'aptitude for *notoriety*,' '*completeness*', and '*justifiedness*' or support by adequate reasons.[92] He planned in detail the tactics for the best presentation of his offer to the American people and anticipated every argument against its acceptance. Even the fact that the code would come from an alien hand is turned into an argument for accepting it since the offer, coming from one who had no power to impose the code and therefore addressed merely to the understanding and not to the will of the American people, could excite no odium. Testimonials are cited, including his correspondence with the Emperor of Russia whose gift of a diamond ring he had sent back.[93]

All was in vain, indeed the most concrete acknowledgements that he received were professions of admiration for his genius and fame, and the report[94] (from Governor Plumer of New Hampshire) that the distinguished American lawyer, Mr Edward Livingstone, had said more than once that his own project of a new penal code for the State of Louisiana had grown out of what he had learnt of Bentham's views in the French translation published by Dumont. In 1830 Bentham, then eighty-two and within two years of his death, made one last gesture. He wrote to President Jackson to express his

[89] Letter from James Madison to Jeremy Bentham, 8 May 1816, in *Works* IV 467-8.

[90] Letter from Jeremy Bentham to James Madison, Sept. 1817, in *Works* IV 507.

[91] *Jeremy Bentham to the Respective Governors of the American United States* (Circular), in *Works* IV 476.

[92] *Letter to the Citizens etc.*, in *Works* IV 478, 480.

[93] See op. cit. n. 91 *supra* 477; and letters to the Emperor, in *Works* IV 514-28.

[94] Letter from Governor Plumer of New Hampshire to Jeremy Bentham, 15 Sept. 1826, in *Works* X 556-7.

intense admiration of his inaugural message to Congress. Here he mentioned his proposals for codification to replace the 'utter inaptitude' of the common law and offered himself as an instrument for Jackson to use in the task of delivering the people from 'the thraldom in which, everywhere, from the earliest recorded days, they have been held by the harpies of the law'.[95] There was apparently no reply.

So ended the curious transition from hostility to almost unqualified admiration of America which Bentham made. Though disappointed, the old man retained no bitterness. Far from rounding on the country that had spurned his offer and allowed five years to pass even before acknowledging it, his references to the 'Anglo-American United States' continued throughout as favourable as ever. If the democracy of America had refused his offer to draft its code of laws, it still remained for him, in spite of its professed ideology of natural rights, the greatest and most successful embodiment on earth of the principles of utility.

[95] Letter from Jeremy Bentham to Andrew Jackson, 26 Apr. 1830, in *Works* XI 39–42.

NATURAL RIGHTS: BENTHAM AND JOHN STUART MILL

I

Bentham's most comprehensive and detailed criticisms of the doctrine of what he termed 'the natural pre-adamitical, ante-legal and anti-legal rights of man'[1] are to to found in the work published after his death under the title of *Anarchical Fallacies*. This subjects to a long minute and sometimes repetitious examination the French Declaration of the Rights of Man and the Citizen of 1791 listing liberty, property, security, and resistance to oppression as natural and imprescriptible rights, and two other documents that grew out of it. It is in this work that the famous saw 'nonsense upon stilts'[2] appears amid much passionate denunciation of a doctrine which Bentham both despised as intellectually disreputable and feared when it was used in political controversy or embodied in public documents, regarding it as a threat to all government and to the stability of society. The vehemence of Bentham's attack culminated in the ugly suggestion that the public assertion of 'anti-legal rights' was a moral crime which now that the French Revolution 'had displayed their import by practical comment' might be made a legal crime as 'hostile to the public peace'.[3]

Plainly much of the panic-stricken rhetoric of Bentham's attack was inspired by the Terror which had already led Bentham to recoil from democracy and to compose, but not

---

[1] *Works* II 491 at 524. See Professor Twining's *The Contemporary Significance of Bentham's Anarchical Fallacies* (*Archiv für Rechts- und Sozialphilosophie* XLI (1975) 315), for an excellent account of the genesis and content of this work. Criticisms of the doctrine of natural and non-legal rights are also scattered through Bentham's *Works* of widely differing subject-matter and date. See *View of a Complete Code of Law*, *Works* III 160-1, 184; *Pannomial Fragments*, *Works* III 218-21; *Supply Without Burden* in *Economic Writings*, 309-10, 332-7; *Comment* in *CW* 62-3, 66, and also Bentham's letter to John Lind in *Correspondence* I, in *CW* 341, as to which see Chap. III *supra*.

[2] *Works* II 501.   [3] Ibid. 524.

to publish, objections to democratic reform of the British parliament.[4] But his hostility to the ideology of natural rights had long ante-dated the French Revolution. Many of the objections elaborated in *Anarchical Fallacies* had appeared in condensed form in his much earlier attack on the American Declaration of Independence which he had provided in 1776 for his friend John Lind to use in his answer to the Declaration of Independence.[5]

Stripped of its rhetoric, Bentham's objections to the doctrine that men possess natural rights fall under two main heads. First, the idea that men possess rights which are not the creature of positive law but could be used in criticism and opposition to it was a gross conceptual confusion; secondly, it was, in Bentham's semi-technical use of the term, a 'political fallacy'[6] as a source of corruption of political argument and thought, especially when embodied in political documents such as those examined in *Anarchical Fallacies* or converted into fundamental laws intended to circumscribe the action of legislatures and government.

In this chapter I shall consider at some length the charge of conceptual confusion together with a modification of that charge at which Bentham hints and which bears a striking resemblance to the account of moral rights, including some that are universal, given by John Stuart Mill in his discussion of Justice[7] as a distinct segment of morality.

Bentham's critique of the doctrine of natural imprescriptible rights as a source of political fallacies which he found manifest in the French documents and examined in *Anarchical Fallacies* has been the subject of an illuminating exchange between Professor Twining and Mr Melvin Dalgarno[8] and I shall not discuss this further here except to make clear the following points. Even in his most panic-stricken moments Bentham remained conscious, as he had been from his earliest writings, of the evils that governments use laws to do, and of

---

[4] See Chap. III *supra*, p. 69.   [5] Ibid., p. 63.

[6] See *The Book of Fallacies, Works* II 379.

[7] *Utilitarianism*, Chap. V, in *10 Collected Works of John Stuart Mill* (ed. Robson, 1969; hereinafter referred to as *Utilitarianism*) 203, 240, et seq.

[8] See Twining, op. cit. (n. 1 *supra*), and Dalgarno, 'The Contemporary Significance of Bentham's Anarchical Fallacies: A reply to William Twining', *Archiv für Rechts- und Sozialphilosophie* XII 357.

the need to keep alive the sense that disobedience to law might in particular circumstances be well justified.[9] So even in *Anarchical Fallacies* he was concerned to make clear that there should be no 'indiscriminate obedience' to the laws of any country, not even in England, where, as Bentham at this period found himself able to say the law was 'probably at least as near perfection upon the whole as the law of any other country'.[10] But Bentham was also always conscious that where a legal system was in force there could be no simple step from the recognition that a particular law would create some particular evil to the conclusion that disobedience to it was automatically justified, as if that evil rendered the law invalid or void.

All laws restricting liberty, Bentham thought, were for that reason evil but before the step from the recognition of the evil to disobedience could be rationally taken a careful calculation and comparison of the consequences of obedience and disobedience was necessary.[11] That this was the rational response of the citizen to bad laws[12] remained Bentham's conviction throughout his life, unaffected by his change from Tory to Radical Democrat and the cooling of the panic excited by the French Revolution. This is to be remembered when reading the intemperate language of his condemnation of the French attempts to embody lists of inalienable and imprescriptible rights in official declarations, and to fashion out of them hugely general, vaguely stated fundamental laws purporting to fetter irrevocably the action of even supreme legislatures. Perhaps the worst of the corrupting fallacies which Bentham found in the Declaration of the Rights of Man and the Citizen was that instead of speaking of what legislatures and governments ought not to do or should not do by way of infringement of these abstractly stated natural rights, it spoke of what governments 'cannot do'[13] thus dealing out in advance of knowledge of particular circumstances 'sentences of nullity'[14] to what legislatures may purport to do. 'Venom', said Bentham, 'lurks under such words

---

[9] *Works* II 528 and *Fragment* Chap. 1, para. 43, in *CW* 444; Chap. IV, para. 21, in *CW* 484.

[10] *Works* II 528.   [11] *Works* III 185, 219.

[12] 'This is the only question to be examined' (*Works* III 185). 'It is an affair of calculation' (*Works* III 219).

[13] *Works* II 494-5.   [14] *Works* II 511.

as "can" and "cannot"'[15] and he feared that their use in the criticism of law would invite insurrection and anarchy, since it would foster the belief that there *was* a simple step to be taken without calculating consequences from the recognition of the evil done by some particular law to the conclusion that it could be disregarded as a nullity.

II

In most of the many different formulations of his criticism Bentham's account of the conceptual confusion which he took to be inherent in the doctrine of natural rights embraced all forms of the belief in rights which were not the 'creatures' of positive law. 'Rights are the fruits of the law and of the law alone; there are no rights without law—no rights contrary to law—no rights anterior to the law.'[16] So his attack was directed not only against political theories of the universal rights of men or human rights according to which all men have rights to the protection of their basic interests such as liberty, security, and the pursuit of happiness, which it is the function of government to protect.

At times Bentham simply asserts that 'right and legal right are the same thing'[17] and that the notion of a right not created by law is a contradiction like 'round square', 'a son that never had a father', 'a species of cold heat', a 'sort of dry moisture', a 'kind of resplendent darkness'.[18] However, sometimes and much more plausibly, he objects to the separation of the idea of a right from that of a law because it introduces not a contradiction but what I shall call 'criterionlessness'. That is, a hopeless indeterminacy since such a separation, Bentham thought, deprives the notion of any criteria for its identification and application. The criterionless character of alleged natural rights means that appeals to them in political argument must either result in unsettleable controversy or worse, will create a gap which men are too often prone to fill by identifying as natural rights whatever 'political caprice' they have to gratify, so disguising in legal-sounding language what is in fact nothing but 'so much flat assertion'.[19]

---

[15] 'the disguised cant of the assassin'; 'words that speak daggers' (*Works* II 500).

[16] *Works* III 221.　　[17] *Econonic Writings* I 334.

[18] Ibid. 334–5.　　[19] Ibid. 335.

When you employ such a word as a 'right', [Bentham wrote] a cloud and that of black hue overshadows the whole field. To any such word as 'right' no conception can be attached but through the medium of a law or something to which the force of *law* is given. Lay out of the question the idea of law and all that you have by the use of the word 'right' is a sound to dispute about.[20]

So he concludes that the only case in which the word 'right' has 'any determinate and intelligible meaning is that in which it has the adjunct "political" attached to it.'[21]

The wholesale condemnation of the idea of a right not created by positive law may now seem to us absurd,[22] and it is not immediately clear how Bentham would have answered the objection that however dubious non-legal natural rights may be as elements in a political theory or when invoked in opposition to the law in public controversy, rights have a firmly established place in ordinary moral assessments which private individuals commonly make of each other's conduct. A man promises to perform some service for a friend: surely, under normal circumstances whether the promise is legally enforceable or not, it creates a moral obligation for the person giving the promise and a right for his friend to the promised service, and to complain if it is not forthcoming. Again, a man may authorize a friend to read his private diary or to supervise his children. Surely the friend can reply to the question 'What right have you to read that man's private diary, or order his children around?' by saying 'I have a right to do these things because he granted me permission to do them.' These seem plain examples of non-legal, moral rights, and their existence seems no more problematical than the moral obligation which is correlative in the right in the case of the promise and the obligations which are qualified or exempted from by the giving of permission in the last two cases. But of course these examples of rights are what may be called moral artefacts; they are created deliberately by human voluntary action which in the

[20] *Works* VIII 557.   [21] *Works* III 218.

[22] But it did not appear so to some Victorian thinkers including some hostile to Bentham's utilitarianism. Thus Matthew Arnold in arguing that greater economic and social equality was desirable in England disclaimed belief in natural rights and said, 'If it is a sound English doctrine that all rights are created by law, certainly that orthodox doctrine is mine' (*Essay on Equality*, in *Mixed Essays, Irish and Others* (1883), 46).

positive or conventional morality of society is recognized as a right-creating event, such as one man giving a promise to another or permission to him to do something which there is in general an obligation not to do. These actions constitute what might be called a title to the right, and this is a legal way of putting the matter which suggests that when Bentham said that to any such word as 'right' no conception could be attached except by law or *"something to which the force of law is given"* he intended to include in the last quoted words the conventional social morality supported by informal social sanctions. Certainly Bentham recognized that conventions supported by what he termed the 'popular or moral sanction consisting of mortifications resulting from ill-will' gave rise to a form of obligation which he calls moral.[23] There seems no reason why his analysis of legal rights as arising from the presence or the absence of legal obligation should not be applied *mutatis mutandis* to conventional morality. It is of course clear that the main target of Bentham's sweeping denials that there are any non-legal rights was the doctrine that men possessed universal rights which were natural in three senses of that word: they are not artefacts, human or divine;[24] they did not depend for their existence on social convention or recognition; and in important ways they reflected or were adapted to certain features of human nature. Bentham could consistently have rejected natural rights of this sort while admitting that there were non-legal rights which were based on coercive social conventions or as the later Utilitarians called it 'positive morality', and which could be created or extinguished by human, voluntary action. In spite of Bentham's unqualified assertion that there are no non-legal rights it seems reasonable to attribute the intention to him to admit what may be called positive moral rights as well as legal rights in view of his reference to 'something to which the force of law is given'. John Stuart Mill in his account of moral rights treats conventional morality, or as he terms it, 'opinion' as playing the same role in relation to

---

[23] *PML* Chap. II, paras. 3 and 5, in *CW* 34–5, and *Fragment* Chap. V, para. 7, in *CW* 496, and see Chap. V *infra*.

[24] Bentham regards the notion of rights arising from divine laws as not open to his criticisms of natural rights which he treats as essentially an atheist doctrine, 'Of all things the farthest from divine rights'; see *Economic Writings* I 310 n. and 334 n.

moral rights as the law though his conception of that role is very different from Bentham's.[25]

A more difficult but more important question is why Bentham, since he nowhere attempted to support the view that a non-legal right is a mere contradiction, was not ready to accept a simple utilitarian theory of non-legal rights as something consistent with his adoption of an unqualified utilitarianism according to which it is 'the happiness of the greatest number that is the measure of right and wrong'.[26] This might seem to supply a criterion for identifying what rights men have in addition to those created by law or arising from social conventions. In his account of legal rights Bentham distinguishes two main types: rights to do some action which arise from the absence of legal obligation not to do it (here called liberty-rights) and rights to positive or negative services which arise from the existence of obligations on others to do or abstain from some action affecting the right-holder[27] (here called rights to services). The question is why should Bentham not have said that men have non-legal rights of these same two sorts based on the principle of utility; that is, liberty-rights when calculations of what would maximize general utility showed no reason for a man to refrain from some action and rights to services when such calculations provided a reason for others to do or to abstain from some action so providing the right-holder with such services. On such a view rights would not indeed appear as they do in formulations of the universal rights of man which Bentham was concerned to attack, at the deepest level of a theory of moral rights, but would be derived from the fundamental goal of maximizing utility. So such a theory would not be right-based, but if the main source of confusion that Bentham found in the notion of non-legal rights was that the separation of rights from law left rights in the air without any identifying mark or criteria (a mere 'sound to dispute about') why should he not have found in what he terms the 'fundamental axiom and measure of right and wrong' an appropriate criterion?

Neither Bentham, who rejected the idea of non-legal rights altogether, nor John Stuart Mill who, on the contrary, held

---

[25] *Utilitarianism*, 250.   [26] *Fragment* Preface in *CW* 393.
[27] See Chap. VII *infra* for the detail of Bentham's analysis of legal rights.

that moral rights (including some which were universal) were essential components of the notions of justice, even consider such a simple direct utilitarian theory of rights, though as I shall show Bentham roughly sketched and Mill takes seriously, an indirect variant of a utilitarian theory. There are, I think, a number of reasons which both thinkers could have given for refusing to regard what I shall call 'utilitarian entitlements', that is, the liberties or services to which an individual would be entitled at any given moment of time on a direct application of the principles of utility, as 'rights'. For the content of such utilitarian entitlements would fluctuate with changing circumstances and have none of the stability over time and consequent availability as guides to action both for the right-holder and others which are strongly associated with the notion of rights wherever the notion is employed. Nor would such a simple utilitarian theory of rights convey the peremptory character evident in the invocation of rights as justifying demands made on others, stating what they must do or not do rather than what they merely ought to do or not to do. Though not absolutely criterionless such a direct utilitarian theory, treating the fluctuating entitlement as rights, would have left them often if not always 'sounds to dispute about'.

However the most important reason for rejecting such a direct utilitarian theory of rights is that it would have broken the connection between the concept of rights on the one hand and coercive obligations on the other which, whatever its precise form, appeared to both Bentham and Mill to be a central feature of the notion of rights. That the connection would be broken if simple utilitarian entitlements were regarded as rights is clear from the fact that neither Bentham nor Mill regarded the direct requirements of the principle of utility as in themselves constituting obligations. Both thinkers tied the notion of obligation to the notion of coercive sanctions, though they differed both as to the form of the connection and as to the possible forms which such sanctions could take.

Though Bentham calls the principle of utility 'the measure of right and wrong' and regards it as constituting the standards by which both the law and the conventional morality of any society should be judged, he plainly does not think that obligations or duties (which he treated, as Mill also did, as equivalent) are generated by the principle of utility.[28] For him, a necessary condition of a man having an obligation to act in a certain way is the likelihood of suffering in the event of failure so to act.[29] In the case of legal obligation, the suffering is administered according to law by officials in the form of legal punishment, and in the case of what he calls moral obligation it takes the form of spontaneous, popular or moral sanctions administered for breach of social conventions by those 'chance persons' with whom the offender is in contact. The content of legal and moral obligations so defined might indeed coincide in civilized societies with the requirements of the principles of utility, and the task, according to Bentham, of both the legislator and the moral educator is to see that they do so as often as possible, and so 'to rear the fabric of felicity by the hands of reason and law',[30] but this coincidence is wholly contingent and frequently not found, so that both legal and moral obligation may conflict with the requirements of utility.

Mill's doctrine follows Bentham here though he uses a different terminology; he calls the principles of utility not axioms or measures of right and wrong but principles of 'expediency',[31] thus making it clear that they do not by themselves constitute a morality or source of moral obligation which like Bentham, though for different reasons, he does not identify with conduct which maximizes general utility. It is probable that so far as legal obligation is concerned Mill would have accepted Bentham's account in terms of legal sanctions or punishment, but his conception of both moral wrong and moral obligation rests on a different form of connection with punishments or sanctions. Morality, for Mill, was a special segment of utility distinguished from mere expediency and does not require men to do every act which would maximize the general welfare. Instead only those actions

---

[28] Bentham, apparently forgetting his definition of all forms of obligation in terms of sanctions occasionally speaks of the requirements of the principle of utility as obligations, *Fragment* Chap. I, para. 36, n.v in *CW* 441, and Chap. I, para. 45, marginal note in *CW* 445.

[29] See Chap. VI *infra*, for variant interpretations of Bentham on this point and a detailed account of Bentham's Theory of Legal Obligation.

[30] *PML* Chap. I, para. 1 in *CW* I.

[31] *Utilitarianism*, 246, 255.

are to be considered morally obligatory if the effect of which on the general welfare is so considerable that there would still be good reason in point of general utility for punishing failure to perform them even when the disutilities involved in regulating and administering punishment are taken into account. Mere conventional or social rules supported by sanctions were not, for Mill as they were for Bentham, a form of morality or source of moral obligation as such but only so to the extent that their requirements happen to coincide with those of morality as Mill defines it: he states this doctrine in the following words:

> We do not call anything wrong unless we mean to imply that the person ought to be punished in some way or other for doing it; if not by law, by the opinion of his fellow-creatures; if not by opinion, by the reproaches of his own confidence. This seems the real turning point of the distinction between morality and simple expediency. It is part of the notion of duty in every one of its forms that a person may be rightfully compelled to fulfill it. Duty is a thing which may be exacted from a person as one exacts a debt; unless we think that it might be exacted from him we do not call it his duty . . . I think that there is no doubt that this distinction lies at the bottom of right and wrong; that we call any conduct wrong or employ instead some other terms of slight or disparagement according as we think the person ought or ought not to be punished for it.[32]

The connection which both Bentham and Mill make between the notion of duty or obligation and sanctions (and in Mill's case between moral wrong and sanctions) though they differ as to the form of connection, is enough to explain why no direct utilitarian theory of non-legal moral rights were entertained by either thinker. But it also explains why an indirect utilitarian account of moral rights was looked upon by Bentham (though only with some grudging tolerance) as a possible interpretation of natural rights and is taken very seriously by Mill in his account of moral rights as essential for the notion of Justice, which he regards as distinct from morality in general, because it involves respect for the moral rights of individuals.[33] At various points in his attack on natural rights Bentham allows that, at its most respectable, talk of non-legal and natural rights may be understood as an obscure way of asserting that men ought to have certain legal rights. 'If I say that a man has a natural

---

[32] Ibid. 246.   [33] Ibid. 247.

right to this coat or to this land, all that it can mean, if it mean anything and mean true, is that I am of opinion that he ought to have a political right to it: that by the appropriate services rendered on occasion to him by the appropriate functionaries of government he ought to be protected and secured in the use of it.'[34] Here Bentham adds: 'He ought to be so—that is to say that the idea of his being so is pleasing to me—the idea of the opposite result is displeasing to me.'[35] But in other passages Bentham contemplates that the speaker who resorts to the obscure language of natural rights in order to assert that there ought to be a certain legal right may have good reasons for the assertion, and that these good reasons are reasons of general utility. Yet even so Bentham thinks such language is to be deplored as mischievously obscure and encouraging dangerous confusion. 'In proportion to the want of happiness resulting from want of rights a reason exists for wishing that there were such rights'. 'But reasons for wishing there were such things as rights are not rights: a reason for wishing that a certain right were established is not that right —want is not supply—hunger is not bread.'[36] It is with this indirect utilitarian explanation of non-legal rights in mind that Bentham was able to say 'I know of no natural rights except those which are created by general utility but even in that sense it were much better that the words were never heard of.[37]

Though I know of no evidence that Mill had these passages of Bentham in mind in giving his own account of moral rights, that account seems like an echo of what Bentham says is 'all that can be meant' by the assertion of a natural right. But instead of deprecating as Bentham does the sense thus given to the notion of a non-legal right and condemning it as a source of confusion Mill thinks it essential for his account of Justice as distinguished from the rest of morality, since an unjust action is distinguished from actions that are merely morally wrong by the fact that it infringes the moral right of some 'assignable' individual. Mill insists that his doctrine is not one of 'abstract right'[38] and he does not use the expression 'natural right' but thought it possible while rejecting

---

[34] *Works* III 218.   [35] Ibid.   [36] *Works* II 501, cf. *Works* III 221.
[37] *Economic Writings* I 333.
[38] *On Liberty*, in *18 Collected Works of John Stuart Mill* (ed. Robson), 224.

traditional doctrines of abstract and natural rights to reach the conclusion that there are certain moral rights which all men have, protecting their most vital individual interests and which are 'natural' in all senses of the word which I have distinguished. For such rights, for Mill, are not human or divine artefacts; they are independent of social or conventional recognition and they are adapted to certain features of human nature. Mill's formulation, which seems so closely to resemble Bentham's language quoted above, is as follows: 'When we call anything a person's right we mean that he has a valid claim on society to protect him in the possession of it, either by the force of law or by that of education and opinion' and 'to have a right, then, is as I conceive to have something which society ought to defend me in the possession of.'[39] These formulations like Bentham's quoted above[40] do not themselves specify the reason why such claims as constitute rights should be enforced by society, but Mill adds this as a separate point: 'if the objector goes on to ask why it ought, I can give no reason other than general utility'[41] and this addition seems parallel to Bentham's 'in proportion to want of happiness resulting from want of rights a reason exists for wishing there were such rights.'[42]

Whether or not I am correct in thinking that Mill's analysis of moral rights is an echo of Bentham's brief and deprecatory observations, it certainly merits critical study. For if this account were successful it would answer what is surely the most serious charge, namely that of 'criterionlessness' which Bentham makes against the doctrine of natural rights and to which contemporary philosophers who have opposed to utilitarianism right-based political and moral theories are still struggling to find an answer.[43] Not only would Mill if his analysis were successful have found an answer to Bentham's most formidable charge but it is one which would have a special appeal to Bentham as a utilitarian though it involves a special and indirect form of that doctrine.

[39] *Utilitarianism*, 250.   [40] *Supra*, pp. 88–9.
[41] *Utilitarianism*, 250.   [42] *Supra*, p. 89.
[43] See among others Dworkin, *What Rights do we Have?* in *On Taking Rights Seriously* (op. cit. *supra*, p. 28, n. 25) criticized in my 'Between Utility and Rights', *Columbia Law Review* (1980).

In considering Mill's accounts of moral rights it is important to distinguish the general form of the analysis from the specific utilitarian reason ('general utility') which Mill offers for enforcing individual claims by law or social pressure which he thinks must exist if such claims are to constitute moral rights. For whatever the defects of the latter the general form of the analysis does reproduce some important features inherent in the conception of universal rights as used in the criticism of law and society or as elements of a political theory. The first of these features is the fact that according to the general form of Mill's analysis for an individual to have a moral right there must be reasons of special weight why he should have the liberty or other advantage to which he has a right. These reasons must be weighty enough to justify not only coercion in individual cases but the use of legal and social forms of enforcement with all the costs suffering and other disutilities which enforcement regulated in such ways inevitably entails. So if the reasons are reasons of general utility, as they are according to Mill's specific criterion, the kind of utility concerned is, as he says, 'extraordinarily important and impressive': 'the essentials of human well being', something which 'no human being can possibly do without'; 'it is a claim we have on our fellow-creatures to join in making safe for us the very groundwork of our existence.'[44] So Mill insists that the utilities involved in moral rights and 'the moral rules which forbid men to hurt one another in which we must never forget to include wrongful interference with each others' freedom are more vital to human well-being than any maxims, however important, which only point out the best mode of managing some department of human affairs.'[45]

Secondly, Mill's form of analysis well reproduces the peremptory character of moral rights: to have a right is to have a moral justification for demanding some liberty of action for oneself or some 'service' as Bentham called it, from others on the footing that even legal or social pressure is appropriate. Thirdly Mill's analysis reproduces, though I think ultimately in a misleading form, the idea that fundamental moral rights have weight even relative to existing law

---

[44] *Utilitarianism*, 251.   [45] Ibid. 255.

or established conventions of society. So if the existing law or conventions of society ignore such rights that is a moral case not for acquiescence but for demanding change and in certain circumstances for resistance.

None the less there are defects both in Mill's formal analysis of fundamental rights and the suggested utilitarian criterion of identification. It is plain that an acceptable analysis of moral rights must be such as to allow sense though not necessarily truth to the statement that the existence of such a right is a good moral reason for having and maintaining a law or social convention conferring a right. It must leave room for the assertion for example that the justification for a law conferring a legal right to worship as one pleases is that individuals have a moral right to this freedom, though there may also be other good reasons for such a law, and of course there are laws for which the protection of individuals' moral rights is no part of their justification. But if as Mill's form of analysis requires, to say that men have a moral right to worship as they please already means that there is a good reason why there should be a legal or conventional right to this freedom, the fact that men have this moral right cannot be advanced as a reason why there ought to be such a legal or conventional right. For if the existence of a moral right is to function as such a reason, the fact that such a right exists must be distinct from its being such a reason. If it were not so distinct, the statement that the fact that a moral right exists is a reason why there ought to be a legal right, would when spelt out, amount to the statement that the reason why there ought to be a certain legal right is that there ought to be a legal right.

It is no doubt theoretically possible that there should always be a good reason for enforcing by law any moral right. But if so this must be a contingent fact which might be otherwise; it cannot be something secured by the meaning of a moral right if we are to regard the existence of moral rights as providing moral reasons why there should be certain legal rights. It has been conceded by Professor David Lyons, to whose important defence of Mill's account of rights[46] I later refer, that Mill's analysis in terms of sanctions of moral

[46] David Lyons, 'Human Rights and the General Welfare' in *Philosophy and Public Affairs* 6 (1977).

wrong and moral obligation explained above may be inadequate since it seems to put the cart before the horse. If punishments are morally justified only if it is the case that something morally wrong has been done by the person punished, that he has done something wrong must be determined, contrary to Mill's account of moral wrong, independently of calculating whether punishment is justified. So another way of presenting the criticism made in the last paragraph of Mill's account of rights is that it too puts the cart before the horse. The legal enforcement of individual claims may be justified if the claims rank as moral rights but they cannot rank as moral rights because their legal enforcement is justified. Mill's analysis would, to use Bentham's satirical phrase which he addressed to Blackstone, 'serve the same thing dished up as a reason for itself'.[47]

A second objection to Mill's analysis is that there are certainly very important rights which only governments as a whole can give effect to because it requires the enactments and maintenance of laws; yet not all rights even those which Mill recognized as universal are rights only against governments or society as a whole calling for the creation or maintenance of appropriate laws or conventions, but Mill at times speaks, perhaps only carelessly, as if all such rights or claims are claims only on society for their protection. Clearly some fundamental rights such as those of security of the person may also call for non-interference or possibly active assistance by individuals.

Both the two defects which I have mentioned would be avoided if the reference to enforcement by law or opinion which appears in Mill's analysis is not treated as a defining feature of moral rights or as indicating that they are rights exclusively against governments or society as a whole but simply as a *measure* of the great weight or importance of the reason why individuals should have the particular liberty or service which is the content of his moral right. On this footing to say that men have a right to worship as they please is to say that, judged by whatever may be the appropriate criteria, freedom of worship is of such importance that it outweighs even the burdens, disadvantages, and other disutilities of maintaining law to protect it, and so *a fortiori*

[47] *Fragment* Preface in *CW* 407 n.

outweighs whatever general reasons individuals have for suppressing or interfering with such freedom. So if men have a moral right to worship as they please this will be a right which individuals as well as governments must respect. But it is the importance or weight of the right identified as a right independently of its being a reason for legal or social enforcement that makes it possible to say that it is a reason for such enforcement.

IV

But the most important defect in Mill's account of moral rights is the part general utility is made to play in the identification of those individual claims which are to constitute moral rights. Not only must an acceptable theory of rights be such, as I have already said, as to make sense of the statement that the fact that men have a particular moral right is a reason why they ought to have a certain legal right, but it must also permit us to distinguish between different types of moral justification for the creation of legal rights. It is plain that general utility and the existence of antecedent moral rights are different justifications even if in some cases both justifications could be offered for the creation of the same legal right. If these two types of justification were the same the result would be that to add to the statement that men have a moral right, say, to worship as they please, the further statement that it will maximize general utility to secure this freedom by law would be a tautology, and to add that it would not maximize utility to secure this by law would be a contradiction. On such a view there could never be a conflict between rights and utility.

Concrete examples may bring home the difficulties inherent in any unqualified identification of the existence of moral rights with the existence of reasons of general utility for the creation or maintenance of legal rights. At the end of the last war in England it was decided that the needs of the economy were such that for the benefit of the country as a whole two steps should be taken. The first was that farmers should be paid certain sums by way of subsidy for turning over to certain types of farming, and the second that coalworkers from abroad willing to work in English pits should be allowed into the country to do so. These changes were made into law, so out of considerations of general utility farmers and foreign coalworkers were given legal rights to subsidies in the first case and to the liberty to come to England to work in the second case. Yet no one who argued for, or approved of, this legislation on such grounds did so on the footing that they showed that the farmers or immigrant miners had moral rights to subsidies or to work here. To conclude from the facts that they had would be to confuse the notion of a moral right with the notion of the right thing to do. If the justifying reason for conceding certain legal or other positive social rights is general utility we can on the basis of utilitarian morality say that to create and maintain such rights is the right thing for the government to do. But this does not carry with it the notion that the person receiving these legal rights has any moral rights to the advantages secured by them. The statement that persons have moral rights to the creation or maintenance of legal rights means that the latter is something to be justified not by reference to considerations of aggregate general welfare but by reference to the separate good in some form of the individuals who are to receive these rights and on the footing that that good is not merely of value as a contribution to pooled or aggregate welfare.

Mill in fact in his identification of certain universal moral rights comes very near though not near enough to recognizing the difference illustrated by these simple examples between justifying the creation of legal rights by reference to general utility and justifying them by reference to antecedent moral rights. He comes nearest to this when he stresses the difference between reasons of what he terms 'ordinary expediency' and those 'vastly more important utilities' which he treats as alone relevant to the identification of universal moral rights 'protecting every individual from being harmed by others either directly or by being hindered in his freedom of pursuing his own good'.[48] The increased benefits to the economy and the general welfare secured by legal subsidies to farmers and permission to foreign miners to work here are certainly what Mill called 'reasons of

[48] *Utilitarianism*, 256; cf. Mill. *On the Subjection of Women* (London 1869), Chap. 2, para. 12.

ordinary expediency', and the case for granting such rights is discovered by enquiring what benefits this would bring to the economy as a whole not to assignable individuals. But the utilities which according to Mill are the stuff of those universal rights to which all individuals are entitled are forms of the individual good of those who have such rights. They are the essentials of individual human wellbeing and things no individual human being can possibly do without. They are identified quite independently of general utility as if the criterion was to do exclusively with individual good, not general utility. Yet Mill is committed to the view that the reason for protecting such individual goods by legal enforcement is general utility and that their status as moral rights is dependent on this being the case. He is therefore committed to a criterion for the identification of moral rights which has two components: essential individual good and the general utility of legal or social enforcement. If his theory is to avoid contradiction it must be shown not merely that these two halves of the criterion may coincide but (exceptions for particular cases apart) that they cannot diverge, so general utility must always require general rules providing legal or social protection of such forms of individual good for all men.[49] This could be shown vacuously if general utility were merely a name for the state of affairs in which all the essential individual goods of all persons were fully protected by law or social convention; but in that case general utility could not be a reason for such legal or social protection. If on the other hand general utility does stand for some pooled or aggregate welfare which may vary in amount or degree, Mill to preserve the consistency of his double-barrelled criterion would have to show that rules denying to some minority of persons the protection of essential individual goods could never result in a greater degree of aggregate welfare than the protection of such individual goods of all persons alike. Mill nowhere attempts to demonstrate that such general sacrifice of some individuals could never be called for by general

---

[49] Mill does allow that moral rights, which he regards every human being as possessing, are not absolute: they may 'in particular cases be overridden by other social utilities which may in the particular case be more important though not as a class (*Utilitarianism*, 259). For his view on the necessity of public rules to secure basic individual interests, see the essay on *Whewell on Moral Philosophy* in *10 Collected Works*, 192.

utility. Even those writers most concerned to show how different Mill's conception of utility is from Bentham's and that by happiness he did not mean, as Bentham did, anything as simple as a surplus of pleasure over pain or of want-satisfaction over want-frustration but rather the development and realization of individuality,[50] do not suppose that this of itself would entail that the freedom and protection from harm to which Mill thinks every human being has a moral right should be extended to every human being alike. For the possibility remains even on this non-Benthamite characterization of utility that a greater realization of individuality summed up over all would be secured if the individuality of some were suppressed so as to permit its greater realization by others. Not only is this a theoretical possibility but it is arguable that in great cultures where minorities have been suppressed, or which have flourished on the dunghill of slavery, the oppression of the individuality of some could be justified in this way. Bentham was not faced with this problem since he was in no way committed to any doctrine of universal rights and was content to let objections to slavery rest on what Mill would have called reasons of ordinary expediency. Thus Bentham's objections were not to the condition of slavery as such but to the consequences of mass slavery and specifically that slave labour in the absence of security and incentives was likely to be less productive than paid free labour. He claimed that though the evil of the condition of a single slave might not in itself be great and might on utilitarian grounds be offset by its advantage to the slave owner, slavery once established, was always likely to be the lot of large numbers. 'If the evil of slavery were not great its extent alone would make it considerable.'[51]

It is of course true that even in its Benthamite form utilitarianism has an egalitarian aspect which might appear to support the belief that a doctrine of universal rights could rest on utilitarian foundations. For utilitarianism is, in a benign sense of the expression, 'no respecter of persons'. This is so because if the only elements of value and disvalue

---

[50] See C.L. Ten, *Mill on Liberty* (OUP 1980), especially Chap. 5 on 'Individuality'. I am much indebted to this work and to conversations with its author.
[51] *Works* I 345.

are pleasures and pains or experiences of want-satisfaction and want-frustration, then in the determination of what would most advance aggregate happiness, the equal pleasures and pains, satisfactions and frustrations of different persons must be given equal weight. Differences of status, race, sex, religion, age, and intelligence are morally irrelevant except when they affect as they may sometimes do the amount or intensity of pain or pleasure caused by human conduct. Suffering is suffering no matter whose it is and if suffering is equal, it is equally bad to inflict it on blacks or white, women or men, Jews or Christians, the stupid and intelligent. 'Everybody is to count for one.' Bentham himself urged the extension of this egalitarian principle to all beings capable of suffering, including non-human animals, and not merely to exclude, racial, religious, or sexual prejudices against giving equal consideration to the equal pains and pleasures of all human beings. His words in effect identifying speciesism as a vice as objectionable as racism are memorable:

The French have already discovered that the blackness of the skin is no reason why a human being should be abandoned without redress to the caprice of a tormentor. It may one day come to be recognized that the number of the legs the vellosity of the skin or the termination of the *os sacrum* are reasons equally insufficient for abandoning a sensitive being to the same fate. What else is it that should trace the insuperable line? Is it the faculty of reason, or perhaps the faculty of discourse? But a full grown horse or dog is beyond comparison a more rational, as well as a more conversable animal than an infant of a day or week, or even a month old. But suppose they were otherwise what would it avail? The question is not can they reason? nor can they talk? but can they suffer?[52]

But this egalitarian aspect of Bentham's utilitarianism though it serves to exclude irrelevant prejudices in the computation of the general welfare as the measure of right and wrong cannot serve as a foundation for individual rights. As many contemporary philosophers, hostile to utilitarianism, have been concerned to show, it in principle licenses the imposition of sacrifices on innocent individuals when this can be shown to advance net aggregate welfare. Such sacrifices may be licensed because the egalitarianism embodied in the maxim 'everybody to count for one and nobody for more

[52] *PML* Chap. XVII, para. 4, in *CW* 283.

than one' is only a weighting principle, to be used in calculating what will maximize aggregate happiness; it treats
persons as equals by securing that in the determination of
what measures are required by the general welfare equal
weight must be given to the equal happiness of all persons.
But it is not a principle requiring the equal treatment of
different persons and it may yield grossly inegalitarian results,
though in certain circumstances it will tend to favour the
equal distribution of economic resources owing to their de-
clining, marginal utility. Individual persons and the *level* of
an individual's happiness are for the utilitarian only of in-
strumental, not intrinsic importance. Persons are merely the
'receptacles' for the experiences which will increase or
diminish aggregate welfare. So utilitarianism is 'no respecter
of persons' in a sinister as well as a benign sense of that
expression, and its egalitarian aspect provides no foundation
for universal moral rights.

Mill, in his discussion of Justice, cites and stresses the importance of Bentham's maxim 'everybody to count for one
and nobody for more than one' regarding it as part of the
meaning of the Greatest Happiness Principle and says that
'It might be written under the principle of Utility as an explanatory commentary.'[53] He rejects Herbert Spencer's
contention that if the principle of Utility is to have egalitarian implications it must presuppose an 'anterior principle
that everyone has an equal right to happiness',[54] and he says
correctly that the Benthamite maxim is only the weighting
principle 'that equal amounts of happiness are equally desirable whether felt by the same or different persons.'[55] Yet
Mill's treatment of this weighting principle is I think confused and certainly at odds with the rest of his account of
moral rights. He claims that as a consequence of this principle
all persons have a right to equality of treatment 'except when
some recognised social expediency requires the reverse'.[56] It
is not clear what the quoted words include but presumably
they do not mean that individuals may be treated unequally
whenever the general welfare would be advanced more by un-
equal than by equal treatment, but if this is so Mill is using

[53] *Utilitarianism*, 258 n.
[54] Ibid.   [55] Ibid.   [56] Ibid.

the maxim 'everybody to count for one and nobody for more than one' as more than a mere weighting principle merely 'making the truths of arithmetic applicable to the valuation of happiness as to all other measurable qualities'.[57]

Secondly, the idea that the principle of utility itself confers a moral right to equal treatment or indeed any sort of moral right conflicts with Mill's formal analysis which ties the idea of a moral right closely to the specific idea of a reason for enforcement by law or social convention. The right to equal treatment which Mill speaks of here exists as a right, in his view, independently of any question of enforcement: it rests solely on the distributive and egalitarian aspect of the principle of utility as Mill and Bentham both interpret it. So Mill says of the correlative duty to treat all equally well who have deserved equally well that this is 'a direct emanation from the first principle of morals involved in the very meaning of the principle of utility.'[58] This is indeed satisfactory to the extent that this would allow non-tautologous sense to the statement that the existence of a moral right to equal treatment is a good moral reason for enforcing equal treatment by law. But it cannot be reconciled with Mill's formal analysis of rights which incorporates being a good reason for enforcement into the very meaning of 'a moral right'.

V

Though Bentham's maxim 'everybody to count for one and nobody for more than one' will not serve the purpose, certainly Mill has, as Mr Ten has argued,[59] resources in the form of his principle of liberty with which to meet such arguments against universal rights, and to show that the sacrifice of minorities to the general welfare could not be justified. But these resources are available to Mill, I think, only at the cost of abandoning his account of universal moral rights in terms of the general utility of legal or social enforcement. The principle of liberty allows interference with individual liberty (which the suppression of individuality would of course involve) only to prevent harm to others, and it is plain that,

---

[57] Ibid.   [58] Op. cit. 257.
[59] C.L. Ten, op. cit. (n. 50, *supra*) 78–9.

however vague that phrase is, it would prohibit the suppression of one person's individuality simply to secure a greater increase in its realization by others. Individual liberty, 'not to be hindered in the pursuit of one's own good' satisfies the first part of Mill's double criterion for being a moral right since it is in Mill's view one of 'the essentials of human happiness', not just a reason of ordinary expediency. But the principle of liberty is not an aggregative principle of general welfare but a distributive principle and it is this which constitutes individual liberty a universal right, not the general utility of its enforcement by law or social convention. Because it is such a right independently of the general utility of its enforcement by law the existence of such a right may coherently be said to be a reason for such enforcement. This will be consistent with treating the statement that the existence of a particular moral right, e.g. to worship as one pleases, is a good reason for creating a legal right as an informative statement of a reason for creating that legal right, and not as the empty tautology that the existence of a good reason for creating a legal right to worship as one pleases is a good reason for creating such a legal right.

What is true of the right to liberty thus secured by the distributive principle of liberty is true of those other essentials of human happiness which Mill treats as universal rights but cannot plausibly be regarded merely as aspects of liberty. These include what Mill calls 'the moralities which protect every individual from being harmed by others directly'. The moral rules, as Mill calls them, which secure these for every man as being essential to human happiness and so satisfying the first part of his double criterion, are also distributive principles like the principle of liberty and so exclude the denial of such rights to some simply to secure an increase in the welfare of others.

If what constitutes individual liberty and the other forms of individual goods as universal rights is a conjunction of the fact that as essentials of human happiness they satisfy the first part of Mill's double criterion together with distributive principles such as the principle of liberty, then no part in the constitution of such rights is played by general utility as the second part of Mill's double criterion would require. This conclusion can, I think, only be avoided if it could be shown that the distributive principles required to support universal rights were either derived from aggregate principles of utility or were justified as the best practical means of giving effect to them. That this is so has been argued by Professor Lyons[60] who thinks that the contrary view springs from the mistake of thinking that Mill is an act-utilitarian concerned to justify particular acts by showing that they maximize utility. Mill, Lyons argues, is concerned with the utility not only of acts but of rules and policies which may require particular acts which do not maximize utility, but the consistent practice of which will none the less advance utility further than fallible attempts to calculate in each particular case which of all possible acts will secure the greatest utility. To follow such principles therefore though they are distributive in form will be an indirect way of securing the best possible advance in general utility. They are distributive principles which a concern for general welfare in the circumstances of practical life will require us to follow.

This interpretation of the status of Mill's principle of liberty certainly deserves serious consideration but I believe it to be mistaken. Though Mill's consistency and the extent of non-utilitarian tendencies in his work, especially the essay *On Liberty* is controversial, those tendencies cannot be ignored. Professor Lyons says that it is unnecessary to 'hypothesise' them; but if the principle of liberty requiring that all men be free to do what is not harmful to others were merely a device for avoiding the errors, which would beset the act-utilitarians' attempts to calculate and compare the effects on general welfare of interfering with liberty and leaving it unrestricted, Mill could not have argued, as he does, for a principle qualified only by the exception 'harm to others' or for the exclusion of so many different utilitarian considerations relevant to the restrictions of liberty.

Thus, if as Professor Lyons argues, what was fundamentally at stake in framing the principle of liberty was the general welfare, exceptions could certainly be made for forms of paternalistic legislation with clear defined limits. In fact Professor Lyons says that Mill 'could easily' have accepted this;[61] but the point is that Mill's failure to provide for

---

[60] Op. cit. n. 46 *supra*.   [61] Op. cit. 118.

something so obvious shows that the principle qualified only by the exception of 'harm to others' is not, for Mill, an indirect way of securing the general welfare itself resting on purely Utilitarian foundations. Similarly the exclusion from the ambit of the exception of 'harm to others' of the distress, dislike, moral 'indignation', or other painful reactions felt by those who object to non-conforming religious or sexual practices, would remain inexplicable on Professor Lyons's view of the status of the principle of liberty.[62] That principle with its one exception is therefore, for Mill, a constraint on the pursuit of aggregate welfare at the cost of individuals and not merely an indirect way of securing it.

So Mill's account of moral rights fails at two points. First, his general form of analysis puts the cart before the horse and allows no sense to the statement that the fact that men have a moral right e.g. to worship as they please, is a good reason for protecting this freedom by law. Here Bentham's repeated warning 'a reason for a right is not a right, hunger is not bread, want is not supply' seems to be vindicated. Secondly the second part of Mill's double criterion for Universal Moral Rights, which was perhaps suggested to him by Bentham's casual and contemptuous remarks and which identifies as rights those forms of individual good the protection of which by law or social convention is required by general utility in fact plays no part in the identification of such rights and should be discarded both as irrelevant and as a source of confusion except as an indication of the weight and importance of such rights. What is left is the first part of the double criterion identifying universal rights as those forms of individual good which are 'the essentials of human happiness', 'the groundwork of our existence', things 'no human being can do without'. Such descriptions even when interpreted in the light of the specific rights which Mill mentions are no doubt vague and controversial, but are I think more than 'mere sounds to dispute about'. They at least narrow the area of dispute and point to the direction in which it might be further narrowed. They suggest that what is wanted to make sense of the notion of universal moral rights is a theory of what individuals need and can reasonably demand from

---

[62] Cf. Ten op. cit. n. 50 *supra*, 54, 78.

each other (by way either of restraint or of active provision) in order to pursue their own ends through the development of distinctive human powers. Some contemporary philosophers have advanced right-based political and moral theories which attempt to derive basic rights from allegedly uncontroversial premisses, such as that human beings are entitled to equal concern or respect[63] or to the preservation of their 'separateness' as individuals.[64] I have considered two such attempts elsewhere[65] and here merely record my view that I do not think any theory of basic human rights can succeed which does not take the form of a theory suggested by the first part of Mill's double criterion.

---

[63] Dworkin op. cit. (n. 43 *supra*) 272 ff.
[64] Nozick *Anarchy, State and Utopia*, 32–3.
[65] 'Between Utility and Rights', op. cit. (n. 43 *supra*).

V

BENTHAM'S *OF LAWS IN GENERAL*

I

Bentham's *Of Laws in General* is a remarkable work with a remarkable history. I have recounted the history of the work in some detail in the editorial preface to the edition published in 1970 in *The Collected Works of Jeremy Bentham*[1] but the salient features of the story are sufficiently curious and I think sufficiently instructive to justify a brief mention here. *Of Laws in General* is in fact a continuation of Bentham's best-known work *An Introduction to the Principles of Morals and Legislation*. The latter work was printed in 1780 but its publication was held back by Bentham for nine years during which, as he told a correspondent, half the printed sheets were devoured by the rats. At last in 1789, partly as the result of pressure exerted by many friends, Bentham finally published the work, adding a preface explaining the delay and apologizing for its still uncompleted state and also attaching to the last chapter a long note sketching in outline the doctrines needed to complete the work. These doctrines he had already developed in detail and they formed the substance of the work now published under the title *Of Laws in General*, which Bentham used for a list of its intended contents. This title echoes Blackstone's *Of the Nature of Laws in General* for Book I para. 2 of his *Commentaries*.

In explaining the nine-year delay in publishing the *Introduction to the Principles*, Bentham tells us that when the body of that work was complete he found himself 'unexpectedly entangled in an unsuspected corner of the metaphysical maze'.[2] What led him into the maze was the attempt to

---

[1] London 1970, ed. H. L. A. Hart. Since the publication of this text a considerable number of errors of transcription from the MSS have been discovered. None affects the substance of any of Bentham's arguments or the use made of *OLG* in the present work. A list of corrigenda is obtainable from the Bentham Project, University College London, Gower St., London WC1E 6BT.

[2] *PML* Preface in *CW* 1.

answer in the last paragraph of the last chapter which is entitled 'Of the Limits of the Penal Branch of Jurisprudence' an apparently simple question. The question concerned the nature of the familiar distinction between the civil and the penal branch of jurisprudence, and between a civil code of law and a penal code. At first Bentham thought, as he told Lord Ashburton, 'the line of separation between these objects' (that is, between penal and civil laws) 'might be traced within the compass of a page or two[3] but he soon became convinced that this was a mistake. It should be explained that for Bentham 'penal' is a much wider term than 'criminal'; for it covers all cases where the law imposes obligations or duties and provides sanctions for them; it includes, therefore, not only crimes but what are now recognized as civil offences or civil wrongs, such as, torts, breaches of contract, and breaches of trust. All these offences, criminal and civil, had been analysed and classified by Bentham in his enormous sixteenth chapter in his *Introduction to the Principles*, entitled 'The Division of Offences'.[4] And when he came to write the last section of the seventeenth and last chapter of that work the problem to which he turned was whether or not there really were (as the distinction between penal and civil suggests) besides penal laws creating offences, laws of another distinct kind—civil laws not imposing duties or creating offences, and if so, what was the relation between them. The words in which he posed this question are these:

What is a penal code of laws? What a civil code? Of what nature are their contents? Is it that there are two sorts of laws, the one penal, the other civil, so that the laws in a penal code are all penal laws while the laws in a civil code are all civil laws? Or is it that in every law there is some matter which is of a penal nature and which therefore belongs to the penal code, and at the same time other matter which is of a civil nature and which therefore belongs to the civil code?[5]

It is obvious that a great bastion of the imperative theory of law would fall if there were found to be laws which did not impose duties and create offences. But to answer these questions Bentham found it necessary to raise other and more fundamental ones, though he did not at first appreciate

[3] *OLG* 305.
[4] *PML* in *CW* 187–280.
[5] Ibid. Chap. XVII, para. 29, in *CW* 299.

how far it would be necessary to dig down to fundamentals, and to confront 'a multitude of problems' which, as he later said, were 'of the most intricate kind which nobody seem'd hitherto to have thought of solving.'[6] These problems concern the basic structure of laws and what Bentham called the individuation of a law. This is something more specific than the general definition of a law; for to settle the individuation of a law it is necessary to ask not, or not merely, 'what is law'? but 'what is *a* law'? What is to count as a single complete law and what as merely a part or parts of a law? These questions Bentham first proposed to answer in two further sections to be added to the last chapter of *An Introduction to the Principles* as it stood in 1780. But when he set to work on them he found that even whole chapters would not suffice for his purpose. By 1782 he had written chapters enough to make a substantial book and wide enough in scope to make appropriate the title *Of Laws in General* which he chose for it. But by 1789 when he published *An Introduction to the Principles* he thought the topics of the further work 'might require a considerable volume'[7] and that this should be published as the last of a then projected series of ten volumes covering the whole field of legislation.[8]

Alas, none of these plans for publication matured: hence it was that *Of Laws in General* lay buried among Bentham's papers for more than 160 years until 1945 when Professor Charles Everett of Columbia University correctly identified it as a continuation of the *Introduction to the Principles of Morals and Legislation*, and published an edition of it under the title *The Limits of Jurisprudence Defined*. Students of Bentham owe a great debt to Professor Everett for his brilliant discovery and for his labour on the difficult manuscripts, and this debt is not diminished by the fact that in the present edition, published under the title that Bentham chose for it, substantial departures from and additions to the text as formerly printed have been made, where further consideration of the manuscripts or other evidence of Bentham's intentions shows that such changes were required.

---

[6] *OLG* 305.
[7] *PML* Concluding Note, para. 1, in *CW* 301.
[8] Ibid. Preface in *CW* 6.

II

I shall devote the rest of this chapter to expounding as best as I can the main features of this extraordinary work. Its originality and power certainly make it the greatest of Bentham's contributions to analytical jurisprudence, and I think it is clear that, had it been published in his lifetime, it, rather than John Austin's later and obviously derivative work, would have dominated English jurisprudence, and that analytical jurisprudence, not only in England, would have advanced far more rapidly and branched out in more fertile ways than it has since Bentham's days. It is true that in broad outline the theory of law which this book presents is the same as that to be found in Austin's *Province of Jurisprudence Determined* and his *Lectures on Jurisprudence or the Philosophy of Positive Law*. For like Austin's theory, Bentham's is an imperative theory of law in which the central concepts are those of sovereign and command, and the definitions of both sovereign and command are at first sight very similar in the two authors. But Bentham expounds these ideas with far greater subtlety and flexibility than Austin and illuminates aspects of law largely neglected by him. Thus instead of an uncompromising doctrine that there must in every legal system be a single sovereign person or body of persons whose legislative powers are legally unlimited, Bentham carefully canvasses the idea that the habit of obedience on which for him, as for Austin, legal sovereignty rests, might be susceptible of various interesting modifications.[9] It might be, for example, partial, that is not forthcoming at all in relation to certain areas of conduct, or it might be divided; so that habitual obedience was rendered to one person or body sovereign on some matters and to another person or body sovereign on other matters. His conclusion was that while there are normally good practical reasons for vesting unlimited legislative power in a single sovereign person or body, there were no conceptual necessities here—no logical objection to the notion of division and limitation of sovereign power. Indeed he found in certain types of federal constitutions historical examples of such arrangements. Moreover Bentham

[9] OLG 18, n. 6; see the further discussion and criticism of Bentham's theory of sovereignty in Chap. IX *infra*.

accepts under the striking and very un-Austinian title of 'constitutional laws *in principem*'[10] the legal quality of restrictions on the supreme legislative power, imposed by a sovereign on himself by a contract with his subjects, and adopted by his successors. Though he thought that such restrictions would usually be enforced by extra-legal, moral, or religious sanctions, he thought it possible that given the appropriate division of habits of obedience that they might also be enforced in the Courts by legal sanctions.[11] He here, therefore, approaches the notion of judicial review, and though his discussion is cramped by what is, in my opinion, an inadequate conceptual framework of commands and habits of obedience, it is a far more rewarding and thought-provoking discussion than Austin's dismissal of the idea of legal limitations on the sovereign.

Bentham's conception of the relation between laws and legal sanctions is also different and more relaxed than Austin's, and contemporary legal theorists who think the rigid separation of legal from moral obligations misguided will find suggestive matter here. For Bentham thought that the sovereign's commands would still be law even if supported only by moral or religious sanctions[12] and he also accepts as a class of laws which he calls 'praemiary or invitative laws'[13] those issued by the legislator without a threat of punishment but accompanied by the offer of a reward for compliance. Bentham discusses in characteristic detail[14] why such laws unsupported by legal sanctions must be rare and why it is that 'in the nomenclature as well as in the practice of the law' that it is on coercive sanctions or, as he terms them, 'punishments', that 'everything turns'.[15]

However, what chiefly differentiates Bentham from Austin and makes him so interesting a philosopher of law is that he was a conscious innovator of new forms of enquiry into the structure of law, and that he makes explicit his method and the general logic of enquiry in a way in which no other writer on these topics does. Hence it is not only jurists but philosophers and logicians who will find some striking anticipations in this book, not only of modern

---

[10] *OLG* 64–71.
[11] *OLG* 68 n.
[12] *OLG* 70, 248.
[13] *OLG* 136.
[14] *OLG* 134–5.
[15] *OLG* 136 f.

legal theories but of modern methodology and even logical doctrines.

These qualities are manifested in the manner in which Bentham defends in his opening chapter the wide definition of a law which he enunciates in his first sentence 'A law may be defined as an assemblage of signs declarative of a volition, conceived or adopted by the *sovereign* in a state, concerning the conduct to be adopted in a certain *case* by a certain person or class of persons who in the case in question are, or are supposed to be, subject to his power.'[16]

From the outset Bentham insists that his readers should appreciate that this definition of law as an expression of the will is much wider than the term 'law' in ordinary usage;[17] for it covers not only *general* laws made by legislatures supreme or subordinate but particular judicial orders, administrative orders (particular or general) and even domestic orders such as those given by a parent to a child whom the parent is permitted by law to punish for disobedience; it also includes measures which repeal or make exceptions to existing laws, which are of the nature of countermand rather than command. Before choosing his wide definition of a law, Bentham gave considerable, though, as always, critical attention to common usage; indeed he discussed with great insight the different historical and local influences which the extension of the English word 'law' reflects.[18] But as he says elsewhere his concern is not 'to teach' but rather 'to fix' the meaning of terms[19] and he justifies his fixing the expression 'a law' with a much wider extension than that given to it in common usage in a manner which shows that he thought along very modern lines about the criteria which should govern the selection of concepts appropriate for use in a science. Indeed what he says sounds very much like modern conceptions of analysis as a 'rational reconstruction' or refinement of concepts in ordinary use.

Thus Bentham defends his selection in two ways. First he points out that his definition picks out a range of phenomena to all of which, as he says, 'we have continual occasion to apply the same propositions',[20] that is, the definition collects a frequently recurrent cluster of features. Secondly

[16] *OLG* 1.   [17] *OLG* 3-9.
[18] *OLG* 6-10.   [19] *Works* III 217.   [20] *OLG* 10.

he stresses the point that his definition isolates an intelligible unit in terms of which other more complex legal phenomena may be analysed, and to which they may be reduced. To bring out the constructive aspect of his definition, and to show that it is as we should say, a model, Bentham speaks of it as defining an ideal object, 'the logical, the ideal, the intellectual whole',[21] and as 'what must be previously formed in order to serve as a pattern'[22] to which for example the contents of a statute or any number of statutes must be reduced. A law so defined is to be preferred as a tool of analysis to the idea of a statute, for a single statute might contain only a part of a law or parts of different laws or multiples of laws, or any combination of these things. So in a vivid image, Bentham compares the use of these two different concepts (a law, as he defines it, and a statute), for the analysis of legal phenomena, to different ways of dividing up an animal carcass: 'if a coarse allusion may be allowed' he said: 'a law as defined here in comparison with a statute is what a single but entire muscle dissected off by an anatomist is to a steak or joint as cut off by a butcher.'[23]

III

The idea of a law as an expression of the lawmaker's volition which Bentham describes in his opening sentence and chooses to serve as his pattern of analysis at first glance looks like the idea of a command familiar from Austin's jurisprudence. But though Bentham's definition includes the idea of a command, it cannot as I have said be identified with it; for according to Bentham a command is only one of four *aspects* or phases which the legislator's will expressed in a law or 'mandate' may bear to the act or acts concerning which he is legislating, which in Bentham's terms are the *objects* of the law. Between these four aspects of the legislator's will and hence of laws Bentham finds certain 'necessary relations' of 'opposition and concomitancy'[24] or, as we should say, certain logical relationships of compatibility and incompatibility; and he thinks that a grasp of these is necessary if we are to understand the

---

[21] *PML* Concluding Note, para. 2, in *CW* 301.
[22] *OLG* 12.
[23] Ibid.   [24] *OLG* 97.

structure of laws and of a system of laws and the conflicts
which may arise between laws.

To exhibit these relationships Bentham developed and in
fact discovered the foundations of an imperative or 'deontic'
logic. In so doing he anticipated not later than 1782 the ideas
of logicians of our own day to whom his work was of course
unknown since it lay buried in the masses of his papers up
to 1945. Bentham calls this form of logic 'the logic of the
will'[25] or 'the logic of imperation'[26] and rightly says 'that it
was untouched by Aristotle' whose logic is 'a logic of the
understanding' which exhibits 'the several forms of argu-
mentation'; whereas the business of the logic of the will is
to exhibit 'the several forms of imperation; or (to take the
subject to its utmost extent) of sentences expressive of
volition; a leaf which seems wanting in the book of science.'[27]
Bentham says that on this subject he had to make the tools
he needed for his analysis and to begin, as he puts it, *ab
ovo*.[28] His claims to be an innovator in this important matter
are I think justified. For although there are scattered hints of
the possibility of a logic of imperatives in the works of earlier
logicians from Anselm to Leibniz, Bentham's articulation of
it seems to have been quite without a forerunner.

A critical exposition of Bentham's logic of the will and of
his account of what he terms the 'aspects of the will' and
their expression in 'mandates' would involve many techni-
calities, but its main features are I think readily comprehensible. If we start with the idea of a command, taking, for
simplicity's sake, an example of a simple command addressed
to an individual to do a single act, like 'shut the door', we
can form from this, using only the idea of a negative act
(that is the not doing or forbearing from some specific act)
the idea of a prohibition, which, in this case, will be 'do not
shut the door'. For a prohibition against doing something is
equivalent to a command not to do it. Command and prohibition are then two of the four aspects of the will; these
two are termed by Bentham 'decided' aspects of the will and
their expression in relation to any conduct Bentham calls

[25] *OLG* 15, n. h; cf. *PML* Chap. XVII, para. 29, n. b2 in *CW* 299 (300).
[26] *OLG* 15, n. h; cf. *PML* Chap. XVII, para. 29, n. b2 in *CW* 299.
[27] *PML* Chap. XVII, para. 29, n. b2, in *CW* 299.
[28] Ibid.

'decisive' or 'directive' mandates. With these two decided aspects of the will Bentham contrasts the remaining two aspects which he calls 'undecided': these are expressed in what he terms 'undirective mandates'.[29] These two may be formed from the ideas of a command and a prohibition which we already now have, again by the use of the notion of *negation*, though here this notion is used in a different way, not to negate the act but to negate the decided aspect. Thus we can form from the idea of the command 'shut the door' the idea of 'a non-command' (or permission to forbear) expressible as 'you may refrain from shutting the door'; and from the idea of a prohibition 'do not shut the door' we may form that of a non-prohibition (or permission to act) expressible as 'you may shut the door'. These then are the four aspects of the will, or as the modern logician might term them, four imperative operators or deontic modalities.

In terms of these four aspects of the will an account can be given of what can and cannot be said to be the law in a coherent system of law at any given time in relation to a given act. Thus for example a command would exclude both a prohibition and a non-command (or permission to refrain) but will include non-prohibition or permission to act. Similarly, a permission to act will exclude a prohibition and must be accompanied by one of the remaining pair (command and permission to refrain) but since they are, as Bentham says, contradictories, it cannot be accompanied by both. These are instances of the generalization which Bentham states as follows: 'there are upon all occasions, two of these aspects, and on none more than two presented to the act at the same time'.[30] Accordingly mandates expressing these four aspects of the will will form a square of opposition of the same structure as that used to exhibit relationships of inclusion and exclusion between the general propositions of the AEIO

---

[29] *OLG* Chap. X *passim.*

[30] Ibid. 97. For simplicity I have taken as an example above a singular command ('Shut the door') addressed to an individual. Bentham's examples are mainly mandates referring to action-types addressed to classes of persons (e.g. 'Every householder shall carry arms', 'Let no person export corn'). Not only are these more appropriate to the usual business of legislation than singular commands but the relatively simple proof (which I give later (*infra*, pp. 115-17)) that all the relationships between mandates identified by Bentham hold good requires them to be interpreted as referring to action types.

forms familiar from Aristotelian logic. Bentham himself does not draw out the diagram of such a square of opposition but correctly presents all the relationships which it illustrates. Its form is as shown in the diagram.[31]

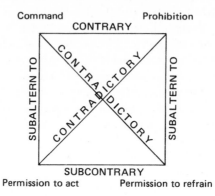

Bentham does not explain or apparently see any need to explain the logical basis of the relationships of what he calls 'opposition and concomitance' between mandates which he identifies. It has been tentatively suggested by Professor Lyons[32] that Bentham may have thought that 'ordinary logic' was sufficient to account for these relationships and no special explanation was necessary since he may have conceived of commands as a specific kind of first-person descriptive statement (which could be true or false) describing the will of the person giving the command. I am more confident than Professor Lyons is that Bentham did conceive of commands and the other forms of imperation as descriptive statements, and I discuss this in Chapter X, but I do not think that if commands are so conceived and are held to be true or false, all the relationships identified by Bentham can be shown to be just an application of ordinary logic. For

[31] See for formalization of Bentham's logic of the will Raz, *The Concept of a Legal System* (Oxford 1970), 54-9, and the general discussion by Lyons (from whose interpretation I differ on certain points) *In the Interest of the Governed* (Oxford 1973), 112-74, and by Lysaght, 'Bentham on the Aspects of a Law' in *Betham and Legal Theory* ed. James (*Northern Ireland Legal Quarterly* offprint: Belfast 1973).

[32] Op. cit. 121.

there is nothing in ordinary logic to show that commands and prohibitions interpreted descriptively (e.g. as 'I wish you to shut the door', 'I wish you not to shut the door' cannot both be true as required by ordinary logic for contraries. If they are treated as contraries this is due to the meaning attached to the expression 'I wish' or, as Professor Lyons puts it in another context, to the substance of what is said, and not to ordinary logical principles.[33] The same is true of the relationships between sub-contraries and between super and subalterns which Bentham also identifies. Only the relationship of contradiction between commands and permission to refrain, and prohibitions and permission to act, all interpreted descriptively, would rest on the formal principles of ordinary logic. It would so rest because permission to act interpreted descriptively, as e.g. 'It is not the case that I wish you not to shut the door', is indeed the simple negation of a command similarly interpreted as 'I wish you to shut the door': this pair of statements are both exclusive and exhaustive as contradictories in ordinary logic are required to be. The same is true of command and permission to refrain, similarly interpreted.

What then accounts, if the principles of ordinary logic do not, for the relationship between mandates which Bentham identifies and what entitles Bentham to use as names for the various relationships he identifies expressions like contraries, and contradictories, so strongly associated with statements that have truth values? A full answer to this question would require a technical logical competence which I do not command but I think the following condensed account[34] which does not treat commands and the other mandates as having truth values displays, in a relatively simple way, the main idea of a distinctive logic of imperatives applicable to the law and reasonably close in spirit to Bentham's logic of the will.

We are to think of the legislator before he starts to legislate with regard to some type of conduct, for example, carrying arms, as making what I shall call 'an exhaustive coherence survey' of the four mandates 'carry arms', 'do not carry arms',

[33] Op. cit. 123.
[34] I owe the main lines of this account to Mr John Mackie's illuminating communications to me on this subject.

'you may refrain from carrying arms', 'you may carry arms', and the six possible pairs of mandates (corresponding to the four sides and diagonals of the square of opposition) which may be formed from these four mandates. Because a legislator wishes his legislation not only to be sound in policy or substance, but to be a *coherent* guide to his subjects as to what they must do, must not do, may do or refrain from doing, he considers in the case of each of the six pairs of mandates whether for the purposes of legislation he can coherently accept both members of the pair, reject both, or accept one and reject the other. The test of coherence is whether it will be logically possible according to the ordinary logic of empirical propositions for his subjects to act in accordance with those mandates which he accepts while not acting on those he rejects.

To act in accordance with a command or prohibition will be always to do or always to refrain from an act of the type in question e.g. always to carry arms, or never to carry arms; to act in accordance with a permission to act or refrain from acting would be at least sometimes to carry arms. Hence in the case of the mandate 'carry arms' and 'do not carry arms' since it will be logically impossible to act in accordance with both but possible not to act in accordance with both or with one of them it will be incoherent for the legislator to accept both for legislation but coherent to reject both or one of them. Though it is the case that acceptance and rejection of mandates are not the same as truth and falsity of propositions, the incoherence of the joint acceptance of 'carry arms' and 'do not carry arms' and the coherence of the rejection of both or one of these mandates mirrors the impossibility which defines the relationships of contraries in ordinary logic of both statements being true and the possibility of both being false or one false and the other true. The same analogies between acceptance and rejection and truth and falsity holds good for all the other relationships of 'opposition and concomitancy' which Bentham identifies and surely justifies his description of these relationships in terms drawn from ordinary logic.

Two points in this account require attention. Bentham sometimes, though rarely, gives as examples of mandates single commands referring to a particular action on a particular occasion (e.g. 'shut that door') and not to action types, like 'always shut that door'. But since acting in accordance with a singular command ('shut that door') would require the same conduct (shutting the door on a particular occasion) as acting in accordance with a singular permission ('you may shut that door'), and similarly acting in accordance with a prohibition would require the same conduct as a permission to refrain (not shutting the door) it will be impossible to show in the same relatively simple way that 'shut the door' and 'do not shut the door' are contraries (permitting the rejection of both) and not contradictories (permitting only the rejection of one). For the same reason it will be impossible to show in this same simple way that 'you may shut the door' and 'you may refrain from shutting the door' are sub-contraries permitting the acceptance but not the rejection of both. If however the mandates are taken to refer to action types so that acting in accordance with permission to act will involve at least sometimes doing an action of a specified type the relationships identified by Bentham will hold good on the tests for coherent acceptance and rejection of mandates.

It should be noted that since on this explanation of Bentham's logic of the will the legislature is assumed to make an *exhaustive* coherence survey of the possibilities of joint acceptance and/or rejection of mandates this account of the logical relationship between mandates will not be vulnerable to the objection that it would always be open to a legislator to refrain from issuing a given mandate so that e.g. the relationship of contradiction between commands and permission to refrain as both exclusive and exhaustive would not hold good.

Bentham's doctrine of the four aspects of the will, or imperative operators, constitutes only the beginning of the account of the logical structure of laws. His 'logic of the will' comprises many other important topics. Among these is an account of the logical structure of human acts or rather of act-descriptions and the relationships between them. He appreciated that laws are very much more complex than unqualified commands addressed to individuals to do a particular act such as 'shut the door'; they are usually conditional, i.e. requiring or permitting certain kinds of act only

under certain circumstances which constitute qualifications
in the scope of the laws, or, as lawyers say, 'limitations' or
'exceptions' to them. Bentham examines with great care the
relationship of an act to its circumstances and in so doing
throws light on a number of different problems. Thus he
investigates the phenomenon which has long intrigued both
philosophers and lawyers, of the substitutability of different
descriptions of the same act: we may say that a man killed
another, or fired a gun with the consequence that the other
died, or pulled the trigger of a loaded gun with that consequence. Bentham compared this relationship of an act to its
circumstance to that of a substance to its properties: 'you
may strip a substance of its properties one by one till you
reduce it to nothing; so you may an act, by stripping it of its
circumstance.'[35] But besides this Bentham shows how the
logical relationship between different laws are in part determined by the type of 'qualifying circumstances' built into
them[36] and how the important legal ideas of excuse, justification and exemption,[37] and even certain procedural forms
or 'pleadings'[38] require for their understanding an analysis
or grasp of the varieties of circumstances and so of conditions
which he classifies.

IV

Bentham's accounts of the basic structure of laws in terms of
the four possible aspects of the law-giver's will commits him
to the view that there are no laws which are not either imperative or permissive. All laws command or prohibit or permit action or refraining from action and all laws except those
which are permissive and the rare 'praemiary' or 'invitative'
laws where the legislator relies on the 'alluring' sanctions of
rewards not on the coercive sanctions of punishment to
provide motives for obedience, create offences in that broad
sense of offence which includes civil wrongs as well as crimes.
Hence with these exceptions all laws are not only imperative
(either commands or prohibitions) but also penal since they
rely for their enforcement on coercive sanctions. Such
sanctions are commonly provided directly by the law through

[35] *OLG* 44.   [36] *OLG* 45, 112-13, 122.
[37] *OLG* 121-3, 145-6.   [38] *OLG* 123, n. h2.

what Bentham terms 'its corroborative appendages' or subsidiary laws addressed to officials or more rarely by the auxiliary religious or popular moral sanctions.

Accordingly for Bentham there is no such thing as a law which is not in some way imperative or permissive. But he recognized that the imperative character of law was not apparent on its face; the law's imperative quality is, he said, 'clouded and concealed from ordinary apprehension'[39] and is not easy to reconcile with the fact that much of the law is phrased, formulated and expounded in statutes, codes, and treatises, not in imperative language but in narrative or 'assertive style', or, as we should say, in descriptive language.[40] This is not merely because the imperative parts of laws are often expressed not in the grammatical imperative mood ('let no man steal') but in forms which look like indicative grammatical forms such as 'whosoever shall steal shall be punished'. The concealment of the imperative character of law with which Bentham is mainly concerned is something different: due not to the use of these grammatical forms but to the absence in many authoritative formulations of the law to any overt reference to the legislator's command, prohibition or permission, and hence to any offence or sanction. So as he says 'in many instances it will be found that the style of imperation is altogether dropped: no intimation being given in the course of many sentences or even pages or even volumes that the will of the legislator or anybody else has any concern in what is delivered, and this may be said of every system of law that has ever yet appeared or is ever likely to appear.'[41]

One of the many important areas of the law where Bentham finds this phenomenon of apparently non-imperative law (i.e. laws which are apparently not commands, prohibitions, or permissions) is the law of property. All developed legal systems contain in their property laws provisions which determine what constitutes a valid title to land or things. These provisions explain what acts or events are sufficient according to law to make a person an owner of some thing, or to invest him with some lesser form of property rights

---

[39] *PML* Concluding Note, para. 14, in *CW* 305.
[40] *OLG* 105-6; 178-9; 180-1; 302-3.
[41] *OLG* 106.

and so they incidentally describe the legal powers which a man has to confer a title on another, that is, power to alienate or transfer his property by such transactions as gift or sale or legacy. Undoubtedly such provisions are law, yet they do not appear to create offences, even in Bentham's extended sense of offence, nor to issue commands or prohibitions or to refer to sanctions. They read like statements of what is the case, or as Bentham puts it, they appear 'to be giving descriptions'.[42] Similar observations could be made concerning many fundamental provisions of constitutional law; those for example which determine who has power to appoint public officials to their offices.

Many of the most fascinating, and it must be added the most difficult pages of Bentham's *Of Laws in General* are devoted to maintaining in the face of appearances to the contrary the thesis that all laws other than merely permissive ones are in part imperative and penal. Bentham in effect offers a demonstration that underlying the surface appearance of the law as it is usually formulated in statutes, codes, or treatises, where it may 'appear as if it were employed solely in giving descriptions'[43] there is always an underlying basic structure which is imperative. Into this, if need be, the surface formulations can be resolved so that every legal provision can be shown to belong to some imperative law.

A full exposition of Bentham's demonstration of this thesis would involve consideration of Bentham's doctrine of the individuation of laws to which Chapter XIV of *Of Laws in General* is devoted, and which is one of the recurrent themes of the book. But the outlines of his theory can be seen best in his discussion of laws relating to title to property as these appear either in codes or in treatises on the law of property. The fundamental law which lies at the root of legal institution of property is an imperative law supported by sanctions; it is one which prohibits interference or, as Bentham calls it, 'meddling' with things or with pieces of land by all except those who have acquired according to law the right to use or occupy them, that is, by all except those persons

---

[42] *OLG* 26.
[43] See the critical discussion of Bentham's doctrine of individuation by Raz in op. cit. n. 31 *supra*, 142-7; and by M.H. James in 'Bentham and the Individuation of Laws' in *Bentham and Legal Theory*, op. cit. n. 31 *supra*, 91.

who have acquired some *title* to the property.[44] The acts or the events which confer a title to property and so bring persons who have such a title within the exception to the law's prohibitions against interference, are in the last analysis simply conditions or exceptions which limit the scope of the basic prohibitory law against 'meddling' and are parts of it. Hence in an ideal complete formulation of the law against wrongful interference with property these conditions would have to be set out *in extenso* by way of explanation of general terms like 'except for the owner' or 'except for those with a title'. But partly because these conditions which define an owner and a good title and which form part of and limit the prohibitory law are very complex and heterogeneous, partly because the same conditions form part of many different laws relating to property, lawyers need to refer to them for many different purposes. It is therefore natural and indeed necessary in the exposition of the law to detach such conditions from the laws which they form part, and hence in codes and treatises they are expounded separately in abstraction from the imperative and sanctioning provisions of the laws of which they form part. This detachment or abstraction for separate exposition of what are in fact parts of such imperative laws generates the illusion that the matter thus extracted or, as Bentham terms it, expository matter, are separate non-imperative laws—civil laws as distinct from imperative and penal laws. But they are according to Bentham parts of laws, not complete laws; and when we assign these abstracted parts of laws to a civil code this is not inconsistent with the fundamentally imperative character of every law. The distinction between penal and civil is a distinction in the exposition of the law not in the law itself. The cause, Bentham says, of the 'seeming inconsistency' between the imperative character of law and appearances to the contrary is 'the want of coincidence or conformity between the typographical arrangement and the logical; between the order of the ideas about which the several laws in question are conversant, and the order of the signs which are made use of to express them.'[45]

In a striking image Bentham compares groups of different

---

[44] *OLG* 26, 201-2, 255-6, 277.   [45] *OLG* 197.

imperative laws which share common conditions to a cluster
of pyramids with a common base.

> Many laws, any two laws, almost, will have a vast portion of their
> substance in common; they will be like contiguous triangles, like the
> diagrams of pyramids represented as standing on the same base, but the
> matter of each will be separately describable as, in pyramids so repre-
> sented, the parts of each are separately assignable.[46]

So in the end Bentham's answer to the initial question
which prompted the writing of this book is that the distinction between imperative and non-imperative law or between
penal and civil law lies in the way in which for convenience
of exposition different parts of the laws, all of which are
imperative, are separated, collected, and arranged. Bentham's
defence of the imperative theory of law is by far the most
powerful, detailed and profound that we have. Many writers
including myself have assailed the idea that laws are essentially or exclusively of the nature of commands imposing
duties. But Bentham's defence of this theory has the supreme
merit that it requires from his critics an exploration of some
quite fundamental issues concerning the various ways in
which human actions may be guided and evaluated by the
standards of conduct which the law sets. It cannot be said
that the exploration of these issues has yet been carried
sufficiently far.

V

In reading this most original work of Bentham's, with its
many illuminating fine-drawn distinctions, it is necessary to
guard against certain misinterpretations which may arise if
insufficient attention is paid to the fact that in the exposition of this logic of the will Bentham uses words such as
'command' and 'prohibition' for the expression of the legislator's will without any implication that these are backed by
coercive sanctions. Bentham says he resorts to this use of
words for 'want of words to remedy it'[47] and he recognizes
that this is a technical use of these expressions which is in a

---

[46] *OLG* 234. See the discussion of 'power-conferring laws' in Chap. VIII *infra*.
[47] *OLG* 134, 298, n. a; cf. *OLG* 95: 'in the former case [i.e. where the wish is
that the act should be performed] the mandate is what in *the most confined sense*
of the word is termed a command' (my italics).

sense 'improper' since a reference to sanctions is embodied in the proper current use of these words, and he himself often throughout his works uses the word 'command' in that ordinary sense. As I attempt to show in Chapter VI the view that Bentham held 'a no-sanction theory of legal obligation' rests in part on neglect of the fact that Bentham uses the word 'command' when expounding the logic of the will in this technical confined sense but otherwise in its ordinary sense.

Attention to Bentham's use of an expression sometimes in its current, ordinary and 'proper' sense and sometimes in a technical sense, also throws light on a feature of *Of Laws in General* which Professor Lyons has much emphasized. It is the case that in many different passages Bentham says quite clearly that all laws are supported by coercive sanctions and speaks of them as 'coercive', 'creating obligations', 'binding persons', 'restricting liberty', and so creating mischief. Thus to cite one of the strongest of such passages, 'a law by which nobody is bound, a law by which nobody is coerced, a law by which nobody's liberty is curtailed, all these phrases which come to the same thing would be so many contradictions in terms.'[48]

Such passages certainly seem to conflict with Bentham's admission both of permissive and of the so-called praemiary laws. However this appearance of conflict dissolves if account is taken of the fact that in such passages stressing the necessary coercive, sanction-backed character of law, Bentham is using the expression 'law' in what he takes to be its ordinary meaning from which he departs at other times. Thus in discussing praemiary laws[49] he acknowledges that such expressions of the legislator's will are not those which beyond dispute are entitled to the appellation of law, since the idea of coercion is inseparably connected with law in the ordinary use of that expression. He thinks, however, that praemiary laws because of their analogies with ordinary coercive laws should not be denied the title of law.

As for permissive laws, Bentham warns us at the very opening of *Of Laws in General*[50] that he is using the word

---

[48] *OLG* 54; cf. *OLG* 248.
[49] *OLG* 136.
[50] *OLG* 3.

'law' with a latitude 'greater than what seems to be given to it in common'. And when he comes to his highly technical chapter expounding in detail the variety of mandates he expressly states that 'to the making up of a law there are no other essential requisites' than an act and an aspect of the legislator's will.[51] I do not therefore think we are faced in Bentham's work with any inconsistency of doctrine as to the coercive character of law but simply, as with Bentham's use of the word 'command', with the use of an expression drawn from ordinary languages sometimes in a technical and sometimes in its ordinary sense.

Professor Lyons[52] does not explain the apparent inconsistency he detects in Bentham as to the coercive character of laws in this relatively simple way, but makes a number of different and very interesting suggestions leading to a discussion of Bentham's conception that a whole legal system could at any moment be viewed as if it contained only coercive laws together with an assumed permissive background principle so that, as Bentham says, every efficient law may be considered as a limitation or exception grafted on a pre-established law of liberty. For this Bentham uses the splendid metaphor of 'a boundless expanse in which the several efficient laws appears as so many spots; like islands and continents projecting out of the ocean'.[53] But I think that Professor Lyons draws too sharp a contrast when, because of Bentham's recognition of permissive laws, he challenges the received view that Bentham paved the way for Austin's conception of law as consisting of coercive commands. There are of course many important differences between Bentham and Austin on other issues but I do not think that they differed concerning the admission of permissive laws. Austin does not of course share Bentham's interest in the fine-grained analysis of the logical structure of laws, and does not use the word 'command' in Bentham's technical sense nor discriminate between different types of permission. But he not only has a place for permissive laws but says of them that they are laws 'improperly so called'[54] yet forming part of the subject

---

[51] *OLG* 93.   [52] Op. cit. (p. 114, n. 31 *supra*) 108 ff.
[53] *OLG* 120.

[54] Op. cit. (p. 59, n. 23 *supra*) 27: 'laws to repeal laws and to release from existing duties'.

matter of jurisprudence. This surely is an echo of Bentham's use of the expression 'impropriety'[55] to describe his own departures from ordinary established or, as he calls it, 'undisputed' uses, in order to develop his general theory.

Two final comments. First, Bentham's lifelong concern was with the substance of the law and with the construction of reforms designed to make law an instrument of human happiness. Yet this book is concerned not with the substance of the law but with its form and structure. Bentham explains how these two facts are reconciled in his final chapter which is devoted to exhibiting the practical uses of the book. He was convinced that no reform of the substance of the law could be effective without reform of its form; and that clear, rationally articulated and comprehensive codes must replace the 'trackless wilds' of legislation and case law. This task, in its turn, he believed could only be accomplished if the discussions in his book, abstract though they are, concerning the fundamental structure, the unity and the completeness of laws, had first been understood.

I would say a word about the style in which this book is written. It is not easy reading: Bentham said that the truths of the science of law 'grow among thorns; and are not to be plucked, like daisies, by infants as they run.'[56] Some may feel that this understates the difficulties of part of this book; Bentham himself was well aware of this and apologized for what he termed 'the long-winded and abstruse discussions' contained in the book,[57] which, in writing to Lord Ashburton, he referred to as a 'dry cargo of speculative metaphysics'.[58] But on the whole the style of the book is limpid and vivid, and abstract ideas are elucidated by felicitous metaphors. Not least Bentham's wit is often very diverting, especially when English law or the lawyers of his day are its target. Consider this perhaps still relevant comment on the statute book:

At present such is the entanglement that when a new statute is applied, it is next to impossible to follow it through and discover the limit of its influence. As the laws amidst which it falls are not to be distinguished from one another there is no saying which of them it repeals or qualifies; nor which of them it leaves untouched; it is like water poured in the sea.[59]

[55] *OLG* 134, 298.   [56] *PML* Preface in *CW* 10.
[57] *OLG* 232.   [58] *OLG* 304.   [59] *OLG* 236.

Again, speaking of remedies for the slow and haphazard publication of legal decisions of importance, an abuse which was profitable to lawyers, Bentham says 'not to put in practice the only means of remedying this grievance, out of tenderness to the lawyers, would be like bringing up half the people in the state for the sake of the undertakers.'[60]

There are in *Of Laws in General* many such shafts of wit, daisies among the thorns, to adorn its important contributions to analytical jurisprudence.

---

[60] *OLG* 71.

LEGAL DUTY AND OBLIGATION

I

THE GENERAL THEORY OF OBLIGATION

'Whatever business the law may be conversant about, may be reduced to one sort of operation viz that of creating duties.'[1] 'The notion of duty is a common measure for every article of law.'[2] Though Bentham came to admit some exceptions[3] to these generalizations they express very well his deep conviction that the notion of a legal duty or obligation was fundamental both for the understanding of the legal regulation of conduct and for the analysis of other concepts used in the description and exposition of the law, such as (to take Bentham's own examples) rights, powers and trusts, property, possession and conveyance.

'Obligation' and 'duty' are frequently used in reference both to law and to morals, and also to matters which do not fit into either of these two categories. But many philosophers (even as diverse in outlook as O.W. Holmes[4] and Kelsen[5]) would deny that there is any unitary concept of obligation and insist that only confusion arises from treating 'legal obligation' and 'moral obligation' as species of a single genus. Others (including Bentham and John Stuart Mill[6]) have insisted that there is a common element determining the meaning of obligation in both legal and moral contexts, and that the differences do not affect the *meaning* of obligation

---

[1] *OLG* 249.   [2] *OLG* 294.

[3] These include 'praemiary' and permissive laws (see *supra*, pp. 123-4, and *infra*, pp. 139-40). Bentham also states that nothing else is 'requisite for a law beside an act and the expression of the legislator's will in relation to it' (*OLG* 93, 156). There are also observations appearing to make 'coercion' or 'punishment' also requisite (*OLG* 54, 248). For the explanation of these apparent divergencies see Chap. V *supra*, pp. 122-5, and also p. 139 *infra*.

[4] 'The Path of the Law' in *Collected Legal Papers*, 173-4.

[5] *General Theory of Law and State* (Harvard 1949), 60; *Théorie pure de droit* (Paris 1962), 161.

[6] *Utilitarianism*, in *10 Collected Works of J. S. Mill* (Toronto) 246.

but constitutes different species of obligation reflecting the different standards used in determining what acts are obligatory. There is also the stronger view, advocated by some contemporary writers, which I consider at the end of this chapter, that not only is there a common element in legal and moral obligation but the former is a species of the latter or at least in some sense presupposes it.

Though it is scattered untidily through his vast works, Bentham does offer a comprehensive and generally, though not wholly, consistent account of a generic idea of obligation within which he distinguishes legal obligation as one specific variant. But his first step in the analysis was to insist, influenced here, perhaps, by a hint dropped by Beccaria[7] that in a sense obligations and duties (and he thought the distinction between these two was unimportant[8]) were what he termed fictions or fictitious entities and were indeed the basic or primary kind of such entities. By this he did not mean that obligations are products of the imagination like centaurs or fairies or other fabulous beings, nor did he mean that they incorporated false beliefs.[9] What he did mean by referring to such notions as obligations as fictions, 'fictions in the logical sense,'[10] he elaborated in a general theory of the language of abstract entities which contained elements closely resembling much later logical doctrine and most notably Russell's theory of logical constructions, incomplete symbols, and definitions in use.[11]

The general bearing of Bentham's theory of fictions may be conveyed by a simple modern example. There are in our language many expressions which at first sight look as if they were the names of real things in the world but are not such names; yet none the less they are used in making statements about real things in the world which are perfectly meaningful and often true. So, to take a modern example, the expression

---

[7] *On Crimes and Punishments*: translated by Paolucci (Indianapolis 1963), 15 n. 20, discussed in Chap. II *supra*.

[8] 'Duties, or what is another word for the same thing, obligations' *OLG* 294.

[9] *A Fragment on Ontology, Works* VIII 199; *Chrestomathia, Works* VIII 126 n.

[10] *Fragment on Ontology*, loc. cit.

[11] B. Russell and A. N. Whitehead, *Principia Mathematica* (Cambridge 1910), I Chap. III; but see John Wisdom, *Interpretation and Analysis in Relation to Bentham's Theory of Definition* (London 1931), especially 78 ff. for a detailed critique of Bentham's theory of fictions.

'the average man' does not name or refer to stand for any particular body or any thing, yet the sentence 'In America the average man is 5 feet 6 in height and weighs 135 lb.' has certainly a meaning and it may be true; and we can say perfectly well what this meaning is in sentences which dispense with the expression 'the average man'. The sentence means that the total height and weight of all male adult Americans divided by their number is the height and weight given. So for Bentham 'the average man' would be the name of a fiction: and it is in this sense that 'obligation' and 'duty' are fictitious entities.

The following three elements contain, I think, the substances of his theory.

(i) First, we have an ontology. Real entities for Bentham include corporeal substances and material things, sensory impressions or ideas.[12] All languages, says Bentham, besides names for such real entities, contain expressions grammatically indistinguishable from names, like the nouns 'right' and 'duty' and 'obligation', but they are not names of real entities. They are the names of fictitious entities, and we must understand this to mean not that there are two classes of entity but two classes of name.[13] Rights and obligations are said to 'exist' and although when we say this we do not ascribe to them existence 'in truth and reality'[14] as we do to real entities, there is a connection between the names of fictions and reality which accounts for the fact that statements made by the use of such names like 'I have an obligation to report for military service' are meaningful and often true. A modern logician would say that what Bentham calls names of fictions are disguised descriptions.

(ii) Secondly, if we are to avoid mystification and obscurity, Bentham insists that in the case of a fiction we must use a special mode of definition or analysis.[15] We cannot, he thought, explain the meaning of a fictitious entity like right or duty by using the standard modes of definition of single words *per genus et differentiam*. It is no use trying to

---

[12] *A Fragment on Ontology, Works* VIII 197.

[13] Op. cit. 198 n.

[14] Op. cit. 197.

[15] *Fragment* in *CW* 494-6; *OLG* 294-5; *PML* Chap. XVI, para. 25, in *CW* 205 (206); *Chrestomathia, Works* VIII 126 n; *Essay on Logic, Works* VIII 246-81.

complete a definition 'a right is a . . .' or 'a duty is a . . .'[16] any more than you would complete a definition of 'average man' by saying 'an average man is a . . .'. Bentham's reason for this is that in the case of such notions as right and duty or any other fictitious entity there is no higher genus of which they are species or sub-classes.[17] He must mean, I think, what Austin,[18] his disciple, says (in claiming in very similar terms that such notions will not admit of definition in the regular manner), namely that there is no higher genus which is not as much in need of definition or analysis as the fictitious entity of which a definition or analysis is sought.

(iii) Thirdly, Bentham urges the use, in the case of fictions such as obligation, of three novel methods of 'exposition' or analysis tailored to fit their special feature. The first is 'phraseoplerosis',[19] that is to find a sentence in which the word to be defined appears and which could be used to make a meaningful true or false statement on a particular occasion. So we must consider not the word 'obligation' but a complete statement such as 'X is under an obligation to pay Y £10'. The second step is 'paraphrasis',[20] that is to find a translation of this whole sentence into one or more sentences in which the word 'obligation' does not appear. Plainly these two steps are very similar to what Russell urged nearly 150 years later as the right way to analyse 'incomplete symbols' which were the names of logical constructions, and in effect Bentham is putting before us the method of analysis later known as definition in use. To these two methods Bentham adds a third which does not reappear in later philosophy, and yet may have a certain importance. This step (called 'archetypation')[21] consists in making explicit the more or less confused imagery which is buried in our use of these expressions. Bentham says that in the case of obligation one 'archetypal

---

[16] *Fragment* Chap. V, para. 8, n. 6, in *CW* 495–6.

[17] Ibid.

[18] *The Province of Jurisprudence Determined and the Uses of this Study of Jurisprudence*, ed. Hart (1954), 370–1.

[19] *Essay on Logic*, Works VIII 246–8.

[20] Ibid. and *Chrestomathia, Works* VIII 126 n.

[21] *Chrestomathia* 126 n, where the material image is said to be 'the image of a cord or any other tie or bond (from the Latin *ligo* to bind) by which the object in question is *bound* or fastened to any other, the person in question bound to a certain course of practice'.

image' is that of a man held down by a heavy weight. His account of the function of this image is striking. He says:

> that for the formation of the variety of fictitious propositions of which the fictitious entity in question, viz. an obligation, is in use to constitute the subject, the emblematic or archetypal image is that of a man lying down with a heavy body pressing upon him, to wit in such sort as either to prevent him acting at all or so ordering matters that if he does act it cannot be in any other direction or manner than of the direction or manner requisite.[22]

Here I think Bentham has not clearly separated two points, both dependent on the fact that our words come to us as J. L. Austin once said 'trailing clouds of etymology'. It seems that Bentham's first point is that something of the primitive roots of words colours, or perhaps infects, our thoughts even when the later sophisticated derivatives are used; so that the primitive 'image' is presented to the mind on the use even of a derivative expression. A second point is perhaps more important. It is that the names of fictitious entities are felt to be analogical extensions of words used to describe the primitive situation of the image, and this figure often dictates what ancillary expressions go with the names of fictitious entities so that, for example, we speak of a man being '*under* an obligation' (like a weight) or '*bearing* an obligation', or 'being *relieved* of an obligation'. Bentham's view is, therefore, that we cannot give an adequate account of the concept of obligation unless we command this view of the ancillary expressions that go with it, which depend upon the nature of the buried figures incorporated in the word. This shows that in offering his analysis of fictions he is not consciously proposing a purely stipulative definition, though it is true that he often also speaks of himself as 'fixing'[23] or 'outstretching common usage'[24] rather than 'expounding' or 'teaching' the meaning of such terms as obligation.

Apart from these logical refinements, two ideas are central in Bentham's account of obligation. First, to say that a man has an obligation to conduct himself in a given manner is to say that 'in the event of his failing to conduct himself in that manner, pain (or its equivalent, loss of pleasure) is considered

---

[22] *Essay on Logic, Works* VIII 247.
[23] *Pannomial Fragments, Works* III 217.
[24] *OLG* 9.

as about to be experienced by him,[25] that is that such pain is probable or likely. So pain is said by Bentham to be 'constitutive'[26] of obligation in all its forms. Secondly there are several sources from which the constitutive pain arises, and these sources of pain constitute the different 'sanctions'[27] characteristic of different types of obligation: physical, legal or political, popular or moral, and religious. The sanction is said to be *physical* when pain arises from conduct in the ordinary course of nature without deliberate human or divine intervention; *legal or political* if it is suffered at the hands of officials chosen to administer it according to law; *moral or popular*, if it is suffered at the hands of such 'chance persons' in the community as a person has to do with, and not according to any settled rule; and *religious* if it is expected to be suffered at the hands of a 'superior invisible being'. To all this Bentham adds the statement that for an obligation to be correctly said to be incumbent on a man it is not at all necessary that he should be aware of the relevant probability of suffering,[28] but if he is not aware of it the obligation is not likely to be 'effective'.

Such then is Bentham's general account of obligation in its various forms. The central element in this generalization is a starkly simple idea: it is nothing but the likelihood of suffering in the event of doing or failing to do an action. What differentiates legal obligation from other forms is that the sanction or the suffering which is relevant is suffering at the hands of officials chosen to administer it according to law: to say that a man has a legal obligation to do a particular action is to say that in the event of his failing to do it he is likely to suffer pain at the hands of officials chosen to administer it according to law.

II

BENTHAM'S MIXED THEORY OF LEGAL OBLIGATION

At first sight this general theory of obligation presents an

---

[25] *Essay on Logic, Works* VIII 247.   [26] Ibid.

[27] Ibid. and *PML* Chap. III paras. 2–12 in *CW* 34–7.

[28] *Essay on Logic, Works* VIII 247. This seems to be clearly Bentham's view though there is one obscure inconsistent passage to the contrary (cited *infra*, p. 142).

exceedingly tidy scheme. According to it, the generic element in all obligation is simply the likelihood of pain or suffering in the event of failure to act in a certain way and the specific variants of obligation (physical, moral, legal, and religious) are neatly differentiated simply by reference to the source from which the pain or suffering issues. In fact, however, as far as legal obligation is concerned this neat impression is misleading, for, as Bentham makes clear in his considered account of the legal or political sanction,[29] it is not enough for legal obligation that the source from which the sanction issues should be judges or officials but it must also be the case that they are chosen 'to dispense it according to the will of the sovereign' and this, given Bentham's imperative theory of law, means that the sanction must be provided for by the law. In his many detailed accounts of different patterns of legislation Bentham terms those laws whose function is to provide for legal sanctions as 'subsidiary laws' or 'punitary laws': they are addressed to judges and require them, or at least permit them, to punish contraventions of 'principal laws'[30] which are simple imperative laws which may be addressed to any citizens requiring them to do or to abstain from certain actions.

Bentham's explanation of the legal sanction makes it clear that even in those accounts of legal obligation where he stresses the probability of incurring the sanction as a constituent of the obligation, he also includes as another constituent the feature that the suffering which is the sanction be imposed according to law. But it is also true that in these probabilistic accounts of obligation he makes no explicit reference to the fact that to constitute a legal sanction the pain or suffering must not only be imposed according to law but must be administered as a punishment for failure to comply with the requirements of some principal law. This condition is important, for a legally obligatory act is one that is required by law and not merely one for failure to do which the law provides unpleasant consequences. Unless this condition is included in the definition of legal obligation it will be impossible to distinguish an act which is legally

---

[29] *PML* Chap. II, para. 4, in *CW* 35.
[30] *PML* Concluding Note, para. 6, in *CW* 302; *OLG* 137 ff.

obligatory and punishable, from conduct which is subjected to a tax or other painful or disagreeable administrative measures. This is so because there is nothing in the notion of pain or suffering to be administered by officials according to law which would restrict it to punishment.

In most of the passages where Bentham is concerned with specifically legal obligation he makes it quite clear that a legal obligatory act is one which is required by law, and it is possible that in his probabilistic accounts of legal obligation he made no specific reference to this requirement because he thought this also was implicit in the account of a sanction as dispensed according to the sovereign's will. There are indeed passages where he explicitly states that though simple imperative laws requiring certain conduct and punitory laws are distinct, the latter imply the former.[31]

It seems therefore to be clear that Bentham, notwithstanding some carelessness in expression, even in his probabilistic accounts of legal obligation, intended to include as necessary constituents two imperative elements, namely a principal law requiring the act which is obligatory and a subsidiary law requiring or permitting punishment for breach of the former. Such a theory therefore contains a mixture of imperative and probabilistic elements and I shall refer to it as Bentham's mixed theory. I shall consider later the view that Bentham also held at least two other theories of legal obligation, but I shall first consider the merits and demerits of the mixed theory, since it has echoes in much subsequent Anglo-American jurisprudence. Substantially the same doctrine offered with a similar promise of emancipation from obscuring mystification or confusion is to be found in the work of Bentham's disciple, John Austin,[32] and in Oliver Wendell Holmes's[33] claim to have 'washed the notion of legal duty in cynical acid' by providing a similar theory of obligation.

The most obvious objections to which Bentham's mixed theory of obligation is exposed are based on its divergence, due to its inclusion of a probabilistic relationship between conduct and sanctions, from the standard usage of lawyers

---

[31] *PML* Concluding Note, paras. 8–9, in *CW* 302; *OLG* 143.
[32] Austin, op. cit. (p. 130, n. 18 *supra*), 14–18.
[33] 'The Path of the Law' in *Collected Legal Papers* (London 1920), 174.

and laymen of the expressions 'obligation' and 'duty'. From this point of view Bentham's account is open to two main simple criticisms. First the statement that a person has a legal obligation to do a particular action can be combined without contradiction or absurdity with the statement that it is not likely that in the case of disobedience he would suffer by incurring some sanction. There are many occasions, especially in a legal system in which only maximum penalties are fixed for crimes, where these two statements can be combined. It also may often be the case that it is quite likely that someone who disobeys a law which plainly applies to him will not be detected, or that if he is detected, will escape conviction, or if he is convicted, will not be punished because as in our system the law allows a convicted person to be discharged without any penalty of any kind, yet such a person has a legal obligation to do what the law requires. The same difference in meaning between the statement that a person has a legal obligation and the statement that he is likely to suffer for disobedience to law is manifest in the fact that it would not be redundant or superfluous to add to the statement that a person has a legal obligation to do a particular act the further statement that if he fails to do it he is likely to incur some legal sanction. So these criticisms insist against Bentham's mixed theory that the likelihood of an individual suffering a punitive sanction in the event of disobedience is not a necessary condition of his having a legal obligation. This means that the relevant connection between disobedience and punitive sanctions is not the likelihood of the latter, given the former, but that the courts should recognize disobedience as a reason according to law for its punishment.

The most that can be said for Bentham's mixed theory, taken as an analysis of any actual usage of the expressions 'legal obligation' or 'duty', is that although the probabilistic connection with sanction which it includes is not any part of the meaning of the statement that a man has a legal obligation to do a particular action, it does state certain features which are characteristic of certain quite frequent cases of the use of statements of this form. For the normal context in which it is asserted that someone—and it may be the speaker himself—has a legal obligation is a situation in which usually there *is* a considerable chance of suffering in the event of

disregard of the obligation, because such assertions are normally made in reference to an efficacious system of law in
which the exaction of sanctions is likely. Where this normal
context holds statements of the form 'You have an obligation
to do so and so' may be and often are used simply as a means
of drawing attention to the probability that punishment or
enforced compensation is likely if the action said to be
obligatory is not done. Anyone who makes such an assertion
may intend the statement 'You have an obligation to do so
and so' to be taken as a prediction or warning of likely
suffering. But of course we must distinguish, as Bentham
does not, between the meaning of what a man says and the
way he intends what he says to be taken by those to whom
he speaks. We may distinguish the former as the *conventional
meaning* of a sentence and the latter as the 'force'[34] of its
use on a particular occasion, and illustrate this distinction by
the following, simple parallel. It is clear that the sentence
'There is a bull in the field' may quite often be spoken or
written as a warning of a likely danger to those who attempt
to enter the field; but though the use of this sentence often
has the force of a warning this is not part of the conventional
meaning of the sentence, for the sentence 'There is a bull in
the field' has the same meaning if it is given in answer to the
question 'What animal is there in the field?' The meaning
of the sentence is a constant element controlled by general
linguistic conventions which hold good for all the occasions
of its use, whereas the force of the use of the sentence on a
particular occasion, which may lead us to classify it as
warning or prediction, depends *inter alia* on the intention of
the speaker which may vary from occasion to occasion. This
distinction between the meaning of a sentence and the force
which may be a characteristic feature of many occasions of
its use is important in many attempts to analyse the idea of
obligation or duty; Bentham's mixed theory may be criticized for having presented as part of the meaning of obligation
a feature which is in fact not part of its meaning but a
characteristic of the force which statements of obligation
frequently have.

To all these criticisms, based as they are upon established

---

[34] See J.L. Austin, *How to do Things with Words* (Oxford 1963), 100 ff. and
Chap. X *infra*, p. 244, n. 2.

usage, Bentham would I think have replied in a tough 'rational-reconstructionist' or revisionary manner, since, for all his interest in language, he was no ordinary language philosopher and his standpoint was critical and reformative. 'Our languages, rich in terms of hatred and reproach, are poor and rugged for the purposes of science and reason.'[35] He would, or at any rate could, concede perfectly well that the criticisms based on usage do accurately reflect that usage and so exhibit features of our actual concept of legal obligation. But he could insist that he had a better concept to offer in its place, and he might have invoked in support of its adoption his dual aims and purposes as a utilitarian Censor critical of the law and an Expositor[36] concerned to analyse its structure. In the role of Censor he could argue that the purpose of the analysis of such notions as legal obligation or duty was to provide a set of clear terms to be used in describing a legal system in a way which would focus attention on aspects of prime importance to the critic, and among these aspects of the law to which it was important to the critic to attend are those points at which the legal system itself creates human suffering or makes it likely. Law for Bentham, because it creates suffering, was an evil to be watched and controlled; but it is a necessary evil and one which human beings can, if they are clear-sighted when they watch, control so as to make it contribute to human happiness. What is needed therefore is a cost-benefit account of a legal system's operation. The benefits which the law confers on those whom it favours Bentham equated with legal rights[37] and these could appear on one side of the balance sheet; the likely sufferings at the hands of the law in the form of obligations would appear on the other side. So it was always necessary to consider, as Bentham does in detail, in relation to every law what parties are 'favoured' by it and what parties are 'exposed' by it to suffer.[38] We must continually keep our eye upon this balance sheet and weigh benefit against suffering; otherwise we may

[35] *Rationale of Reward, Works* II 255; cf. *OLG* 12.
[36] *Fragment* Preface in *CW* 397–8, but see for a different interpretation of the distinction between Expositor and Censor Postema 'The Expositor, The Censor and Common Law', *Canadian Journal of Philosophy*, 9 (1979) 643.
[37] See Chap. VII *infra*; *OLG* 57, 63, 84.
[38] *OLG* 53 ff.

be taken by surprise when the law, supposed to be our watch-dog, turns out to be a hyena.

Given this point of view the probabilistic connection included in Bentham's mixed theory between actions which are contraventions of the law and suffering or sanctions is all-important, and is therefore fit to be chosen to be a defining feature of legal obligation in a revised utilitarian concept of obligation, useful to the critic and reformer of the law. Bentham, as I have argued by no means ignored (though he sometimes makes only implicit reference to them) the imperative elements of the mixed theory and he recognizes other forms of connection between disobedience to law and the sanctions besides the probabilistic connection which he sometimes stressed. But he seems to have thought at times that where the sanction or penalty was not a predictable or likely consequence of disobedience it was not worth attention ('the obligation a cobweb, the duty a feather')[39] and accordingly built its likelihood into his revisionary concept of obligation.

III

ALTERNATIVE THEORIES

In his illuminating essay on 'Sanction Theories of Duty',[40] Mr Peter Hacker has argued that besides the Mixed Theory expounded above there are traces in Bentham's works of three other theories inconsistent with the Mixed Theory. One of these is not a sanction theory at all and Mr Hacker cites passages from Bentham where he appears to say that all that is required to constitute a legal obligation is a legislative command and makes no reference to the requirement that this must be supported by some form of sanction for disobedience. I shall call this theory the 'No Sanction Theory'.

A second alternative theory which Mr Hacker finds in Bentham is one which I shall call the 'Dual Imperative Theory'. This departs from the Mixed Theory by eliminating its requirement that if an act is to be obligatory suffering

---

[39] *OLG* 136 n. f.

[40] In *Oxford Essays on Jurisprudence* (2nd series, ed. Simpson), 131. I am much indebted to this essay which has led me to refine the exposition and criticism of Bentham in my 'Il Concetto Di Obbligo': *Rivista di Filosofia* (1966) 125.

must be a likely consequence of failure to do it. In support of his view that Bentham held such a theory Mr Hacker cites passages where Bentham appears to say that all that is required for the constitution of a legal obligation is a principal law commanding or prohibiting certain conduct combined with a subsidiary law prescribing punishment for a breach of the former.

The third alternative which I shall call the 'Single Imperative Probabilistic Theory' is one from which Mr Hacker thinks Austin took his own definition of legal obligation. According to this theory, a legal obligation is constituted by a legislative command when it is likely that the person commanded will suffer in the event of disobedience.

The No Sanction Theory

Bentham certainly recognized that there could be *laws* without coercive sanctions but it does not follow, and I am sure that it is not the case, that he thought that there could be legal obligations without such sanctions. The laws without coercive sanctions which he did recognize include permissive laws which may be either 'uncoercive' or 'discoercive',[41] the most important function of the latter being to revoke some previous legal requirement or prohibition. Such laws do not create but extinguish legal obligations. More important for the present purpose are what Bentham terms 'praemiary' laws or 'invitative' laws[42] where to motivate obedience the legislator holds out the prospect of reward, not that of punishment. Such laws, Bentham says, do not generate obligations for 'to take away punishment' is to deprive words like 'obligation' of all meaning. Such laws generate only analogues of obligations which are of 'flimsy consistence': "the obligation a cobweb, the duty a feather'. For the same reason the expression of the legislator's will in such praemiary laws though it expresses the same 'aspect' of the will as that which enters into a command is not, in the ordinary sense of the word a command, though he thought it dogmatic to refuse to such praemiary laws the title of law on that account.

---

[41] *PML* Concluding Note, para. 3 in *CW* 302; *OLG* 95–100, 119–20. Cf. Chap. IV *supra*, pp. 123–4.
[42] *OLG* 134 ff.; *PML* Chap. XI para. 2 in *CW* 126.

Mr Hacker supports his view that Bentham held a No Sanction Theory with four passages.[43] In the first three of these Bentham appears to state that a command is sufficient to create a duty and makes no explicit reference to sanctions. These passages would only be sufficient to establish that Bentham held a No Sanction Theory if he meant by 'command' in these contexts an expression of the legislator's will unsupported by sanctions. However, it is not only clear from his discussion of praemiary laws that there Bentham restricts the word 'command' to expressions of the legislator's will supported by coercive sanctions but there are also many passages where he goes out of his way to say that in the ordinary and proper use of the expression, 'command supposes punishment'.[44] But what is more important is that Bentham himself drew attention to the fact that his own use of the word 'command' in certain special contexts to denote the mere expression of the legislator's will without regard to coercive sanctions was 'an impropriety'[45] which he found himself forced to adopt 'for want of words to remedy it' in expounding his logic of the will and distinguishing four aspects of the will and the four corresponding types of legal mandate which he calls 'command', 'non-command', 'prohibition', and 'commission'. In using the word 'command' for this technical purpose Bentham tells us that this is 'the most confined sense'[46] of the word and he makes use of it only when he also makes it clear that he is referring only to the aspect of the will. It is therefore quite impossible to ascribe to Bentham a No Sanction Theory on the strength of passages where he says that legal commands impose duties if there is no reason to think that in such passages Bentham himself is not using the word 'command' in what he says is its ordinary and current sense. There remain two passages relied upon by Mr Hacker where Bentham speaks of a legal obligation as imposed when the law 'directs' men to perform or abstain from some action and makes no specific reference

---

[43] *Fragment* Chap. I, para. 12 in *CW* 429 (430); *OLG* 58, 293; *View of a Complete Code of Laws, Works* III 181 (all cited in Hacker, op. cit. 138–9). But note that in *Fragment* Chap. V, para. 7 in *CW* 496 Bentham also states that 'the original, ordinary and proper sense of duty involves liability to punishment'.

[44] *Pannomial Fragments, Works* III 217; *OLG* 134.

[45] *OLG* 134, 298 n. a.

[46] *OLG* 95.

to sanctions, but in the first of these passages Bentham does in fact refer to 'the evil of the obligation'[47] and makes plain that he means by that the punishment prescribed for it, and in the second passage, 'obligation' is described as a 'forced service'.[48]

The Dual Imperative Theory

Here Mr Hacker has a much stronger case, though not, I think, in the end a convincing one. It is true that when Bentham is dealing with legal obligations alone, apart from his generic theory embracing other forms of obligation, he makes no reference to the probability or likelihood of the party under an obligation suffering for disobedience. His standard practice when considering legal obligation alone as he does in *An Introduction to the Principles of Morals and Legislation* and *Of Laws in General* is to refer to the sanction only as something 'appointed' or 'marked out' for the breach of the law, and to the party bound as 'laid under' 'coercion' and thereby 'exposed' to suffer.[49] Certainly this non-probabilistic terminology suggests that he held a theory according to which the combination of a principle and subsidiary law is sufficient to constitute a legal obligation without reference to the probability or likelihood of a sanction issuing and being experienced. I do not however think that this discrepancy between the account of legal obligation given in the context of the generic theory and that given of it apart from that context really represents a change in theory. This would involve on Bentham's part a double change of opinion implausible even in an author as disorderly as Bentham, for the accounts of legal obligation without reference to the probability or likelihood of sanctions are in point of date of authorship[50] between the two statements of the generic theory which refer to such probability. It is I think more plausible to suppose that Bentham thought, when treating of legal obligation alone, that the probability or likelihood of

---

[47] *View of a Complete Code of Laws, Works* III 181.

[48] Op. cit. 159.

[49] *OLG* 56 and Chap. VI *passim*.

[50] The first statement of the generic theory is in the *Fragment* published in 1776; the second is in the *Essay on Logic* (*Works* VIII 217) written after both *PML* and *OLG*, to the first of which (published in 1790) it refers at *Works* III 247 n.

suffering required by the generic theory would be sufficiently
established in the case of legal obligation by the mere fact
that when a legal system is in force the subsidiary law prescribing punishment would be the command of a sovereign
legislator who, as such, is in receipt of habitual obedience
from the judges, and that he overlooked or perhaps thought
irrelevant the fact that in the rare individual cases in special
circumstances the chances of a prescribed punishment being
inflicted might sink to zero.

The Single Imperative Probabilistic Theory

The single reference[51] that Mr Hacker cites in support of the
view that Bentham held this theory is certainly very obscure
and gives no hint as to the source of the suffering for disobedience to which it refers, but this third theory is more or
less well adapted to a special type of case to which Bentham
does frequently refer, when the legislature relies for the provision of a motive for obedience not on legal sanctions at all
but on what Bentham terms 'the auxiliary sanctions':[52] the
popular or moral sanction, and the religious sanction. Bentham is quite clear that there could be and indeed are such
laws and also that unlike praemiary laws they create obligations, though the obligation would be a hybrid constituted
by the legislator's expression of will and the probability that
disobedience to it will be met with manifestations of popular
disapproval or ill will or divine punishment or both. Even a
law forbidding murder was, he thought, both possible and
intelligible   though   supported   only   by   such   auxiliary
sanctions.[53] But a special and important class of obligation
constituted in this way may arise from what he terms 'laws
of a transcendent class'[54] which may limit the powers of the
sovereign. In his interesting but unsatisfactory account of
such limitations Bentham represents the Sovereign as imposing an obligation on himself to respect in the use of his
legislative   powers   certain   voluntary   concessions   which
he has made. Though these will be normally supported only
by the auxiliary sanctions, Bentham settles, after some initial

[51] Hacker, op. cit. 139, citing *Pannomial Fragments, Works* III 217.
[52] *OLG* 133, 248.
[53] *OLG* 142.
[54] *OLG* 64 ff. See Chap. IX *infra*.

doubts,[55] for the view that such auto-limitation by the Sovereign are laws and create obligations.

VI

FUNDAMENTAL CRITICISM

This chapter has so far been mainly concerned with the detailed interpretation of Bentham's theory or theories. The criticism of the 'mixed theory' expounded in Section II above, together with Bentham's imaginary response to it, will seem to many quite superficial, not touching the core of Bentham's strongly positivist conception of legal obligation as quite independent of moral obligation which has influenced so much later thought. For it is true that to avoid the particular criticism so far considered, Bentham would merely have to drop the probabilistic element from the Mixed Theory thus converting it into the Dual Imperative Theory. If that theory were itself acceptable this move would make it possible to conform to ordinary legal and non-legal usage and both to state without contradiction that a person had a legal obligation but was not likely to suffer for failure to fulfil it, and to state without redundancy that a person under such an obligation would be likely to suffer for such a failure. Certainly there are more important criticisms than these to be made of Bentham's conception of legal obligation and contemporary writers have focused on two, touching on points where Bentham has most influenced later theory. These points raise vast issues and I cannot do more in this section than state in summary fashion their main thrust and their main merits or demerits.

The first of these fundamental criticisms, while remaining faithful to Bentham's general positivist spirit, calls in question his imperative theory identifying laws with the command direct or indirect of the sovereign legislator. For many different reasons some of which are elaborated elsewhere in this book,[56] and others are to be found in my *Concept of Law*, the idea of a command and habitual obedience cannot account for the variety of law-creating events and types of

---

[55] *OLG* 16.
[56] Chap. X *infra*.

law recognized as giving rise to legal obligations. The notion of a legal standard mandatorily requiring certain conduct is plainly distinct from and wider than the idea of a command or prohibition expressing a legislator's will, even if in some legal systems such expressions of will are recognized as one kind of mandatory legal standard creating legal obligation, or even as the only one. Laws creating legal obligations whose source is precedent, or custom, or enactment by a legislative assembly involving a complex procedure, cannot be fitted without gross distortion into Bentham's Imperative Theory, even with the aid of his subtle account of the 'adoption' or 'susception' by the sovereign of laws originating from other sources than his own will.[57] The diversity of such sources and types of law is to be explained only by reference to the basic law-identifying rules accepted by the Courts of a legal system, which provide criteria for the recognition of the rules of the system. On this ground alone criticism of Bentham's Imperative Theory which of course enters into his accounts of legal obligation seem well taken.

The Imperative Theory, however, also fails to account for a feature of statements of legal obligation which cannot be characterized by the aid of Bentham's conceptual resources of command and habit of obedience. This feature is what is now called the 'normativity' of such statements and statements *of the law* or the legal position of individuals under the law. To say that a man has a legal obligation to do a certain act is not, though it may imply a statement *about* the law or a statement that a law exists requiring him to behave in a certain way. It is rather to assess his acting or not acting in that way from the point of view adopted by at least the Courts of the legal system who accept the law as a standard for the guidance and evaluation, of conduct, determining what is permissible by way of demands and pressure for conformity. Such statements are not historical or factual statements describing the past, present or future actions, attitudes or beliefs of either subjects or officials of the legal system, but statements of what individuals legally must or must not do; similarly statements of legal rights are statements of what individuals are legally entitled to do or not to do or to have

---

[57] *OLG* 21–7; see also Chap. X *infra*.

others do or forbear from doing. Such normative statements are the most common ways of stating the content of the law, in relation to any subject matter, made by ordinary citizens, lawyers, judges, or other officials, and also by jurists and teachers of law in relation to their own or other systems of law.

Of course other, non-normative, historical, or factual forms and descriptions of the law of any society are also possible and commonly used. Instead of saying that US male citizens have a legal duty to register for the draft on attaining the age of twenty-one we could with equal truth say that on a given date Congress enacted a law requiring this to be done and providing penalties for non-compliance. This would be a historical proposition *about* the law, not a proposition *of* law, but though both forms of statement are true and are intimately connected they do not have the same meaning. The historical statement about the law, that Congress enacted a particular statute, states facts which are part of the truth conditions of the normative statement of law, but that connection between the two statements must not blind us to the difference in meaning between them. Many attempts have been made to 'reduce' normative statements to ordinary historical or factual propositions which are felt to be less problematic. Bentham's efforts to explain legal obligation examined in Section II of this chapter are examples of such reductionism. Viewed as attempts to provide an analysis of the concept of legal obligation used by lawyers and others in describing the content of the law these efforts are unsuccessful in the ways illustrated in that section.

What then is it that explains the use of normative statements as the standard normal form of description of the content of the law? To many theorists an obvious answer is seen to lie in some intimate connection between law and morality since no one could doubt that normative statements asserting rights, obligations, or duties are not merely common but are indispensable to basic forms of moral judgement. This view has many variants but all have the common feature that they regard the expressions 'duty', 'obligations.', 'rights', as having the same sense in both legal and moral contexts and accordingly regard propositions of law asserting the existence of a legal right or duty as a special kind of moral judgement. For theorists who hold such views there is no separate or distinct kind of duty, or obligation or right which is legal but not also moral: a legal right or duty is a moral right or duty differing from others only because it exists only by virtue of the legal system.

Among the many variants of this view the simplest, most extreme, and easily refutable is one that has sometimes been ascribed to supporters of the doctrine of Natural Law. It is that among the truth conditions of any statement of legal duty not only must there be a legal system in force including a rule or set of rules which impose this duty, but these, or at least the system as a whole, must be morally acceptable or justified. To the obvious objection to this extreme view that the history of law is in part a record of morally iniquitous laws, the theorist can only respond by denying that such iniquitous laws are laws and denying that what they require are legal duties. It is precisely on the ground that such a view would deny the title of 'law' and 'legal duty' to what are for many good reasons regarded as law and legal duties that this view cannot be correct. It is indeed rejected by some modern exponents of natural law as a travesty of their doctrine and a misinterpretation of Aquinas's famous dictum 'Lex Injusta non est Lex'.[58]

To all such views there is one general overriding objection. Statements of law in normative terms asserting the existence of legal duties may be made and are held to be true not only when made about the legal system of the person making such statements but also when made about foreign systems or even about systems of law which are no longer in force. Yet in none of these cases need the person making statements of law of this kind regard the law as having any moral justification, or his own statement as a form of moral judgement. He may do so, but also he may not, and frequently such statements of law are quite morally neutral or uncommitted, or may without contradiction, be accompanied by the statement that there is no moral obligation to do what the law in question requires.

The natural inference to draw from these facts is that legal and moral rights and duties are not necessarily related, that

[58] For criticisms of this alleged misinterpretation see Finnis, *Natural Law and Natural Rights* (Oxford 1981).

normative statements of law are not as such forms of moral judgement, and that the expressions 'right', 'duty', and 'obligation' have different meanings though they may share certain common features in legal and moral contexts. This is my own 'positivist' view, but before I expound it and the criticisms made of it, I shall consider two sophisticated modern attempts which seek to preserve the idea that 'obligation' and 'duty' have the same meaning in legal and moral contexts.

V

The first attempt is that made by Professor Dworkin.[59] He is a resolute opponent of the view that legal and moral obligation are conceptually distinct. But he also claims that his theory is not committed to what he takes to be the 'orthodox Natural Law theory'[60] that what is legally right is also always morally right. None the less there is for him a necessary or conceptual connection between law and morality which accounts among other facts for the fact that we describe what legislative enactments require in the normative term of duty. This conceptual connection between law and morality becomes evident if we look at the law as it is seen by judges who have a duty to ascertain it and apply it in deciding cases. A judge coming to his office accepts, according to Dworkin, the settled practices of his legal system as determining part of the law which he has a duty to apply. This settled part of the law includes the mass of constitutional law, statutes, and precedents under which individuals have already been treated as having legal rights and duties. This is the explicit law; but for Dworkin it does not constitute the whole law, for besides the explicit law, there is, so Dworkin claims, the implicit law which consists of the set of coherent and consistent principles which both explain and morally justify the explicit law. This body of explanatory and justificatory principles has two dimensions: one of 'fit' and the other of 'morality'.[61] This is so since it must both explain

<hr>

[59] *On Taking Rights Seriously*, 2nd edn. London 1978, esp. Chap. 4 and pp. 104-8; 124-7; 326-49.
[60] Op. cit. 326, 339, 341.
[61] Op. cit. 339-40.

the explicit law, as a hypothesis inferred from a set of data may explain those data, and it must also do what no merely explanatory hypothesis can do: it must provide the best moral justification of the explicit law.

This set of implicit, explanatory, and justificatory principles is called by Dworkin 'the soundest theory of the law'; but it is important to stress that for him such principles constitute actual parts of the legal system and are as objective as the explicit parts of the system; for though a judge can only state what he believes to be the best justification of the explicit law, whether it is so or not, is a matter of objective moral truth or moral fact. Yet, though this is a matter of objective moral fact,[62] its truth is essentially controversial; there can be no demonstration or public tests of its truth as there can be in the case of the explicit law.[63]

In Dworkin's theory two main purposes are served by the judges' identification of such implicit law. One is to settle what are termed 'hard cases' where the explicit law because it is vague, conflicting, ambiguous, or otherwise indeterminate, fails to dictate a decision either way. In other words the implicit law is a reservoir of principles presupposed by but wider than the explicit law, which will serve to yield a unique decision in all cases left indeterminate or partially unregulated by the explicit law. This is Dworkin's answer to the positivist's theory that the law can fail to regulate some issues and is in that sense incomplete, with the consequence that to decide such issues a judge has to exercise a law-making discretion.[64] The merit of Dworkin's answer on that point is however a separate topic. Here I am only concerned with the second function which Dworkin attributes to the implicit law, namely, its provision of an explanation of how it is that enactments of a legislature requiring citizens to do or to abstain from some action can create rights and duties for them, the existence of which is asserted in normative statements of law.[65]

Dworkin's explanation is one which assumes that the rights and duties which have been recognized under the settled practices of the legal system and whose creation by legislative

[62] Op. cit. 339, 348-9.   [63] Op. cit. 80, 123, 332.
[64] Op. cit. Chap. IV, *passim*.   [65] Op. cit. 105, 108.

enactment has to be explained, are a species of moral right and duty. According to him this is possible only because they have been created in accordance with certain justifying principles of political morality which form part of 'the soundest theory of the law'. Thus in a democracy a legislature's powers to create this species of moral duty, which a legal duty is, may be explained by reference to the general principles which morally justify parliamentary democracy as a form of coercive government.[66] Such justifying principles form part of the implicit law of the system and are a specific form—an institutional form—of morality since they can be seen to be presupposed by and implicit in the settled practice of a particular legal system. Because they are so implicit in such settled practice they are to be distinguished from morality in the abstract or, as Dworkin terms it, from 'background morality' which has no such footing in the already established legal system. A judge must look only to the moral principles so implicit in the established system and would not be entitled to deny the title of legal duty to some requirement of the law simply because it is morally iniquitous according to background morality. This indeed is the point at which Dworkin claims to distinguish his theory from what he terms 'orthodox natural law theory' and to defend it from the objections briefly considered on p. 146 above. It is this that enables him to recognize as he does that what is legally right is not always morally right.[67]

Attractive as a *via media* is, I do not think that this one is coherent. There are a number of different objections to it but in considering these it is necessary to bear in mind two things. The first is the strongly objective character attributed by Dworkin to morality. Since morality for him is an objective matter, moral judgements (including the crucial judgement made by judges as to what is morally the best or soundest justification of the explicit law) are not made true simply because they are believed or accepted by a Judge or by anyone else, though of course those who make such moral judgements can only state what they believe is the case.[68] Secondly, it is Dworkin's view that when different judges coming from different social backgrounds or 'sub-cultures'[69]

---

[66] Op. cit. 108.   [67] Op. cit. 341.
[68] Op. cit. 124.   [69] Op. cit. 127.

differ as to what is objectively the best justification of the explicit law, each judge must make this moral judgement for himself. There is no public test to which he can appeal to show that he is right and he is not in any way bound to co-ordinate his views with that of other judges, even though, for Dworkin, such views are not merely about what the law ought to be but about what the law *is*; this is so because for him, implicit law is as much law as the explicit law.

The most serious objection to Dworkin's form of the theory that legal rights and duties are a species of moral rights and duties appears when we consider how he accounts for rights and duties created by what he terms 'a wicked legal system' and how he reconciles this theory with the admission that what is legally right is not always morally right. He concedes that a legal system like that of South Africa or Nazi Germany may contain explicit laws of great iniquity so that the rights and duties that arise from them may be sharply at variance with any defensible morality. He acknowledges that in the case of such systems the 'soundest theory of the law' would include morally repugnant principles sanctioning an absolute dictatorship or morally odious policies like 'blacks are less worthy of concern than whites'.[70] He agrees that in such systems no set of principles which we could find morally acceptable would fit the explicit law. In such cases, he says, a judge's moral duty may be to lie and conceal what the law is because the least odious of the principles which will fit the system may yet be too odious to be enforced. None the less, Dworkin accepts that under the explicit rules of such wicked systems, legal rights and duties arise as *prima facie* moral rights and duties, though they may conflict dramatically with the true objective background morality which may require the judge to lie, in which case the *prima facie* moral right which is also a legal right would be overridden in conflict with the requirements of background morality.

In my view these conclusions surrender the idea that legal rights and duties are a species of moral right or duties, or reduces the idea to utter triviality with no bite against the positivist or anyone else; for on this view, the justifying

---

[70] Op. cit. 326–7, 341–3.

principles allegedly embedded in the law which generate the alleged moral component of legal right and legal duty impose no restraints at all. If all that can be said of the theory or set of principles underlying the system of explicit law is that it is morally the least odious of morally unacceptable principles that fit the explicit evil law this can provide no justification at all. To claim that it does would be like claiming that killing an innocent man without torturing him is morally justified to some degree because killing with torture would be morally worse.

So on this theory, just as on the positivist's view, when we enquire what legal rights and duties have been established by the settled explicit law of the system, we may disregard 'the alleged dimension of morality' and all questions of moral justification by 'the soundest theory of the law' which fits the system because this is necessarily devoid of any justificatory force. If there are no laws, however evil, which the 'soundest theory' fitting the law could fail to justify, all that survives of the theory, so far as rights and duties under the settled law are concerned, is the truism that in a good system of law the laws and the rights and duties that arise from them would have a moral justification and in an evil system they will not. This seems indistinguishable from legal positivism.

Dworkin's only answer to this criticism is one that seems to me to abandon the original idea that what explains a legislature's powers to create legal rights and duties are principles of political morality forming part of the soundest theory justifying the law. Instead, he seeks to demonstrate the existence of a moral component in all legal rights and duties by appeal to considerations of fairness and what he terms the doctrine of political responsibility.[71] According to this doctrine a judge is always morally bound to consistency as a matter of fairness and to treat like cases alike. If therefore under an established legal system individuals have been accorded rights or held to be under duties in accordance with a settled explicit law, then independently of the moral merits of the law, other individuals have a *prima facie* moral right as a matter of fairness to a similar application of the law

---

[71] Op. cit. 126.

in their case.[72] This is so where the explicit law is clear, settled, and determinate, but if the explicit law is indeterminate, dictating no decision either way, and so leaves for decision what Dworkin terms 'a hard case', fairness and the requirements of consistency under the doctrine of political responsibility will call for a direct application of the implicit principles which explain and best justify the clear explicit law. In either case this right, arising from fairness, though a general moral right is not absolute, and it can be outweighed if the law is sufficiently wicked.

This last-ditch defence designed to show a minimal moral component in all legal rights and duties even in a wicked legal system, seems to me hopeless. How can it be that there is a moral right, even if only a *prima facie* moral right, in point of fairness to the continued application of wicked laws or the principles underlying them? Even if we were to allow the strange moral alchemy which treats the fact that evil has been done in the past as a moral reason for doing it now, this line of argument against the positivist seems full of paradox. Thus in the first case according to the application of some iniquitous statute there could be no legal right with a moral component; for since it is the first case the alleged moral component, based on the fairness of consistency, treating like cases alike, would be absent. Again, when the law is clear the theory seems indistinguishable from positivism. This is so because to establish the clear right in clear cases both Dworkin and the positivist have to point only to the accepted practice of the legal system, and no moral argument is required, for the judge must accept the settled practices of his system. Dworkin's moral terminology here therefore seems to add only a confusing but idle decoration to the positivist simple conclusion. It is as if Dworkin were to say 'Yes, that is how one establishes in clear cases legal rights and duties, but remember that in every such case except the first, there is a moral component due to fairness and the need for consistency, even in wickedness, and that is why we can speak here of legal rights and duties consistently with the idea that they are a species of moral rights and duties.' In the 'hard cases' where the explicit law is not clear, Dworkin, as I

---

[72] Op. cit. 226–7.

have said, treats individuals as having a moral right to the direct application of the principles underlying the explicit law, though this right may be outweighed if those principles are sufficiently wicked. But how can there be in such cases any form of moral right? *Ex hypothesi* the principles themselves being only the least odious of morally unacceptable principles have no intrinsic moral merit, and since *ex hypothesi* such cases are ones where the law is indeterminate no expectations can be aroused to justify their extension to cases not clearly covered by the law.

VI

It is important in considering these criticisms of Dworkin's theory not to confuse it with a theory which also insists that rights and duties have the same meaning in legal and moral contexts, but attributes this not to the fact that there are implicit principles which as a matter of objective moral fact really do justify that law, but to the fact that this is *believed* to be the case, at least by the judges who apply the law and make normative statements of duty in the course of doing so. This theory, unlike Dworkin's, is not troubled by the existence of wicked legal systems because it does not require that the beliefs in moral justification be true but only that they be accepted by those who hold them.

A theory of the kind last mentioned is provided by Joseph Raz[73] in the course of his wide-ranging general account of normativity in terms of reasons for action. It may surprise some that though his theory insists that normative statements of duty have the same sense in legal and moral contexts, the general character of his theory is strongly positivist and indeed quite sceptical about the claims of the law to have any moral authority as such. Unlike Dworkin, Raz does not explain the identity of meaning of normative propositions in legal and moral contexts by arguing that there are implicit principles embedded in the law which actually justify it. Instead, he advances two different distinctions of importance. The first of these is the distinction between a normative

---

[73] See his *Practical Reason and Norms* (London 1975), esp. 123-9, 146-8, 162-77; *The Authority of Law* (Oxford 1979), 153-7; *The Concept of a Legal System* (2nd edn., Oxford 1980), 234-8.

statement which is committed and one which is 'detached'. The second distinction is that mentioned already between the actual moral justifiability of compliance with the law and the *belief*, correct or incorrect, that this is morally justifiable.

Raz's distinction between committed and detached normative statements focuses attention on a little-noticed but important feature of moral discourse. It is a feature of such discourse that normative statements may be made both by those who themselves accept the relevant principles as guides to conduct and standards of evaluation and those who do not so accept them. Statements made by the former are committed statements and are to be contrasted with statements made by those who speak from the point of view of those who accept the principles and so speak as if they themselves accepted them though they do not in fact do so. Such statements are detached. Thus the Christian who says to his Jewish friend about to eat a dish of pork 'You ought to not eat that' speaks from, without sharing, the point of view of one who accepts the Jewish dietary laws. It is, therefore, not a statement merely *about* Jewish laws but a statement *of* the law which in the mouth of this speaker is uncommitted or detached. Similar normative statements of law (not merely statements about the law) may be made from the point of view of one who accepts the laws of some system as guides to conduct, but though made from that point of view are in fact made by one who may be an anarchist and so does not share it. These are detached or uncommitted statements of law which may be made both by subjects of a legal system who do not accept its laws even though they purport to apply to them, or may be made about foreign or even extinct systems of law which do not apply to those who make such statements. It is of course common for a jurist expounding the law of some system for theoretical purposes to do so in the form of detached normative statements. This conception of a detached normative statement is in principle a successful explanation of what is left unexplained in other theories which insist that rights and duties have the same meaning in legal and moral contexts; and it shows how it can be the case that normative statements may be used in describing the law by those who in no way endorse or accept it as guides or standards of conduct. It is moreover a valuable supplementation to my own distinction drawn in *The Concept of Law* between external statements about the law and internal statements made by those who accept the law.[74] Raz shows the need for a third type of detached statement made from the point of view of those who accept the law by those who in fact do not accept it. I would quarrel, however, for reasons I explain later both with Raz's characterization of the legal point of view from which he considers such detached statements are made and with his account of what is involved in the judges' acceptance of the laws of their system. Into both of these Raz injects a moral element which is, I think, unrealistic but is necessary for his account of the normativity of legal statements of duty.

Raz's second distinction between the actual moral justifiability of compliance with the law and the belief correct or incorrect in its moral justifiability is important in determining what the conditions are if a legal system of a particular structure is to constitute the law of a particular society. Raz's final view, after hesitation,[75] seems to be that one necessary condition is that there be on the part of the judges either belief or at least the pretence of belief in the moral justifiability of the law. However, since only belief, however misguided, is required, the existence of wicked legal systems presents no problem for this theory. Nor does this theory treat, as Dworkin's does, whatever moral principles justify compliance with the law as themselves for that reason forming part of the law. The steps by which Raz reaches his conclusions are as follows. He agrees[76] with my argument in *The Concept of Law* that in order for a legal system to be in force it is not enough though it is necessary that in general the behaviour of the population be in conformity with its laws. He holds, as I do, that it is also necessary that the judges of the system should accept or, as he sometimes puts it, should endorse these laws. This involves their accepting and endorsing the rule or rules[77] of recognition

---

[74] *The Concept of Law* (Oxford 1961), *passim*.

[75] Cf. his *The Authority of the Law*, 155 and n. 13 with *Practical Reason and Norms*, 147–8, and *The Concept of a Legal System* (2nd edn.), 235.

[76] *Practical Reason and Norms*, 126.

[77] In *The Concept of Law* I defend the view that every legal system has a single complex rule of recognition. Raz (op. cit. 146) disputes this, but agrees

of the system as customary rules practised by the judges which provide the criteria or sources by reference to which the judges identify the laws which they are to apply as judges in deciding cases. Rules of recognition accepted in the practice of the judges require them to apply the laws identified by the criteria which they provide and of course the laws so identified are the same as those which impose duties and confer rights on individuals.

What then is it for judges to accept or endorse such rules of recognition and so derivatively to accept or endorse the laws which such rules require them to apply? At times Raz writes as if such acceptance does not necessarily involve any moral approval either of a rule of recognition or of the rules which it requires the judges to apply, but only requires the regular and settled use by the judges of the law in guiding and evaluating both their own behaviour as judges and the behaviour of those to whom the laws apply. In his earliest writings on this subject Raz considered that a judge might follow a rule of recognition either without any beliefs as to what justifies judges in doing so or for merely prudential reasons,[78] but in his latest work, correcting this earlier statement, his considered view seems to be that the judges' full acceptance as endorsement of the rule of recognition does involve the belief or the pretence of belief that judges are morally justified in following it and in applying and evaluating behaviour by reference to the laws which it requires them to apply.[79] So a judge who merely believes that he should follow it for some personal or prudential reason must, if what he does is to constitute acceptance of the rule of recognition, *pretend* that he believes that there are moral reasons for compliance with it. Similarly, in his analysis of the notion of effective authority which includes the authority of the law of an effective legal system, Raz claims that the recognition of any authority involves either belief in its moral legitimacy or the 'avowal' or 'the show'[80] of such

---

that every legal system has at least one such rule. For the sake of argument I provisionally concede the point and speak here of 'rules of recognition'.

[78] *Practical Reason and Norms*, 148.

[79] *The Authority of the Law*, 155; and 'La Pureza de la Teoria Pura' in *Analysis Filosofico* (1981) 74.

[80] *The Authority of the Law*, 28.

belief. So that it is enough that those who recognize such authority should 'avow' such a belief. On this view a judge's statements about legal rights and duties express moral approval and make a moral claim though the approval may be pretence and the claim may be insincere.

Raz's shift of opinion in this matter and his watering down with the aid of the idea of pretence and insincerity of the moral approval which he thinks is involved in the judges' acceptance of rules of the legal system strongly suggest to my mind that the inclusion of this as a necessary component of acceptance is a mistake. Insistence on this is I think a consequence dictated by the general reason-based and cognitive explanation of normativity which is a feature of Raz's theory of practical reason and which connects the idea of duty with a special sort of reason for action the existence of which is an objective matter of fact. This theory yields a cognitive account of duty which in skeleton form is as follows. A normative statement asserting that a person has a duty entails that he 'ought' to act in a certain way and that either means or entails that there is a reason for him so to act. But since statements of duty may apply to persons independently of their desires, aims, or purposes, or other subjective motivation, and may require them to defer their interests to others, the reasons for actions which duties entail are objective and not dependent upon those who may be said to have such a reason having some subjective motivation which performance of the duties will advance or implement. Such reasons for action involved in the very notion of duty constitute, at least when the duties are to act in the interest of others as legal duties frequently are, moral reasons for action. Hence it is that a judge who accepts and applies laws imposing such duties and in the course of doing so makes statements of legal duty must either believe that there are such objective moral reasons for complying with the law or at least must pretend to do so. So, as Raz in his last writing on the subject asserts,[81] normative statements of duty made by a judge in the course of applying the law are moral claims, sincere or insincere.

It might seem that the moral component which according

---

[81] See esp. 'La Pureza de la Teoria Pura' op. cit. n. 79 *supra*.

to Raz is necessarily involved in the judge's acceptance of a rule of recognition and hence of the laws of the system identified by it is too small to worry any legal positivist.[82] In fact, Raz's general theory is in other respects a strong positivist one though it holds out some olive branches to the natural law theorist, including the doctrine here criticized that obligation and duty have the same meaning in legal and moral contexts. It is to be noticed that Raz, true to his general positivist account, does not stipulate as a condition of the existence of a legal system that the belief which a judge may either hold or pretend to hold that there are sound moral reasons requiring compliance with the law as such be true and in fact, as we learn from his writing on political obligation, Raz thinks it must be false.[83] This makes the moral component in the judge's acceptance very small indeed.

Small as this moral component is insistence on it to my mind conveys an unrealistic picture of the way in which the judges envisage their task of identifying and applying the law, and it also rests, I think, on a mistaken cognitive account of normative propositions of law.

When a judge of an established legal system takes up his office he finds that though much is left to his discretion there is also a firmly settled practice of adjudication, according to which any judge of the system is required to apply in the decision of cases the laws identified by specific criteria or sources. This settled practice is acknowledged as determining the central duties of the office of a judge and not to follow the practice would be regarded as a breach of duty one not only warranting criticism but counter-action where possible by correction in a higher court on appeal. It is also acknowledged that demands for compliance would be regarded as proper and are to be met as a matter of course. The judges not only follow this practice as each case arises but are committed in advance in the sense that they have a settled disposition to do this without considering the merits of so doing in each case and indeed would regard it not open to them to

---

[82] Bentham, as explained *supra*, pp. 109, 142, held that the Sovereign's commands could be regarded as laws imposing obligation even when they are supported only by the 'auxiliary' sanction of popular morality.

[83] See *The Authority of the Law*, Chap. 12 on 'The Obligation to obey the Law'.

act on their view of the merits. So though the judge is in this sense committed to following the rules his view of the moral merits of doing so (at least so far as the rules are clear and provide him with determinate guidance) is irrelevant. His view of the merits may be favourable or unfavourable, or simply absent, or, without dereliction of his duty as a judge, he may have formed no view of the moral merits. Raz indeed seems to admit as much by conceding that pretending to believe or the avowal of belief in the merits, is enough.

If then it is unrealistic to suppose that the judges must believe in the moral justification of compliance with the law, how can it be that they must at least pretend to believe in it? Raz's argument in the end seems to be that when in the course of applying the law judges assert that someone has a legal duty this, as a matter of the *meaning* of its component terms, *must* amount to a moral claim, sincere or insincere.

Why should such an interpretation of the statement that a person has a legal duty when said by a judge in the course of applying the law be accepted? Of course if Raz's reason-based explanation of normative statements and his cognitive analysis of the notion of duty were correct so that 'X has a duty to act in a certain way' means that there is an objective reason for X to act in that way, this would amount to a moral judgement if we concede, as for the sake of argument we may, that moral judgements are statement of objective reasons. Raz's views on this point are, as I have said, part of a comprehensive theory of practical reason, according to which normative propositions, asserting the existence of duties, committed or uncommitted, true or false, sincere or insincere, assert the existence of such reasons. It may be that this theory holds good for moral judgements asserting a categorical moral duty and that these do carry with them if sincere, a belief in the existence of such reasons. I do not share but will not dispute here this cognitive account of moral judgement in terms of objective reasons for action, though it is currently a matter of great and exceedingly complex dispute among philosophers. But I find little reason to accept such a cognitive interpretation of legal duty in terms of objective reasons or the identity of meaning of 'obligation' in legal and moral contexts which this would secure. Far better adapted to the legal case is a different, non-cognitive theory of duty according to which committed statements asserting that others have a duty do not refer to actions which they have a categorical reason to do but, as the etymology of 'duty' and indeed 'ought' suggests, such statements refer to actions which are due from or owed by the subjects having the duty, in the sense that they may be properly demanded or exacted from them. On this footing, to say that an individual has a legal obligation to act in a certain way is to say that such action may be properly demanded or extracted from him according to legal rules or principles regulating such demands for action. So if a judge in deciding a case before him declares that an individual has a legal obligation, e.g. under some statute duly enacted by the legislature, this will be a committed statement since the judge making it accepts in common with other judges of the legal system the rules of recognition of the system which includes enactment by the legislature as a criterion for identifying the laws which they must apply and enforce. Satisfaction of such a criterion by subordinate laws of the system constitutes for a judge who accepts in common with other judges this rule of recognition a specific kind of reason which I shall call an authoritative legal reason for himself conforming to such laws so far as they require him to act in certain ways, and to treat them as standards for the evaluation of the conduct of others to whom they apply as legally right or wrong, so determining what demands may be properly made upon them.

Given the existence of a legal system whose courts accept specific rules of recognition, detached statements of legal obligation may be made by those who accept neither its rules of recognition nor any of its subordinate laws, either as guides to their own behaviour or as standards for the evaluation of the conduct of others. Such detached statements are made from the point of view of the Courts who accept these things, by academic lawyers and others in describing the content either of their own legal system or foreign systems.

This 'positivist' account of legal obligation as conceptually distinct from moral obligation presents only the bare bones of the matter but I do not think that fleshing it out in an acceptable manner would involve abandoning the essentials of this account. Of course it is true that many judges and many ordinary citizens in most legal systems believe and often assert that they have a moral obligation to conform to law as such, and unless this were true and generally believed to be true, legal systems might be much less stable than they are. Nothing I have said, in defending an account of legal obligation as conceptually distinct from moral obligation in a way which avoids the pitfalls of Bentham's unsatisfactory reduction of them, is inconsistent with these important, but as I see it, still contingent truths about the connections of law and morality. I have only argued that when judges or others make committed statements of legal obligation it is not the case that they must necessarily believe or pretend to believe that they are referring to a species of moral obligation.

Again, it is true but also consistent with the account of legal obligation which I have given that the Courts are not always not merely passive mouthpieces of clearly settled law. Frequently and in many important cases the law is not clearly settled and dictates no results either way. In such cases in my view, which is hotly challenged by Dworkin and others, the judges have an inescapable though restricted law-making function, which standardly they perform by promoting one or other of those moral values or principles which the existing law can be regarded as instantiating. I am aware that the full defence of this account of obligation against its modern critics would involve a large-scale scrutiny of many different strands of argument, but perhaps I have said enough in considering the views of two leading critics to show that the debate is not yet at an end.

VII

LEGAL RIGHTS[1]

I INTRODUCTORY

Most English students of jurisprudence learn to take the first steps towards the analysis of the notion of a legal right from Hohfeld's *Fundamental Legal Conceptions*.[2] In my view Bentham is a more thought-provoking guide than Hohfeld, and indeed than any other writer on the subject, though unfortunately his doctrine has to be collected from observations scattered through his voluminous and not always very readable works. Bentham certainly anticipated much of Hohfeld's work and he has moreover much to say about important aspects of the subject on which Hohfeld did not touch. But his account of legal rights is by no means free from objections; for at some important points his utilitarianism gets in the way of his analytical vision. Bentham's doctrine has however the supreme merit of confronting problems ignored by other theories, even where as in the case of 'interest-theories' of rights, they are similar to his own.

The notion of a legal right has proved in the history of jurisprudence to be very elusive: how elusive may be judged not only from the well-known division of theories into 'Will theories' and 'Interest theories' but also from some of the interesting though also strange things that jurists and others have said about rights. They have on the whole hammered rights with sceptical doubts much harder than obligations or duties. Duguit, for example, held that there were legal

---

[1] The present account of Bentham's doctrine of rights is collected from *PML*, *OLG*, and passages in *Works* III. A brief exposition and criticism of part of Bentham's doctrine based mainly on *Works* III was given in my lecture on Bentham published in *British Academy Proceedings* xlviii (1962). This was criticized by Professor David Lyons in 'Rights, Claimants and Beneficiaries', *American Philosophical Quarterly* 6 (1969) 173, and the present fuller and, I hope, more precise account and criticism of Bentham owes much to the stimulus of his article.

[2] 1919 (3rd reprint 1964).

duties but no legal rights;[3] Austin,[4] Bentham,[5] and in our own day, Ross,[6] while apparently admitting that there may be non-legal obligations or duties insist that 'strictly' the only rights are legal rights. It has moreover often been observed that the concept of a right, legal or moral, is not to be found in the work of the Greek philosophers, and certainly there is no noun or noun phrase in Plato or Aristotle which is the equivalent of our expression 'a right', as distinct from the 'right action' or 'the right thing to do'. Jurists of stature[7] have even held that lawyers of some sophisticated systems of law, including Roman Law, never achieved a clear concept of a legal right. Thus Maine wrote: 'singular as the fact may appear to those unacquainted with it, the Romans had not attained, or had not fully attained, to the conception of a legal Right, which seems to us elementary'[8] and 'The clear conception of a legal right . . . belongs distinctively to the modern world.'[9] He added that 'unquestionably a clear and consistent meaning was for the first time given to the expression "a right" by the searching analysis of Bentham and Austin.'[10]

Maine's reference to Bentham not as discovering or revealing the meaning of the expression 'a right', but as *giving* a clear meaning to it is accurate; and raises a methodological issue of some importance. When we ask for the analysis of such notions as that of a legal right, what precisely is it that we are seeking and by what criteria should success or failure be judged? Bentham's views on these matters are astonishingly modern and are still worth attention. He thought that the expression 'a right' was one of a fairly short list of terms including the term 'law' which were the subject matter of 'universal expository jurisprudence',[11] and its task was to

---

[3] *Traité de droit constitutionel* (1911), I 64, 130–45, discussed by Allen, *Legal Duties* (1931), 158, and Ross, *On Law and Justice* (1958), 186.

[4] *Lectures on Jurisprudence* (5th edn.), Chap. XII, 344.

[5] *Works* II 501; III 221. See also Chap. IV *supra*.

[6] Ross, op. cit. 248, 365.

[7] Besides Maine (see n. 8 *infra*) Buckland, *Text Book of Roman Law*, 2nd edn. (1950), 58 and Villey, *Leçons d'histoire de la philosophie de droit* (1957), Chaps. XI and XIV.

[8] *Early Law and Custom* (1891), 365; cf. 366.

[9] Op. cit. 390.

[10] Op. cit. 366.

[11] *PML* Preface in *CW* 6, and Chap. XVII, para. 24, in *CW* 295.

expound the ideas annexed to these terms. But he did not think that in discharging this task he was strictly bound by common usage, or that definitions, if they were to be useful in jurisprudence, should merely follow or reflect that usage, which at points he found to be confused, arbitrary, and vague and in various other ways unsatisfactory. Quite frequently and explicitly, he departed from usage in order to construct a meaning for a term which, while generally coinciding with usage and furnishing an explanation of its main trends, would not only be clear, but would pick out and collect clusters of features frequently recurrent in the life of a legal system, to which it was important to attend for some statable theoretical or practical purpose. Hence Bentham spoke of himself as expounding the meaning of terms by 'fixing' rather than 'teaching' their import;[12] and when he came in *Of Laws in General* to elaborate his definition of a law he spoke of 'rather a meaning which I wish to see annexed to the term law than one which it has any settled and exclusive possession of already'.[13] In modern terminology, Bentham's conception of analysis is that of 'rational reconstruction' or refinement of concepts in use: his general standpoint is critical and corrective, and in the sequel I shall appeal to it in criticism of part of Bentham's own doctrine concerning legal rights.

II SURVEY OF BENTHAM'S DOCTRINE

Bentham distinguishes three principal kinds of right which correspond roughly to Hohfeld's 'claim-right', 'liberty' or 'privilege', and 'power', though he does not include an element corresponding to Hohfeld's 'immunity'. In spite of this rough correspondence there are many differences of which perhaps the most important is that unlike Bentham, Hohfeld considers that the very common use of the expression of a right to cover all the four cases which he distinguishes is a 'loose'[14] and even 'nebulous'[15] usage: the 'proper meaning'[16] of the term according to Hohfeld is to designate the element

---

[12] *Works* III 217.
[13] *OLG* 11.
[14] Hohfeld, op. cit. 42, 51.
[15] Op. cit. 54.
[16] Op. cit. 38, 39.

which he terms a claim-right, and the broad or loose use is described as 'unfortunate'[17] because it leads to confusion of thought. Notwithstanding these strictures Hohfeld recognizes that the use of the term to cover claim-right, liberty, power, and immunity is a use of the term in a 'generic'[18] sense and hints that the characteristic common to the genus is 'any sort of legal advantage'[19] though he does not explain this idea further. Bentham does not express any similar misgivings concerning the wide extension of the term in ordinary usage, and though in the cases of other terms he is prepared to distinguish what is 'strictly and properly so called' from what is not, he does not do so in the case of rights.

Bentham starts by making what he says is a fundamental distinction between two sorts of rights distinguished by different relationships to the idea of obligation or duty.[20] The first sort of rights owe their existence to (or as he says 'result from') the absence of legal obligation:[21] the second sort result from obligation imposed by law.[22] Rights of the first sort are rights to do or abstain from some action, and rights of the second sort are rights to what Bentham calls 'services',[23] i.e. the actions or forbearance, of others. Corresponding to these two different sorts of rights are two different sorts of law or states of the law. Rights resulting from obligation are conferred by (or as Bentham puts it, 'have as their base') coercive laws; rights resulting from the absence of obligation have as their base discoercive or permissive laws.[24] In this last phrase Bentham includes three different cases. These are (i) *active* permission[25] or countermand: where the law permits some action, previously legally prohibited or obligatory, to be done or not done; (ii) *inactive* or original permission:[26] where the law simply declares that some action not previously prohibited or obligatory may be done or not done; (iii) the case where the law is silent.[27] Such permissive

---

[17] Op. cit. 51.   [18] Op. cit. 42.   [19] Op. cit. 71.
[20] Obligation and duty are treated as synonymous terms by Bentham: see *OLG* 294.
[21] *Works* III 181, 217-18; *PML* Chap. XVI, para. 26, in *CW* 212.
[22] *Works* III loc. cit.; *OLG* 57-8, 294.
[23] *Works* III 159; *OLG* 57-8.
[24] *Works* III 181; *PML* Concluding Note, paras. 3-7, in *CW* 302.
[25] *OLG* 57-8.   [26] Ibid.
[27] *OLG* 98-9, *Works* III 159.

laws or legal silence leave the individual who is the right-holder free or at liberty to do or not to do some action; I shall use the expression 'liberty-right' instead of Bentham's more explicit though clumsy circumlocution for this sort of right, and I shall use instead of Bentham's expression 'right resulting from obligation' the more familiar 'right correlative to obligation' for his second sort of right, which arises when the law imposes a duty not on the right-holder, but on another and thus restricts the other's freedom to act as he chooses.

A. Liberty-rights

Bentham in my view was certainly justified in regarding liberty-rights as of very great importance. Some later theorists have thought that so negative an idea could be of little significance for jurisprudence and could not represent 'a legal relation'.[28] This I am sure is a great mistake. Without attention to this negative and apparently insignificant element there cannot be any clear understanding of such important ideas as that of ownership, or of the legal character of the sphere left open by the law to economic competition, or any clear formulation of many legal problems to which that has given rise.[29] Indeed in the sequel I shall claim that this element of a liberty-right is involved in all the most important kinds of legal right at least in the civil law. But the notion of a liberty-right needs some further characterization beyond that given to it by Bentham's phrase, 'right resulting from the absence of obligation'. The following points in particular deserve attention.

The bilateral character of liberty-rights

In England and in most other countries a man has a right to look over his garden fence at his neighbour; he is under no obligation not to look at him and under no obligation to look at him. In this example the liberty is therefore bilateral; both the obligation not to look and the obligation to look are in Bentham's phrase 'absent'. Most of Bentham's examples of a liberty-right and his general account of them represents them

---

[28] e.g. Pollock, *Jurisprudence* (2nd edn. 1902), 62, but see Hohfeld, op. cit. 48 n.

[29] See *infra*, p. 172, n. 53.

as bilateral; they are, he says, such rights as men have in the
state of nature where there are no obligations. But he occasionally speaks as if a unilateral liberty, that is the absence of
either an obligation not to do something *or* an obligation to
do it, were enough to constitute a right of this kind.[30] On
that footing a right to do an action would merely exclude an
obligation not to do it, and men always have a right to do
what they have an obligation to do. Hohfeld's 'liberty' or
'privilege' is by his definition a unilateral liberty,[31] and, in
some special contexts, to treat unilateral liberties as rights
accords with a common and intelligible usage for which I
offer an explanation below.[32] But I shall treat Bentham as
committed to regarding bilateral liberties as the standard type
of liberty-right.

Liberty-rights and correlative obligations not to interfere
The fact that a man has a right to look at his neighbour over
the garden fence does not entail that the neighbour has a
correlative obligation to let himself be looked at or not to
interfere with the exercise of this specific liberty-right. So
he could, for example, erect a screen on his side of the fence
to block the view. But though a neighbour may do this if he
wishes, and so has himself a liberty-right or bilateral liberty
to erect or not to erect such a fence, there are other things
that, in most countries, he cannot legally do to prevent his
tormentor looking at him. For he has certain legal obligations
or duties, civil or criminal, or both, which preclude some,
though not all forms of interference, and these in practice
more or less adequately protect the exercise of the liberty-
right. Thus he cannot enter the next-door garden and beat up
his tormentor, for this would be a breach of certain duties
not indeed correlative to his tormentor's liberty-right to look
at him, but correlative at least in the case of civil duties to
certain other rights, which his tormentor has and which are
not mere liberties. These are the tormentor's rights not to be
assaulted and his right that others should not enter on his
land without his consent. These are rights correlative to
obligations and to Bentham's account of these I now turn.

[30] e.g. *Works* III 218 but cf. III 159.
[31] Hohfeld, op. cit. 39.
[32] *Infra*, pp. 173-4, 188, n. 93.

B. Rights Correlative to Obligations

The right not to be assaulted and the right of an owner or
occupier of land that others should not enter on it without
his consent are rights to what Bentham terms a negative
service,[33] that is to the abstention from 'hurtful action';[34]
in other cases of rights correlative to obligations, where the
obligation is to *do* something rather than abstain from
action the right is to an 'affirmative' or 'positive' service,[35]
or, as Bentham paraphrases it, to 'a useful action'.[36] All
rights correlative to obligations are rights to services which
consist in the performance of their correlative obligation and
with two exceptions all legal obligations or duties have correlative rights. One exception is the case of 'self-regarding
duties'[37] where the duty is imposed by law solely for the
benefit of the agent on whom they are imposed. Bentham's
examples of self-regarding duties include duties to abstain
from suicide, from 'indecency not in public', incest, idle-
ness, gaming, and 'other species of prodigality'.[38] The other
more important exception to the principle that all legal
obligations have correlative rights is where the legislator has
disregarded entirely the dictates of utility and created obligations by which no one at all benefits. Such obligation
Bentham terms 'ascetic', 'pure', or 'barren', or 'useful to no
one'[39] and he thought they had been all too numerous in the
history of human law. But apart from these two cases, whenever the law creates civil or criminal obligations, it always
thereby creates what Bentham terms 'an enforced service'
negative or positive, for the benefit of others; and to have a
right correlative to an obligation is to be the person or persons intended to benefit from the performance of the obligation.[40] But not only individuals have rights; the public and
also distinct classes included in it have, according to Bentham, rights in those cases where the persons intended to
benefit are what he terms 'unassignable individuals'.[41]

---

[33] *Works* III 159; *OLG* 58-9.   [34] *Works* III 159.
[35] *OLG* 58-9; *Works* III 159.   [36] *Works* III 159.
[37] *OLG* 58, 294; *PML* Chap. XVI, para. 25, n. e3 in *CW* 206.
[38] *PML* Chap. XVI, para. 33, n. x2, in *CW* 225; para. 34, n. a3, in *CW* 226;
para. 35, n. m3, in *CW* 232; and para. 36, n. o3 in *CW* 233.
[39] *Works* III 181, 221.
[40] *PML* Chap. XVI, para. 25, n. e2, in *CW* 206; *OLG* 58.
[41] See *infra*, pp. 177-9.

Accordingly, with the two exceptions mentioned, every offence, crime or civil wrong, is a violation of some right and a case of 'wrongful withholding of services'[42] so that 'there is no law whatsoever that does not confer on some person or other a right'.[43] I shall call this identification of a right-holder by reference to the person or persons intended to benefit by the performance of an obligation 'the benefit theory' of rights; and when I come to criticize it I shall try to make precise the sense not only of benefit but of a person intended to benefit and to clarify the distinction which Bentham makes between assignable and unassignable individuals.

C. Powers

Legal powers are for Bentham a species of right[44] and his works contain a most elaborate taxonomy of the different kinds of legal powers together with a sophisticated analysis of the idea of a legal power and of the legal provisions by which powers are conferred on individuals.[45] The simplest kind of power is that which a man has when he is allowed by law to interfere with or physically control things or the bodies of persons or animals. Bentham subsumes such interference (which of course may take a great variety of forms such as touching, holding, moving, confining) under the general notion of handling and he calls such powers 'powers of contrectation': examples are an owner's power to make physical use of his property or a policeman's power of arrest. Such powers are in fact liberty-rights differing from other liberty-rights in two respects: first the action which, in such cases, there is liberty to do is restricted to actions physically affecting things or bodies; secondly in such cases the liberty is exclusive or exceptional[46] in the sense that it is a liberty to do something that others are generally under an obligation not to do. Such powers are conferred by permissive laws,[47] but like other liberty-rights they may be

---

[42] *PML* Chap. XVI, para. 35, n. g3, in *CW* 228.
[43] *OLG* 220.
[44] *OLG* 84, 220, n. a but see *infra* p. 195 n. 1.
[45] See *OLG, passim*, esp. Chap. IX; and Chap. VIII *infra*.
[46] For an examination of Bentham's notion of powers of contrectation as exclusive or exceptional liberties see Chap. VIII *infra*.
[47] *OLG* 81, 86-7, 137 n.

protected or 'corroborated'[48] by duties imposed on others not to obstruct, or even requiring them to assist, their exercise. If they are not so corroborated, they exist as 'bare' liberties: and then like other liberty-rights their existence does not entail the existence of any correlative obligations.

More important for our present purpose is the kind of power which Bentham calls 'investitive' and 'divestitive'.[49] These are the powers which a man has when he is enabled by law to change the legal position of others, or of himself and others as he does for example when he alienates property or makes a will or contract. In entering into such legal transactions he does an act (usually the writing or saying of certain words according to more or less strictly prescribed forms) which manifest certain intentions as to future rights and duties of himself and others. Such acts, or acts in the law, are not only *permitted* by the law but are *recognized* by the law as having certain legal consequences: given certain circumstances, a duly executed conveyance of land is 'valid', i.e. legally effective in divesting the transferor of certain rights and duties and in investing the transferee with similar ones. Bentham's elaborate account of the legal provisions by which such investitive and divestitive powers are conferred is designed to reconcile their existence with his general 'imperative' theory of law according to which all laws either impose duties or grant permissions.[50] There is not according to Bentham a further special kind of laws which confer powers; but powers are conferred when laws imposing duties or granting permissions are 'imperfect mandates',[51] i.e. incomplete in some respects and so contain 'blanks'[52] left to 'power-holders' to 'fill up', and when they do this they thereby determine or vary the incidence of existing 'imperfect' laws.

---

[48] *PML* Concluding Note, para. 7, in *CW* 302; *OLG* 260-1.

[49] *OLG* 82-4; cf. *PML* Chap. XVI, para. 27, n. n2, in *CW* 217; *Works* III 186-90 on 'collative and ablative events'.

[50] *OLG* 95-9 and *passim; PML* Concluding Note, para. 3, in *CW* 302. See also Chap. V *supra*, p. 119, and Chap. VIII *infra*, p. 210.

[51] *OLG* 26, 80-91.

[52] *Works* III 222; cf. III 197.

III CRITICISM OF BENTHAM'S DOCTRINE

A. Liberty-rights

Liberty-rights and their protective perimeter
Those who have doubted the importance of liberties or mere absence of obligation for the analysis of legal rights have felt that so negative a notion without some positive correlate is not worth a lawyer's attention. This is a mistaken way of presenting the important fact that where a man is left free by the law to do or not to do some particular action, the exercise of this liberty will always be protected by the law to some extent, even if there is no strictly correlative obligation upon others not to interfere with it. This is so because at least the cruder forms of interference, such as those involving physical assault or trespass, will be criminal or civil offences or both, and the duties or obligations not to engage in such modes of interference constitute a protective perimeter behind which liberties exist and may be exercised. Thus, to take a trivial example, my right to scratch my head is protected, not by a correlative obligation upon others not to interfere with my doing an act of that specific kind, but by the fact that obligations to refrain from assault or trespass to my person will generally preclude effective interference with it. In most cases the protection of my liberty afforded by this perimeter of obligations will be adequate but it may not be complete: if others could stop me scratching my head without any breach of these obligations e.g. by hypnotizing me, they may do so. This makes clear the difference between a liberty-right to do an act of some kind protected by a strictly correlative obligation upon others not to interfere with it, and a liberty-right protected only by a normally adequate perimeter of general obligations.

It may be that jurists who have doubted the importance of the negative notion of absence of obligation or liberty have done so because the protective perimeter has obscured their view of it; but it is in fact important not to lose sight of either the liberty or the perimeter. Both are required in the analysis of many legal phenomena including that of economic competition. Two people walking in an empty street see a purse lying on the pavement: each has a liberty so far as the law is concerned to pick it up and each may prevent the other doing so if he can race him to the spot. But though each has this liberty there are also several specific things which each has a right that the other should not do; these are rights with correlative obligations and these correlative obligations together with the duties of the criminal law protect (and also restrict) each party's liberty. Thus neither of the competitors may hit or trip up the other, or threaten him with violence in order to get the prize. The perimeter of obligations to abstain from such actions constitutes the ring within which the competitors compete in the exercise of their liberties. Of course where competition is not in question, as in the case of 'fundamental' human rights or liberties, great importance may be attached to their unimpeded exercise and in such cases the law may protect the liberty by a strictly correlative obligation not to interfere by any means with a specific form of activity. But most liberties are not so protected.[53]

Bentham appreciated the importance of this combination of a liberty with a protective perimeter of obligations, but his formulations on the point are casual and somewhat ambiguous. He distinguishes between a 'naked' right and a 'vested' or 'established' one.[54] A naked right is a liberty unprotected by any obligation such as the rights which men have in the state of nature; a man has a vested or established right when he has a right that others should abstain from interfering with a liberty which he has. This language suggests that Bentham thought of rights as vested only where there was a strictly correlative obligation not to interfere, but in other passages in discussing liberty-rights he envisages their protection by a perimeter of general obligations not strictly correlative to the liberty. 'I may stand or sit down—I may go in or out—I may eat or not eat etc.: the law says nothing

---

[53] Thus the famous cases *Allen* v. *Flood* (1898) A.C. I, *Mogul Steamship* v. *Macgregor & Others* (1892) A.C. 25, *Quinn* v. *Leathern* (1901) A.C. 495, and (in part) *Rookes* v. *Barnard* (1964) A.C. 1129, are best understood as raising the question whether an individual's liberty-rights to trade or employ labour or sell his labour are protected by a perimeter consisting only of duties corresponding to the specific torts of conspiracy, intimidation, and inducement of breach of contract, or by a perimeter consisting also of a duty corresponding to a more general tort of interfering with the trade, business, or employment of a person without lawful justification or excuse.

[54] *Works* III 218.

upon the matter. Still, the right which I exercise I derive
from the law because it is the law which erects into an offence
every species of violence by which one may seek to prevent
me from doing what I like.'[55]

Notwithstanding his appreciation of the importance of the
combination of liberties with a perimeter of protective
though not correlative obligation, Bentham, like Hobbes in
describing the state of nature, treats liberties even when
'naked' as rights. But it is not at all clear that lawyers or anyone else would speak of a completely naked or unprotected
liberty as a right, or that any useful purpose would be served
if they did. The state of nature, if worth describing at all, can
be described adequately in other terms. So far as organized
society is concerned there would be something not only
strange but misleading in describing naked liberties as rights:
if we said, for example, that a class of helots whom free
citizens were allowed to treat as they wished or interfere with
at will, yet had rights to do those acts which they were not
forbidden by the law to do. All the very important points
in Bentham's doctrine distinguishing between liberty-rights
and rights correlative to obligations can be preserved by
treating bilateral liberty as an essential *element* in the analysis
of liberty-rights but only constituting a liberty-right in conjunction with a perimeter of some protecting obligations or
duties. It is not necessary, nor I think useful for any purpose,
to treat liberties without any such protection as a distinct
kind of legal right.

Unilateral liberty-rights

Bentham, as I have said, occasionally speaks as if a unilateral
liberty were sufficient to constitute a liberty-right. On this
footing a liberty-right to do an act would be compatible with,
and indeed entailed by, an obligation to do it. The right-
holder would not, as in the case of bilateral liberty, be free
to choose whether to do an act or not; he would be at liberty
to do an act only in the sense that he was not under an obligation not to do it. Bentham does not discuss the appropriate-
ness or otherwise of extending the notion of rights to include
unilateral liberty; but it seems clear that a general extension

[55] *Works* III 159–60.

to include all unilateral liberties would neither accord with usage nor be useful. In the ordinary case, where the law imposes general obligations, e.g. to pay taxes, or to abstain from assault or trespass, it would be pointless or even confusing to describe those who had these obligations as having rights to pay taxes or to abstain from assault. Yet there undoubtedly are certain specific contexts where unilateral liberties are intelligibly spoken of as rights to do actions even where there is also an obligation to do the same action. Among these are cases where individuals by way of exception to a general rule are not merely permitted but also legally required to do some act generally prohibited.

Thus a policeman ordered to arrest a man might be asked 'What right have you to arrest him?' and might well produce his orders as showing that he had a right to arrest. In general the query 'What right have you to do that?' invites the person addressed to show that some act of his which is *prima facie* wrongful because generally prohibited is one which in the particular case he is at liberty to do. The questioner is not concerned to know whether the liberty is unilateral, i.e. accompanied by an obligation, or bilateral; so the form of his question covers both.[56]

B. The benefit theory of rights correlative to obligation

The most striking feature of Bentham's analysis of legal rights is his benefit theory of rights correlative to obligation: the view that with the exception of 'barren' and 'self-regarding' obligation *all* obligations, civil or criminal, have correlative rights held by those intended to benefit by their performance. In considering this doctrine certain features of Bentham's elaborate classification of offences[57] must be kept in mind, since, according to him, every offence, i.e.

---

[56] Further examples of unilateral liberties spoken of as rights are afforded by cases where duties in Bentham's phrase, are 'superadded' to liberty-rights (*OLG* 270-1, 296). Thus a trustee who has equitable duties to put the trust property to a certain use may be said to have a right to do this since the equitable duty is for historical reasons conceived as something distinct grafted on to his still persistent legal bilateral liberty-rights, though its actual effect is to render the liberty unilateral.

[57] *PML* Chap. XVI in *CW* 187 ff.

every breach of obligation with the two exceptions mentioned, violates a right. Bentham distinguishes between offences which are primarily or in the first instance detrimental to 'assignable persons' (which he terms 'offences against individuals' or 'private offences')[58] and offences detrimental only to unassignable individuals.[59] Of the latter there are two kinds, viz. public offences against a whole community or state, or semi-public offences against classes of persons within the community distinguished either by some class characteristic or by residence in a particular area. Offences of the first kind violate individual rights: examples of them are murder, assault, theft, and breach of contract:[60] offences of the second kind violate the rights of the public or a class, and examples of them are failure to pay taxes or desertion from the army (public offences)[61] and violation of health regulations imposed for the protection of a particular neighbourhood (semi-public offences).[62]

Intended benefits to assignable versus *unassignable individuals*
Before attempting any general criticism of Bentham's benefit theory, it is necessary to explore the ambiguities of the central ideas involved in it. These ambiguities are, I think, involved in all theories which attempt to define the notion of an individual's right in terms of benefits or interests, and they concern (a) the ideas of benefit and detriment, (b) the distinction between assignable and unassignable persons, and (c) the idea of a person intended by the law to benefit. These are difficult notions requiring fuller investigation than is attempted here, but the following may suffice for the present purposes.

(*a*) *Benefit and detriment.* Bentham, though committed to the doctrine that pleasure and pain are the only things good and bad in themselves,[63] does not in his account of rights and offences simply identify benefit with pleasure or avoidance

---

[58] *PML* Chap. XVI, para. 6, in *CW* 188.
[59] *PML* Chap. XVI, para. 7, in *CW* 189.
[60] *PML* Chap. XVI, para. 33, in *CW* 223-4.
[61] *PML* Chap. XVI, para. 55, n. r4 in *CW* 262.
[62] *PML* Chap. XVI, para. 13, n. o, in *CW* 194; and para. 33, n. x2, in *CW* 225.
[63] *PML* Chap. VIII, para. 13, in *CW* 88-9; and Chap. X, para. 10 in *CW* 100.

of pain or detriment with pain or loss of pleasure. Hence, for him, as for others, theft of £1 from a millionaire indifferent to the loss constitutes a detriment to him and an offence against him; while forbearance from such theft constitutes a negative service and a benefit to which he has a legal right. So, too, security of the person or of reputation are benefits, even if in some cases the particular individual concerned would have welcomed an attack or found it pleasurable or otherwise desirable. So in general the idea of benefit or services, positive or negative, includes the provision or maintenance of conditions or treatment which are regarded by human beings generally, or in a particular society, as desirable or 'in their interest' and so to be sought from others. Correspondingly the idea of a detriment or harm includes the loss of such benefits and conditions and treatment generally regarded as undesirable and to be avoided. No doubt Bentham thought also that what makes anything a benefit or desirable is its general tendency to produce pleasure or to avoid pain,[64] and if, in a particular society, the notion of benefits or detriments had no such connection with pleasure and pain, this was an aberration to be deplored.

Given this conception of benefits and detriments, it follows that in the case of those offences which Bentham calls offences against individuals and regards as violating the rights of assignable individuals, the breach of the law necessarily, and not merely contingently, constitutes a detriment to individuals, and compliance with the law in such cases necessarily, and not merely contingently, constitutes a benefit to individuals. This feature is secured simply by the definition of the offence in terms of actions which constitute in themselves detriments to individuals even if they do not always cause pain. For killing or wounding or slandering an individual or thieving from him or false imprisonment or 'wife-stealing' (abduction), given the above account of detriments, necessarily constitute detriments and do not merely contingently cause them or make them more likely. Since it is perfectly reasonable, without further investigation of 'legislative intent', to ascribe to laws prohibiting offences which thus necessarily constitute a detriment to individuals,

---

[64] *PML* Chap. XVI, para. 11, in *CW* 191-3; *Works* III 214.

an intention to benefit them, it is by reference to this feature that Bentham's central conception of assignable individuals intended to benefit from the law is mainly to be explained.

In such cases we may call the benefit or detriment 'direct' and it is to be observed that in the case of Bentham's public and semi-public offences benefits and detriments are not involved in the same direct way. As Bentham points out[65] compliance with laws requiring payment of taxes will make funds available to a government, but whether or not benefits as above defined will result for any individuals is a contingent matter, depending on what Bentham terms 'a various and remote concatenation of causes and effects',[66] including the nature of the government's policies for use of the funds and their skill or even luck in implementing them. The same is true of laws requiring military service or prohibiting treason. General compliance with such laws will constitute certain conditions without which it would be impossible or less likely that various benefits will be ultimately received by individuals, and in that sense these conditions may be said to make their receipt more likely than would otherwise be the case. Such contingently beneficial laws may be said to provide indirect benefits.[67]

(*b*) *Assignable and unassignable individuals.* This distinction

---

[65] *OLG* Chap. XII, para. 17, in *CW* 62-3; *PML* Chap. XII, para. 17 in *CW* 149.

[66] *OLG* 62.

[67] Of course the distinction between direct and indirect benefits will present disputable borderline cases, since whether anything is to be counted as in itself a benefit or only making the receipt of benefits more likely will often depend on degrees of likelihood, numbers of contingencies and also on analogies with standard direct individual benefits. Thus compliance by an employer with a duty to provide each of his workmen working in dangerous conditions with protective clothing might, like a law requiring him to pay each of them a sum of money, be considered as constituting a direct benefit, and its breach as constituting a direct detriment; whereas a law requiring him to fit a fence or guard on dangerous machinery while men are at work, might be considered not as constituting a direct benefit for them but only as making the avoidance of harm more likely, and so constituting an indirect benefit. It is also to be noted that if provision of such a fence or guard is treated as constituting a direct benefit it would be a *common* benefit, in contrast with the *separate* or *individual* benefits constituted by the provision of each workman with protective clothing. It seems likely that Bentham would regard all laws providing such common benefits as intended to benefit classes not 'assignable individuals'. (See *infra*, p. 179, n. 74, with regard to statutory duties.)

appears in many places in Bentham's works[68] and he uses it to explain what is meant by saying that certain offences are against the public or against a class, and that the public or a class are intended to benefit by a law and so have rights resulting from the obligations which it imposes. Bentham does not conceive of the public or of a class as an entity distinct from its members, and for him to speak of the public or class of persons as having rights is still to speak only of individuals, but of individuals who cannot be 'individually assigned' included in the community or class.[69] What then is it for an individual to be 'assignable'? Bentham's most explicit statement on this subject is in a footnote which merely tells us that an individual may be assignable 'by name or at least by description in such manner as to be sufficiently distinguished from all others'.[70] This leaves the notion of a law intended to benefit assignable individuals still obscure; because the various laws, such as the laws forbidding murder or assault which he does in fact regard as intended to benefit assignable individuals (and so as conferring rights upon them), do not refer to individuals either by name or by some uniquely applicable description, nor on any account of legislative intent does it seem that they are intended only to benefit individuals so identified,[71] if that means identified at the time when the law comes into existence.

None the less Bentham's brief explanation of his distinction can be used indirectly to determine whether or not the individuals intended to be benefited by a law are assignable, since the corresponding question whether or not an *offence*[72] is against assignable individuals can be answered by direct reference to it. Thus the laws which Bentham regards as creating offences against assignable individuals and so as

[68] e.g. *PML* Chap. XII, para. 3, in *CW* 143; Chap. XVI, para. 6, in *CW* 188-9; *OLG* 37. It also appears in John Stuart Mill's account of rights in *Utilitarianism*, Chap. V.

[69] *PML* Chap. XVI, para. 8, n. e, in *CW* 189.

[70] *PML* Chap. XVI, para. 4, n. c, in *CW* 188.

[71] Of course they may be said to be intended to benefit 'each individual' in the community but this does not make the individuals 'assignable' in Bentham's sense.

[72] Bentham observes that rights may best be 'expounded' by considering the corresponding offences: *PML* Chap. XVI, para. 25, n. e2, in *CW* 206 and see *OLG* 58.

conferring rights upon them are such that to establish that the offence has been committed it must be shown that an individual who *is* 'assignable' in Bentham's sense, i.e. distinguished from others in some way and so uniquely identified, has suffered some individual detriment from the commission of the offence. It seems therefore that we may interpret the statement that a law is intended to benefit assignable individuals (and so confers rights upon them) as meaning no more than that to establish its breach an assignable individual must be shown to have suffered an individual detriment.[73] This seems to give the required contrast with those laws creating offences which Bentham classes as against unassignable individuals, such as failure to pay taxes or military desertion; for in such cases it is not necessary to show that any individual has suffered any detriment and it may often be the case that no individual has suffered or will suffer thereby. On this footing, an offence may be said to be against unassignable individuals, and so one which violates the rights not of individuals but of the public or a class, if (a) it is not an offence against assignable individuals, and (b) general compliance with the law creating an offence is intended to constitute an indirect benefit for any one or more individuals who are or may be included in the community or in a class within it but who are not otherwise identified.[74]

[73] This interpretation is not I think inconsistent with Bentham's remark (*PML* Chap. XVI, para. 7, n. d, in *CW* 189) that the divisions between private, semi-public, and public offences are liable to be 'confounded'. He points out that 'the fewer the individuals of which a class is composed . . . the more likely are the persons to whom an offence is detrimental to *become* assignable.' This seems merely to point out that though an offence (e.g. breach of health regulations imposed for the benefit of a particular area) is correctly regarded as one against a class in accordance with the interpretation offered above, it will in the case of small *closed* classes be possible to determine which individuals ultimately suffer from a given offence even though proof of their suffering is not, as in the case of offences against individuals, necessary to establish that the offence has been committed. But Bentham's point here is certainly not clear.

[74] It should be observed that Bentham's distinction between laws which confer rights on individuals and those which confer them on the public or classes, based as it is on assignability as interpreted above, is *not* the same as the apparently similar distinction which has sometimes been invoked by English courts in their attempts to formulate tests for determining whether breach of a statutory duty, such as the duty to fence dangerous machinery or provide specified forms of fire-escape, gives rise to an action for damages on the part of individuals for injuries caused by the breach. Breach of most such statutory duties would, according to

(c) *Intended by the law to benefit.* If the statement that a
law intends to benefit an individual and so confers a right
upon him is interpreted as meaning no more than that its
breach constitutes a direct individual detriment, then we have
a criterion for determining when laws confer individual rights
which avoids difficult enquiries into 'actual' legislative
intent. Moreover this criterion will give a decisive and at least
an intelligible answer to some questions which have confronted theorists who, within the general framework of an
interest- or benefit-theory of rights, have wished to limit, in
some reasonable way, the class of intended beneficiaries who
should count as having rights. Thus, to take an example,
famous from Ihering's[75] discussion of it, in a similar context,
should a law, forbidding in general terms the importation of
manufactured goods, which was in fact enacted solely in
order to benefit a particular domestic manufacturer be taken
to confer a right upon him? Ihering was anxious to distinguish
such a case as a mere *'Reflexwirkung'* (reflex operation) of a

---

Bentham's assignability test, not be offences against individuals and so would not
confer a right upon them to performance of the statutory duty; since to establish their breach it would not be necessary to show that any individual had suffered
any individual detriment, but only that e.g. the machinery had not been fenced
as required: such an offence, for Bentham, would either be against a class (e.g. of
workmen) or against the public. It is on the other hand true that in determining
whether the legislature in creating such statutory duties also by implication
created a statutory tort, courts have flirted with the idea that this depended on
whether the statutory duty was 'owed to' individuals or imposed in their interests and not merely imposed for the general welfare of the public (see *Solo-
mons* v. *R. Gertzenstein* [1954] 2 Q.B. 243). This test has been rejected by some
judges (see per Atkin L.J. in *Phillips* v. *Britannia Hygienic Laundry* [1923] 2
K.B. 832) and indeed the finding that a statutory duty was owed to or for the
benefit of individuals seems rather to be a conclusion from a finding, made on
other grounds, that the statute conferred a right of action upon individuals, than
a reason for such a finding. But whatever this distinction is it does not, for the
reasons stated above, turn, as Bentham's does, upon assignability. It appears
rather to be a distinction (which the Courts have found very difficult to apply
in practice) between the cases where, on the construction of the statute, it can be
said that its main purpose was to secure to each individual of a specific class
some specific benefit or protection from some specific harm and those cases
where either there was no such discernible purpose, or, if there was, this was
merely ancillary to a dominant purpose to create or maintain conditions (e.g.
the conservation of manpower or resources) whereby all or any unspecified
members of the public might benefit in various unspecified ways.
   [75] *Geist des römischen Rechts* (1924 edn.), III 351-3, discussed by Kelsen
in *Haupt probleme des Staatrechts* (1960 edn.), 578-81, and Ross in *Towards
a Realistic Jurisprudence* (1946), 167-8, 179 ff.

duty and not as a right, and he sought for, but never clearly formulated, some criterion which would distinguish a right violated by a demonstrable 'individual breach of the law' (*Individuelle Rechtsverletzung*) from a mere reflex operation of duty.[76] Kelsen believed that no such distinction could be drawn; but Bentham's conception of a direct detriment to an assignable individual, interpreted as above, might well have served this purpose and the test later suggested by Ross[77] in discussing Ihering's case is in substance identical with it.

For the purpose of criticism of the benefit theory I shall assume that the above interpretation of Bentham is correct.[78] I do so because this is the strongest form of the benefit theory and if it is vulnerable to criticism it is not likely that a theory depending on a more extended sense of 'intended by the law to benefit' is likely to be successful. For the same reason I shall not consider further Bentham's account of rights of the public or a class.[79]

Absolute and relative duties

The principal advocates of benefit or 'interest' theories of rights correlative to obligations have shown themselves sensitive to the criticism that, if to say that an individual has such a right means no more than that he is the intended beneficiary of a duty, then 'a right' in this sense may be an unnecessary, and perhaps confusing, term in the description of the law;

[76] Ihering's earlier account of rights (op. cit., 2nd edn., III 339) had avoided this problem since it restricted rights to cases where the enforcement by legal proceedings of duties protecting interests was left to the individual concerned ('Selbstschutz des Interesses').

[77] Op. cit. (n. 75 *supra*) 179 ff. Lyons's account of the 'qualified beneficiary theory' which he favours and considers may be attributable to Bentham (op. cit. (p. 162, n. 1 *supra*) 173-4, 176-80) is very close to the above interpretation of Bentham.

[78] There are certainly passages in Bentham (e.g. *OLG* 55-6) where he seems to contemplate that if the legislator intended an 'assignable' individual to benefit even very indirectly from the performance of an obligation this would confer a right to its performance on him. On this view the favoured manufacturer in Ihering's case would have a right that the goods should not be imported.

[79] In fact Bentham seems to have made very little use of his idea that in the sense explained the public or a class within it have legal rights. Nearly all of his examples of rights are rights of individuals. Austin expressly confines legal rights to the rights of 'determinate persons' (op. cit., p. 163, n. 4 *supra*, Lecture XVII, 401).

since all that can be said in a terminology of such rights can
be and indeed is best said in the indispensable terminology
of duty. So the benefit theory appears to make nothing more
of rights than an alternative formulation of duties: yet
nothing seems to be gained in significance or clarity by trans-
lating, e.g. the statement that men are under a legal duty not
to murder, assault, or steal from others into the statement
that individuals have a right not to be murdered, assaulted,
or stolen from, or by saying, when a man has been murdered,
that his right not to be killed has been violated.[80]

Ihering as I have said was visited by just such doubts.
Bentham confronted them in his codification proposals in the
form of an inquiry whether the law should be expounded at
length in a list of rights or a list of obligations. The test which
he proposed was 'Present the entire law to that one of the
parties that has most need to be instructed'[81] and he thought
that the law should generally be expounded at length in
terms of obligations but need 'only be mentioned' in a list of
rights; his principal reason for this was that, because of the
penalties imposed, the party on whom the law imposed the
obligation had most need for instruction.[82]

(a) *Criminal* versus *civil law*. The most cogent criticisms of
the benefit theory are those that on the one hand press home
the charge of redundancy or uselessness to a lawyer of the
concept of right correlative to obligation defined simply in
terms of the intended beneficiary of the obligation, and on
the other hand constructively presents an alternative selective
account of those obligations which are for legal purposes
illuminatingly regarded as having correlative rights. This latter
task amounts to a redrawing of the lines between 'absolute'[83]
and relative duties which for Bentham merely separated
'barren' and self-regarding duties from duties 'useful to others'.

---

[80] Under the American Civil Rights Act 1964 suits were brought in the Federal
Courts against white men who had murdered negroes alleging 'that they had de-
prived their victims of their civil rights'. This desperate expedient was necessary
because murder is a state, not a federal, crime and prosecutions in such cases
were not likely to succeed in Southern state courts. I owe this point to Mrs
Carolyn Irish.

[81] *Works* III 195.

[82] Ibid.

[83] So Austin (op. cit., Lecture XVII, 401-2).

This has been done sometimes in too sweeping a fashion as a distinction precisely coinciding with that between the criminal and civil law, and on the assumption, which seems dogmatic, if not plainly mistaken, that the purpose of the criminal law is not to secure the separate interests of individuals but 'security and order', and that all its duties are really duties not to behave in certain ways which are prejudicial to the 'general interests of society'.[84]

None the less a line may be drawn between most duties of the criminal law and those of the civil law which does not depend on this assumption, but would, on principles quite distinct from those of the benefit theory, reserve the notion of relative duties and correlative rights mainly for the obligations of the civil law, such as those which arise under contracts or under the law of tort, and other civil wrongs. For what is distinctive about these obligations is not their content which sometimes overlaps with the criminal law, since there are some actions, e.g. assault, which are both a crime and a civil wrong; nor is the only distinction of importance the familiar one that crime has as its characteristic consequence liability to punishment, and civil wrong liability to pay compensation for harm done. The crucial distinction, according to this view of relative duties, is the special manner in which the civil law as distinct from the criminal law provides for individuals: it recognizes or gives them a place or *locus standi* in relation to the law quite different from that given by the criminal law. Instead of utilitarian notions of benefit or intended benefit we need, if we are to reproduce this distinctive concern for the individual, a different idea. The idea is that of one individual being given by the law exclusive control, more or less extensive, over another person's duty so that in the area of conduct covered by that duty the individual who has the right is a small-scale sovereign to whom the duty is owed. The fullest measure[85] of control comprises three

---

[84] Allen, *Legal Duties*, 184-6.

[85] The right-holder will have less than the full measure of control if, as in the case of statutory duties, he is unable to release or extinguish the duty or if principles of public policy prevent him, even after breach of the duty, making a binding agreement not to sue for injury caused by its breach (see e.g. *Bowmaker Ltd.* v. *Tabor* (1942) 2 K.B. I). In such cases the choice left to him is only to sue or not to sue. There are suggestions, never fully developed, that such a choice is a necessary element in a legal right in Bentham's *Fragment* Chap. V, para. 6, n. b. S. 2. in *CW* 495.

distinguishable elements: (i) the right holder may waive or extinguish the duty or leave it in existence; (ii) after breach or threatened breach of a duty he may leave it 'unenforced' or may 'enforce' it by suing for compensation or, in certain cases, for an injunction or mandatory order to restrain the continued or further breach of duty; and (iii) he may waive or extinguish the obligation to pay compensation to which the breach gives rise. It is obvious that not all who benefit or are intended to benefit by another's legal obligation are in this unique sovereign position in relation to the duty. A person protected only by the criminal law has no power to release anyone from its duties, and though, as in England, he may in theory be entitled to prosecute along with any other member of the public he has no unique power to determine whether the duties of the criminal law should be enforced or not.

These legal powers (for such they are) over a correlative obligation are of great importance to lawyers: both laymen and lawyers will need, in Bentham's phrase, 'to be instructed' about them; and their exercise calls for the specific skills of the lawyer. They are therefore a natural focus of legal attention, and there are I think many signs of the centrality of those powers to the conception of a legal right. Thus it is hard to think of rights except as capable of *exercise* and this conception of rights correlative to obligations as containing legal powers accommodates this feature.[86] Moreover, we speak of a breach of duty in the civil law, whether arising in contract or in tort, not only as wrong, or detrimental to the person who has the correlative right, but as *a wrong to* him and a breach of an obligation *owed* to him;[87]

---

[86] Where infants or other persons not *sui juris* have rights, such powers and the correlative obligations are exercised on their behalf by appointed representatives and their exercise may be subject to approval by a court. But since (a) what such representatives can and cannot do by way of exercise of such power is determined by what those whom they represent could have done if *sui juris* and (b) when the latter become *sui juris* they can exercise these powers without any transfer or fresh assignment; the powers are regarded as belonging throughout to them and not to their representatives, though they are only exercisable by the latter during the period of disability.

[87] Lyons (op. cit. (p. 162, n. 1 *supra*), 178) assumes that 'rights under the civil law' arise only from 'special relations or transactions between the parties' (e.g. contracts) and that only in such cases are the right holders 'claimants' to whom duties are 'owed'. But individuals have rights corresponding to the primary

we also speak of the person who has the correlative right as *possessing* it or even *owning* it. The conception suggested by these phrases is that duties with correlative rights are a species of normative property belonging to the right holder, and this figure becomes intelligible by reference to the special form of control over a correlative duty which a person with such a right is given by the law. Whenever an individual has this special control, as he has in most cases in the civil law but not over the duties of the criminal law, there is a contrast of importance to be marked and many jurists have done so by distinguishing the duties of the criminal law as 'absolute duties' from the 'relative' duties of the civil law.[88]

It is an incidental, though substantial merit of this approach that it provides an intelligible explanation of the fact that animals, even though directly protected by the duties of the criminal law prohibiting cruelty to them, are not spoken or thought of as having rights. However it is to be observed that if the distinction between absolute and relative duties is drawn as above suggested, this does not entail that only duties of the civil law have correlative rights. For there are cases made prominent by the extension of the welfare functions of the state where officials of public bodies are under a legal duty to provide individuals if they satisfy certain conditions, with benefits which may take the form of money payments (e.g. public assistance, unemployment relief, farming subsidies) or supply of goods or services, e.g. medical care. In such cases it is perfectly common and natural to speak of individuals who have satisfied the prescribed conditions as being legally entitled to and having a right to such benefits. Yet it is commonly not the case that they have the kind of control over the official's duties which, according to

duties in tort which do not arise from such special relations or transactions and such duties are 'owed' to them.

[88] It is sometimes argued that in the case of persons not *sui juris* e.g. infants, it is only the fact that they are direct beneficiaries of the correlative duties which explains the ascription of rights to them, rather than to their representatives who alone can exercise the powers over the correlative duties. But the explanation offered above (p. 184, n. 86) seems adequate; even if it is not, this would only show that being the direct beneficiary of a duty was a *necessary* condition of a person not *sui juris* having a right. Hence it would still be possible so far as this argument goes, to distinguish the duties of the criminal law (over which there are no such powers of control exercisable by the beneficiaries' representatives) as not having correlative rights.

the view suggested above, is a defining feature of legal rights correlative to obligations. For though such obligations are not always supported by criminal sanctions they cannot be extinguished or waived by beneficiaries, nor does their breach necessarily give rise to any secondary obligation to make compensation which the beneficiaries can enforce, leave unenforced or extinguish. None the less there are in most of such cases two features which link them to the paradigm cases of rights correlative to obligations as these appear in the civil law. In most cases where such public duties are thought of as having correlative rights, the duty to supply the benefits are conditional upon their being demanded and the beneficiary of the duty is free to demand it or not. Hence, though he has no power to waive or extinguish the duty he has a power by presenting a demand to substitute for a conditional duty not requiring present performance an unconditional duty which does, and so has a choice. Secondly, though breach of such duties may not give rise to any secondary duties of compensation, there are in many such cases steps which the beneficiary if he has suffered some peculiar damage may take to secure its performance, and in regard to which he has a special *locus standi* so that on his application a court may make a peremptory or mandatory order or injunction directing the official body to carry out the duty or restraining its breach.[89] These two features of the case differentiate the beneficiary of such public duties from that of the ordinary duties of the criminal law. This explains why, though it is generally enough to describe the criminal law only in terms of duties, so to describe the law creating these public welfare duties would obscure important features. For the necessity that such beneficiaries, if they wish the duty to be performed must present demands, and the availability to them of means of enforcement, make their position under the law a focus for legal attention needing separate description from that of the duties beneficial to them.[90]

[89] Difficult questions may arise concerning the nature of the interest which a successful applicant for such relief must possess. See *R.* v. *Manchester Corp.* [1911] I K.B. 560.

[90] But so far as such public welfare duties are thought of as providing for essential human needs they may on that ground alone be regarded as constituting legal rights. See *infra*, pp. 192-3.

(b) *Contracts and third parties.* The identification of a right-holder with the person who is merely benefited by the performance of a duty not only obscures a very important general dividing line between criminal and civil law, but is ill adapted to the law relating to contract. Whereas in the last paragraph it was urged that to be an intended beneficiary of an obligation is not a satisfactory *sufficient* condition of having a right, the present criticism is that it is not satisfactory as a *necessary* condition. For where there is a contract between two people, not all those who benefit and are intended to benefit by the performance of its obligations have a legal right correlative to them. In many jurisdictions contracts expressly made for the benefit of third parties, e.g. a contract between two people to pay a third party a sum of money, is not enforceable by the third party and he cannot waive or release the obligation. In such a case although the third party is a direct beneficiary since breach of the contract constitutes a direct detriment to him, he has no legal control over the duty and so no legal right. On the other hand the contracting party having the appropriate control has the legal right, though he is not the person intended to benefit by the performance of the contract.[91] Where, however, the law is modified as it is in some jurisdictions so as to give the third party power to enforce the contract then he is consistently with the view presented here spoken of as having legal right.[92]

The analysis of a right correlative to obligation which is suggested by the foregoing criticisms of the benefit theory is

[91] It is sometimes argued that the fact that in some jurisdictions a third-party beneficiary may sue shows this point against the beneficiary theory of rights to be mistaken. But of course a third party entitled to sué or not to sue would on *that* account be recognized as having a legal right and this does nothing to confirm the beneficiary theory.

[92] Lyons, op. cit. 183–4, argues that 'one of the conditions of a valid and binding promise and thus a condition of a right accruing to a promisee is that he really wants what is promised' (even if this is true of 'promises' it scarcely seems applicable to legal contracts). He then suggests that performance of a contract for the benefit of a third party must 'assure a good' to the promisee, since this satisfies his want to have what is promised done, and that it is this, not his control over the promisor's obligation, which accounts for the ascription of a right to him. But if the performance of the obligation beneficial to the third party is not sufficient to lead lawyers to recognize the third party as having a legal right, surely the secondary benefit to the promisee consisting in gratification of his wish to benefit the third party is not sufficient to account for his right.

that for such a right to exist it is neither sufficient nor necessary for the person who had the right to be the beneficiary of the obligation; what is sufficient and necessary is that he should have at least some measure of the control, described above, over the correlative obligation.

IV THE LIMITS OF A GENERAL THEORY

If the arguments of the last section are accepted and if we substitute for the utilitarian idea of benefit, as a defining feature of a right correlative to obligation, the individual's legal powers of control, full or partial, over that obligation, a generalization may be made concerning all three kinds of right distinguished by Bentham. This is attractive because it imposes a pattern of order on a wide range of apparently disparate legal phenomena. Thus in all three kinds of right the idea of a bilateral liberty is present and the difference between the kinds of right lies only in the kind of act which there is liberty to do. In the case of liberty-rights such as a man's right to look at his neighbour, his act may be called a natural act in the sense that it is not endowed by the law with a special legal significance or legal effect. On the other hand in the case of rights which are powers, such as the right to alienate property, the act which there is a bilateral liberty[93] to do is an act-in-the-law, just in the sense that it is specifically recognized by the law as having legal effects in varying the legal position of various parties and as an appropriate means for varying it. The case of a right correlative to obligation then emerges as only a special case of legal power in which the right-holder is at liberty to waive or extinguish or to enforce or leave unenforced another's obligation. It would follow from these considerations that in each of these three types of case one who has a right has a choice respected by

[93] As in the case of liberty-rights, duties may be superimposed on rights which are powers and such duties will render the liberty to exercise the power unilateral (a simple example from property law is where an owner of property binds himself by contract either to sell it or not to sell it). In general where there is a duty to exercise a power the resultant unilateral liberty is not described as a right nor is there usually any point in so describing it. Exceptions to this are again cases such as that of a trustee whose legal rights are theoretically distinguishable from his equitable duties (see *supra*, p. 174, n. 56) and are thought of as coexisting even where they in fact conflict.

the law. On this view there would be only one sense of legal right—a legally respected choice—though it would be one with different exemplifications, depending on the kind of act or act-in-the-law which there is liberty to do.

The merits of this analysis are therefore threefold. First, it coincides with a very wide area of common and legal usage. Secondly it explains why liberty-rights, powers, and rights correlative to obligations are all described as rights and does so by identifying as common to three superficially diverse types of case, an element which, on any theory of law or morals, is of great importance; namely an individual choice respected by the law. Thirdly, the concept which it defines is well adapted to a lawyer's purpose; for it will lead him to talk in terms of rights only where there is something of importance to the lawyer to talk about which cannot be equally well said in terms of obligation or duty, and this is preeminently so in the case of the civil law.[94]

However, in spite of its attractions, this theory, centred on the notion of a legally respected individual choice, cannot be taken as exhausting the notion of a legal right: the notion of individual benefit must be brought in, though *not* as the benefit theory brings it in, to supplement the notion of individual choice. Unless this is done no adequate account can be given of the deployment of the language of rights, in two main contexts, when certain freedoms and benefits are regarded as essential for the maintenance of the life, the security, the development, and the dignity of the individual. Such freedoms and benefits are recognized as rights in the constitutional law of many countries by Bills of Rights, which afford to the individual protection even against the processes of legislation. In countries such as our own, where the doctrine of legislative sovereignty is held to preclude limiting the powers of the legislature by Bills of Rights, they are, though given only the lesser measure of legal protection in the form of duties of the criminal law, thought and spoken of as legal rights by social theorists or critics of the law who are accustomed to view the law in a wider perspective than the lawyer concerned only with its day-to-day working.

---

[94] But not exclusively: see p. 184 *supra*.

IMMUNITY RIGHTS

Both the benefit theory of rights and the alternative theory of a right as a legally respected choice are designed primarily as accounts of the rights of citizen against citizen; that is of rights under the 'ordinary' law. From that point of view the benefit theory was criticized above (*inter alia*) for offering no more than a redundant translation of duties of the criminal law into a terminology of rights, e.g. not be murdered or assaulted. But this accusation of redundancy is no longer pertinent when what is to be considered are not rights under the ordinary law, but fundamental rights which may be said to be against the legislature, limiting its powers to make (or unmake) the ordinary law, where so to do would deny to individuals certain freedoms and benefits now regarded as essentials of human well-being, such as freedom of speech and of association, freedom from arbitrary arrest, security of life and person, education, and equality of treatment in certain respects.

The various elements which the benefit theory uses to analyse rights correlative to obligations and those which the rival 'choice' theory uses to analyse these and other kinds of right (that is: duty, absence of duty, benefit, act, and act-in-the-law) are not sufficient to provide an analysis of such constitutionally guaranteed individual rights. These require for their analysis the notion of an immunity. Bentham, unlike Hohfeld, did not isolate this notion in distinguishing different kinds or meanings of legal right, and indeed his attention was never seriously given to the analysis of fundamental legal rights. This was, no doubt, because, although, unlike Austin, he did not think that there were logical or conceptual objections to the notion of legal limitations of a sovereign legislature[95] he viewed with extreme suspicion any legal arrangements which would prevent the legislature enacting whatever measures appeared from time to time to be required by the dictates of general utility; and suspicion became contempt at the suggestion that such arrangements should be used to give legal form to doctrines of natural or fundamental individual rights. Hohfeld, who identified among

---

[95] See for his discussion of such limitations, *OLG* 18, 64–71, 306; *Fragment* Chap. IV, paras. 23–36 in *CW* 484–90; and Chap. IX *infra*.

the various 'loose' uses of the expression 'a right' its use to refer to an immunity, defined an immunity as the correlative of 'disability' or 'no power';[96] so that to say that a man, X, had a certain immunity meant that someone else lacked legal power to alter X's legal position in some respect. But, plainly, even in the loosest usage, the expression 'a right' is not used to refer to the fact that a man is thus immune from an *advantageous* change; the facts that the City Council cannot legally, i.e. has 'no power', to award me a pension, and my neighbour has no power to exempt me from my duty to pay my income-tax, do not constitute any legal rights for me. An individual's immunity from legal change at the hands of others is spoken and thought of as a right only when the change in question is *adverse*, that is, would deprive him of legal rights of other kinds (liberty-rights, powers, rights correlative to obligations) or benefits secured to him by law.

The chief, though not the only employment[97] of this notion of an immunity from adverse legal change which we may call an 'immunity right' is to characterize distinctively the position of individuals protected from such adverse change by constitutional limitations or, as Hohfeld would say, by disabilities of the legislature. Such immunity rights are obviously of extreme importance to individuals and may usually be asserted in the form of justifiable claims that some purported enactment is invalid because it infringes them. There is here an illuminating contrast with the redundancy of rights as defined by the beneficiary theory; for whereas, as I have urged above, nothing is to be gained for the lawyer, either in clarity or the focusing of legal attention, by expounding, say, the law of murder or assault in terms of rights, the case is altered if a constitutional Bill of Rights precludes the legislature from depriving individuals of the protections of the criminal law. For then there is every reason why lawyers and others should have picked out for them, as rights to life or security of the person, legal immunities the assertion of which on behalf of the individual calls for their advice and skill. That is why I said above that though

[96] Hohfeld, op. cit. 60.

[97] Immunities against divestment of various kinds of rights are involved in the notion of ownership. See A. M. Honoré, 'Ownership' in *Oxford Essays on Jurisprudence* (1st series 1961), 119.

certain legally secured individual benefits would have to be
brought in to any adequate account of legal rights, they
would not be brought in as the benefit theory brings them in.

WIDER PERSPECTIVES

Law is however too important a thing to leave to lawyers—
even to constitutional lawyers; and the ways of thinking
about rights common among serious critics of the law and
social theorists must be accommodated even though they are
different from and may not serve any of the specific purposes
of the lawyer. Here also a concept of legal rights limited to
those cases where the law, in the ways described above,
respects the choice of individuals would be too narrow. For
there is a distinct form of the moral criticism of law which,
like the constitutional immunity rights already described, is
inspired by regard for the needs of the individual for certain
fundamental freedoms and protections or benefits. Criticism
of the law for its failure to provide for such individual needs
is distinct from, and sometimes at war with, the criticism
with which Bentham was perhaps too exclusively concerned,
that the law often fails to maximize aggregate utility. A critic
of the former, individualistic, kind will of course not address
himself only to those legal systems in which there are immunity rights guaranteed by Bills of Rights; but in scrutinizing
systems like our own, where the maximum form of provision
for such individual needs must fall short of constitutional
immunity rights, he will count the measure of protection
afforded by the ordinary criminal law as a provision for those
needs, together with the duties to provide for them which fall
on public bodies or officials. Viewed in this light the law
against murder and assault will be considered and described
quite properly as securing rights to life and security of the
person; though if it were a question simply of expounding
the criminal law this would be redundant and even confusing.
    Hence in cases where the criminal law provides for such
essential human needs the individualistic critic of the law
would agree with the benefit-theorist in speaking of rights
corresponding to certain duties of the criminal law. They
would however differ in two ways: first the critic need entertain no *general* theory that every direct beneficiary of a legal

obligation had a corresponding legal right and he could therefore consistently subscribe to all the criticisms of the beneficiary theory made above; secondly the individualistic critic
implicitly draws a distinction quite foreign to the letter and
the spirit of the beneficiary theory between the legal provision
of benefits simply as a contribution to general utility and as
a contribution to the satisfaction of individual needs. It is
the latter which leads him to talk of rights secured by the
duties of the criminal law.

The upshot of these considerations is that instead of a
general analytical and explanatory theory covering the whole
field of legal rights I have provided a general theory in terms
of the notion of a legally respected individual choice which is
satisfactory only at one level—the level of the lawyer concerned with the working of the 'ordinary' law. This requires
supplementation in order to accommodate the important
deployment of the language of rights by the constitutional
lawyer and the individualistic critic of the law, for whom the
core of the notion of rights is neither individual choice nor
individual benefit but basic or fundamental individual needs.
This result may be felt as distressingly untidy by some, and
they may be tempted to combine the perspectives which I
have distinguished of the ordinary lawyer, the constitutional
lawyer, and the individualistic critic of the law in some
general formula embracing all three. Such a general formula
is suggested by Hohfeld's statement that the generic sense of
a right means 'any legal advantage'.[98] But I fear that, behind
the comfortable appearance of generality, we would have
only an unilluminating combination or mere juxtaposition of
the choice theory together with the benefit theory; and this
would fail to be sensitive to the important reasons for describing only some legally secured benefits, only in some
contexts, as legal rights.

---

[98] Op. cit. 42, 71. Cf. also Bentham's discussion in *OLG* 55–9 of the inclusion
in the idea of a 'party favoured by the law' of two kinds of favour: favour in
'point of interest' and 'in point of agency'. A party is 'favoured in point of agency'
when he has an *exceptional* liberty, i.e. a liberty to do some act generally
prohibited.

VIII

LEGAL POWERS

I INTRODUCTORY

The expression 'legal power' is not very familiar in our jurisprudence. Yet we need it or some equivalent expression to refer to a range of situations, familiar in the ordinary working of a modern legal system, where persons are enabled by the law either to do actions physically affecting other persons or things, or to bring about changes in the legal positions of others or of themselves, or of both themselves and others. Some of the cases that fall within this wide characterization of legal powers are in fact quite commonly referred to in the terminology of 'powers' by judges, lawyers, legal writers, and others. Thus we speak of a policeman's powers of arrest, of the legislative powers of a parliament, of a minister's powers to make rules, regulations, or orders, of a Corporation's powers to make by-laws, of a judge's power to make an order or to sentence a convicted person or to vary a settlement, or of the Lord Chancellor's power to appoint county court judges. These are all cases where the powers mentioned are held by officials or public bodies. It is somewhat less common to speak of private citizens, who are enabled by law to change the legal positions of others or of themselves or to do actions physically affecting things or persons, as having 'powers' to make such changes or to do such actions. Some of these latter cases are so described; we speak of a private individual as having a power of appointment over trust property or a power to appoint new trustees, or of a tenant for life's powers of sale, a landowner's powers of alienation. It is, however, more usual to use words like 'right'[1] or 'capacity' or 'competence' rather than 'power' to refer to the fact that an owner of a property can (that is, can legally) walk

---

[1] Legal powers are for Bentham a species of right. See *OLG* 84, 137 n. h (139); 220 n. a. But cf. for a qualification *PML* Chap. XVI, para. 25, in *CW* 205 n. e2. Hence Bentham speaks indifferently of a 'power of conveyance' (*OLG* 78 n. c (79)), and 'a right of alienation' (*Works* III 183).

over it or lease it, or that a person can make a will or a contract to marry.

Analytical jurisprudence is often said to be concerned with the analysis of fundamental legal concepts, but the limelight of Anglo-American jurisprudential attention has been mostly directed onto duties, obligations and rights and has been very little concerned with the concept of legal power. Yet, as I have said elsewhere,[2] the structure of a modern legal system, and indeed some most important aspects of law, cannot be understood unless the notion of legal powers and of the rules which confer them are understood. Bentham alone among analytical jurists has attempted a detailed analysis of this notion. He did this mainly in *Of Laws in General*,[3] and this chapter is in part an exposition of the main features of the analysis of legal powers provided by this work.

Before I begin this exposition I should mention that the idea of a legal power does figure in the work of one well-known and relatively modern analytical jurist and is reproduced in most modern textbooks on jurisprudence. I refer of course to W.N. Hohfeld, who identifies under the name of 'power'[4] one of the four fundamental legal conceptions which, according to him, the word 'right' is loosely used to express. For Hohfeld, a man has a legal power whenever he is able by some voluntary act of his to vary the legal position of another person, who is in this case said by Hohfeld to have a corresponding 'liability' to have his legal position varied by the other. A simple example is the power of a man to alienate his property to another. As I have said, such a power in private hands is often referred to as a right; and Bentham indeed regarded a power as one species of right but not all rights as powers. It was of course an achievement on Hohfeld's part to have got so far, though in fact much of his work was anticipated by Bentham's analysis of rights and powers. But much more than Hohfeld gives us is needed to display the notion fully and to analyse legal powers in their variant

---

[2] *The Concept of Law*, 32 ff.

[3] See Chap. V *supra*.

[4] *Fundamental Legal Conceptions* (1919), 51-7. Hohfeld considers that the term 'right', though frequently and loosely used for, *inter alia*, powers, is an unfortunate term for the purpose (ibid. at 51).

forms, and to exhibit the character of the laws which create
or confer them.

In my own previous inadequate approach to the subject I
touched it only sufficiently to emphasize how important an
element in a legal system powers are, and how great a need
there is to provide an analysis of rules which confer powers
before venturing upon any general definition or analysis of
law. I suggested a division between public powers, such as
powers of legislation and adjudication, and private powers,
where my main examples were powers to make wills or
contracts.[5] This account therefore left out many of the
powers listed above. Furthermore, I attempted no close
analysis either of the notion of a power or of the structure
of the rules by which they were conferred, save to insist that
they were different from rules which imposed obligations or
duties, and to reject theories such as those of Kelsen who refused to recognize in a rule conferring a legal power anything
more than a fragment of a rule imposing a duty and directing
an official to apply a sanction under certain conditions.[6]
Hence, so far as I was concerned, there was much unfinished
business concerned with legal powers, and I was astonished
when I subsequently came to study in detail Bentham's *Of
Laws in General* to find how much of it had already been
attempted by Bentham.

II POWERS OF CONTRECTATION

Bentham starts his analysis with the reduction of all legal
powers to two main kinds,[7] the second of which, though
different from the first, is dependent upon it. These two
kinds at first sight seem only to reflect the notion that there
may be power over inanimate things as well as power over

---

[5] *The Concept of Law*, 28 ff. For criticism of my approach see D.N. Mac-
Cormick, *Law as Institutional Fact* (Edinburgh 1973), 14 ff. and *H.L.A. Hart*
(London 1981), Chap. 6.

[6] See H. Kelsen, *General Theory of Law and State* (1945), especially 143-5,
where laws conferring power to legislate are described as 'not independent complete norms' and as 'intrinsic parts' of norms made on their basis. It is not clear
to me whether or not Kelsen's later recognition in *The Pure Theory of Law* (trans.
Knight 1967) of a class of 'dependent authorizing norms' modifies his earlier
doctrine.

[7] *OLG* 81.

persons. But Bentham is too perceptive to make what would, in this context, be a misleading distinction, because he sees that persons up to a point *are* like inanimate things: they have after all physical bodies which can be handled or interfered with, moved or confined like things. The power to interfere physically in this way either with things or with persons' bodies Bentham subsumes under a general notion of a power of *handling* or, as he calls it most frequently, 'power of contrectation'.[8] His other variants for this power are 'impressive' power or 'autocheiristic' power[9] which convey the idea of physically affecting bodies with one's own hands. It is, so far as human beings are concerned, a power over what Bentham calls their 'passive faculties', which means their capacity to be affected by physical handling or 'contrectation'.[10]

Legal examples of this first kind of power are a policeman's or an ordinary citizen's power of arrest, or an owner's power to handle and use the things which he owns, or to walk over and cultivate the land he owns. In these cases the power is legal because it is provided or conferred by the law and Bentham's account of the way in which this is done is simple and, I think, fundamentally correct, though it is at points vague and incomplete. The central idea in Bentham's explanation of such powers is that of a legal permission to do acts of the kind which fall under the general head of 'contrectation'. A permission is simply the absence of legal prohibition and hence the absence of a legal duty not to do a certain act. For Bentham such permissions constitute a species of legal *right* which he terms 'rights arising from absence of obligation' or sometimes more simply 'liberties'. But not all such liberty-rights, as we may call them, even when the acts which the right holder has liberty to do are acts of contrectation, are regarded by Bentham as legal powers. Sometimes he contrasts 'liberty' with 'power',[11] and sometimes he makes the same contrast by distinguishing those powers of contrectation which are 'properly speaking . . . the

---

[8] *OLG* 81; 137-9, n. h.

[9] *OLG* 57, n. e; 87.

[10] The above is an account of what Bentham calls 'the power of physical contrectation' or 'power of contrectation properly so called'. But he also recognizes the power to affect sensation ('the passive faculty' of the mind) and calls it the power of 'hyperphysical contrectation' (*OLG* 137-9 n. h).

[11] *OLG* 255.

work of the law' from those that are not.[12] Unfortunately
Bentham nowhere clearly or exhaustively explains what it is
that distinguishes a mere liberty of this sort, or a power
which is not 'the work of the law', from a legal power, but
the general character of this distinction may be gathered
from his illustrative examples and his rather vague observations.[13] The distinction seems to be as follows: a legal
permission only constitutes a *legal* power if it is in some way
an exception to or contrasts with general duties imposed by
law and so can be regarded as a kind of legal favour or advantage and not merely as an absence of duty. Bentham's
simplest example is again the power of an owner to use the
thing or land which he owns; he is at liberty to do this while
persons generally are under a duty not to do it. Hence in
relation to the particular thing or piece of land owned he
enjoys an advantage as compared with those subject to the
general duties, though of course owners of other property
enjoy similar advantages and hence have a similar legal power
over their property.

In the example just given the power is said to be 'exclusive'.[14] It is so in the sense that a particular person is permitted to do acts in relation to a particular thing or piece
of land which others are generally prohibited from doing.
Bentham, however, recognizes that this does not exhaust the
notion of legal favour or advantage, which for him differentiates a legal power from a mere liberty. Not all legal powers
are exclusive; for there are legal powers which are enjoyed
by everyone and so are 'inexclusive'. One example is illuminatingly discussed by Bentham[15] and contrasted with an
owner's exclusive powers: this is the ordinary citizen's power
of arrest, which is regarded as an *exception* to a general rule
prohibiting 'meddling' with the persons of others. It is important that this is regarded as an exception to such a general
rule, and not as a mere boundary condition or limitation of a
more narrowly framed rule prohibiting interference with the
persons of non-criminals and non-suspects. Bentham insists
that an owner's powers to use his property are not to be regarded as exceptions to a similar general rule prohibiting

---

[12] *OLG* 57 n. e; see also 256-7.
[13] The principal passages are at *OLG* 27; 56-7; 255-6.
[14] *OLG* 255-6.   [15] *OLG* 200-1.

meddling with property: for in his view there is no such general rule, the rule in the case of property being that there is always some person who is at liberty to meddle. In the case of property therefore the liberty to meddle is not an *exception* but a *limitation* or boundary condition of a rule prohibiting non-owners from meddling. What then is the difference between exceptions and limitations? As Bentham was well aware the criterion is not a formal one[16] but depends on what are taken to be the reasons for having a rule and on the scope of such reasons. He argues very persuasively,[17] in the case of powers of arrest or 'meddling' with the persons of others, that it is because we think that the general reasons for prohibiting interference with the persons of others apply also to the cases where arrest is permitted, but are in such cases outweighed by other reasons, that we look upon the power as an *exception* to a general rule prohibiting interference. We do not look upon an owner's powers in this light; for we do not think that there are reasons for having a general rule prohibiting all 'meddling' which are outweighed in the owner's case. So the owner's powers appear as merely the boundary conditions or limitations of a more narrowly framed rule prohibiting non-owners from meddling, for which rule of course there are good reasons.

Bentham's examples of inexclusive powers include the powers of members of a community over land which is the common property of all.[18] Here everyone has the same liberty to use the land, but Bentham recognizes this liberty as a *legal* power because it is an exception to the general rule restricting the use of land in the community and so is a 'favour' or advantage conferred by law.

Considering that [the law] might have commanded us all, you and me and others not to exercise any act upon that land and that such are the commands which to you, to me and to everyone but one or few it actually does give with respect to by far the greatest part of the land under its dominion, it is on that account frequently spoken of as if it had done something in favor of those whom it has thus left at liberty: it is spoken of as having given them or rather left them a *power over the land* . . . .[19]

---

[16] Bentham discusses the logical equivalence of exceptions and limitations at *OLG* 114-16.

[17] *OLG* 200-2.   [18] *OLG* 255-6.   [19] *OLG* 255.

Bentham's concept of a legal power of contrectation naturally invites comparison with what Hohfeld terms 'a liberty'. A legal power of contrectation is in fact more specific than Hohfeld's liberty in two respects. First, it is characterized as an exclusive or exceptional liberty to do something generally prohibited, and this feature does not enter into Hohfeld's definition of liberty, which is defined as a mere absence of a duty of opposite tenor, though it is rather vaguely and confusingly suggested by the synonym of 'privilege' which Hohfeld offers for liberty. Secondly, the kind of act which can constitute an exercise of the power of contrectation 'strictly so called' is restricted by Bentham to acts involving physically handling or affecting things or animate bodies. It should, however, be observed that, though exclusive or exceptional permissions constitute, according to Bentham, the minimum step which the law takes to confer powers of contrectation, very often the law goes further and strengthens or, as Bentham says, 'corroborates'[20] the mere permission in various ways. Thus the law corroborates a legal power to arrest by making it an offence to resist arrest or for third parties to interfere with the arrest or even to withhold their assistance if it is called for. The power to inflict punishment[21] or to seize goods in execution and, of course, an owner's power to use his property are other examples of powers of contrectation which are normally corroborated in such ways.

III POWERS OF IMPERATION

So much then for the first of the two kinds of powers to which according to Bentham all legal powers are in the last analysis reducible. The second kind Bentham calls the 'power of imperation'. This is distinguished from the power of contrectation not because it is a power only over persons (for as we have seen the power of contrectation can be that) but because it is a power over the active as distinct from the passive faculties of persons.[22] This means that it is a power to procure persons to act in conformity with a command or

---

[20] *OLG* 261-4.
[21] *OLG* 137 n. h (139).
[22] *OLG* 18 n. b; 137 n. h.

prohibition by providing motives influencing their will, and it does so in either of two main ways: by threatening punishment if the act is not done or by offering reward if it is done. These two forms of motivation or influence, the stick and the carrot, Bentham calls, in his quaint terminology, 'coercive' and 'alluring' influence.[23] Obviously for the law the stick is more important than the carrot as a method of securing conformity, though among Bentham's lesser known works there are some important contributions to jurisprudence, and indeed to social science, advocating and studying various forms of carrot or reward as a method of social control.[24] Here, however, I shall confine attention to the form of the power of imperation which relies upon the stick, that is, coercive influence. The first thing to observe is that it is dependent upon the power of contrectation for its efficacy; it is no good telling people to do things and threatening pain or punishment for disobedience unless there is power actually to inflict punishment.[25] This in the last resort will usually involve physical interference with the body of the disobedient person or his property, though it is not, of course, necessary or even usual that these two interdependent powers be exercised by the same persons.

If we accept the general imperative theory of law which Bentham held (though in a far subtler and more plausible form than Austin did), it is plain that the power of imperation as defined by Bentham is an apt description of legislative powers, both of the sovereign law-making body and of subordinate law-making agencies, at least where the legislation creates legal duties backed by sanctions. Bentham, however, thinks that the same notion also explains the whole range of legal powers which enable a person to vary the legal position of himself or others. This, I shall argue, is a mistake, though there are some simple cases besides general legislative powers which yield quite easily to this analysis. Thus a parent's or guardian's powers over a child include powers to give orders, to threaten punishment and himself to inflict it for disobedience. The law, according to Bentham, provides this power essentially by permitting a parent or guardian to do

---

[23] *OLG* 259–60 and 262. See the discussion of 'praemiary laws' in Chap. VI, p. 139 *supra*.

[24] See also *Works* I 533 ff.   [25] *OLG* 137 n. h.

these things in the case of the child, though they are generally forbidden. Like the policeman's power of arrest such private powers of imperation as the parent or guardian has over the child may be strengthened or corroborated in various ways by the law: it may, for example, prohibit third parties from interfering. A slightly more complex variant of the power of imperation is to be seen in the power of a military officer to give orders to his men. It is more complex only because, though the officer gives the orders and may threaten punishment, the punishment would normally be inflicted by other persons, who are either ordered to inflict it specifically by the officer or are under standing orders to inflict punishments directed by some other person or body. Such cases are fairly obvious applications of the notions of imperation and contrectation. The person having a power in these cases issues commands or prohibitions, but it is not obvious how, as Bentham thought, the notion of imperation also explains the general run of cases where a person is enabled by law to vary his own or other persons' legal position, as he does when he makes a contract or conveys property or, to take an example from public life, where he exercises a power to appoint a judge. What a man does when he exercises such powers seems at first sight very unlike issuing commands or prohibitions or threatening punishment for disobedience. How does Bentham's notion of a power of imperation explain these various and important transactions whereby individuals can, by saying or writing or doing certain things, change legal rights and duties of themselves or others?

To understand Bentham's theory here we must turn to what I think is one of his greatest insights into the structure of a legal system. This is his distinctive doctrine that in a modern legal system the power of imperation must be divided or, as he puts it, 'broken into shares'.[26] He does not mean by this merely that, as well as a supreme legislative authority with power to make general laws, there must also be subordinate legislative authorities with delegated powers to make general laws in restricted fields, but rather that there must be a division of legislative power in respect of scope or extent, that is in respect of generality and particularity, and

[26] *OLG* 26, n. h.

general powers and particular powers must be as a practical matter assigned to different persons. Bentham devotes a whole chapter[27] to this topic, which he calls 'The Generality of a Law', and he thinks, rightly in my view, that a grasp of the distinction and interconnection between what he calls general and particular laws or 'mandates' and the corresponding powers to make such laws is vital for the understanding of many features of law. It is, he says, 'a clue without which it would be scarce possible for us to find our way through the labyrinth . . . .'[28]

In Bentham's terminology there must be not only powers to make general laws applicable to classes of persons, powers, as he calls it, to legislate *de classibus*, but there must be also powers to legislate *de singulis*, that is, concerning identifiable individual persons, or identifiable individual things, times, or places. He does not mean by this that we must on occasion find it necessary to give individuals an order, as the policeman does when he says 'move on', but, and this is a more fundamental point, that the legislature must frequently leave it in some cases to others (who may be officials or private persons) to settle the membership of those general classes of persons on whom the legislator imposes duties (or confers rights) when legislating *de classibus*. To illustrate this necessity I take, as a very simple example, a legislative provision for the appointment of an official, say a judge.[29] The legislature, by general legislation, may settle the rights, duties, and powers which judges are to have, and the penalties if any which may be imposed upon them for violation of their duties. But the membership of the class of judges must be left to others who will make appointments of individuals as occasion requires. When someone has such a power to appoint individuals to a class upon which the law has imposed duties or conferred rights he has according to Benthem a *share* in the entire power of imperation.

To grasp Bentham's point fully, we must, as he tells us, appreciate a difference between two kinds of classes[30] with which general legislation may deal. The membership of some classes (let us call them *natural* classes) is determined by

---

[27] *OLG* Chap. IX.   [28] Ibid. 80.
[29] Bentham gives this as an example: *OLG* 87.
[30] *OLG* Chap. IX, 82–3.

natural events, not by human choice nominating or appointing its members. The class of pigs, or men aged twenty-one, are plain instances of this type of class. Other classes may be called *artificial* because their membership is determined by human choice nominating individuals as members of that class.[31] Examples of such artificial classes are the class of Judges of the High Court, or the class of Prime Ministers. Plainly an act of choice referring to an individual is required to constitute him a member of the class. No complex civilization could dispense with the need to make general arrangements (and hence also general laws) concerning classes of both these kinds. But since there must be artificial classes as well as natural classes, there will naturally be a division of the total legislative power into shares. The legislature legislating *de classibus* will settle what the rights and duties of the class of judges are to be, while some other individual or body of persons will nominate individual judges from time to time and so will have power to appoint judges. Similarly, the general law may settle what the rights and duties of an owner of land are to be; but it will be for individuals, by doing certain acts, including such things as executing conveyances or transfers or by entering into various transactions, to settle who from time to time is to be the owner.

Bentham shows how the two kinds of power, general powers of legislation *de classibus* and particular powers of legislation *de singulis*, are complementary and that however extensive one of them was it could not do the work of the other. Thus, if a man was given power to legislate concerning any identifiable individual but only concerning such individuals and not classes he could not, as Bentham points out,[32] address himself to 'posterity' since this could only be done by the use of general terms. Conversely, a legislator even with the most extensive powers of legislating about classes could not with such powers make the appointments required for maintaining artificial classes.

With this outline account of Bentham's distinction between legislation *de classibus* and legislation *de singulis* in mind, let us look a little more closely at some of the simpler cases which Bentham treats as falling under the general head of

---

[31] Ibid.   [32] *OLG* 91.

the power of imperation although, at first sight, the person exercising the power does not himself appear to be issuing commands or prohibitions, still less to be making threats of punishment either at his own hands or at the hands of others. Take again the case of the power to appoint judges. When someone is given this power, certain formalities may be required by law for its exercise; generally a warrant or document must be signed of which the central operative clause would be something like 'Y is hereby appointed to be one of Her Majesty's Judges'. When the document is signed the person becomes one of the judges and thenceforth has certain specific duties, rights and powers which constitute what Bentham calls the legal 'condition', or as we might say, the *status*, of a judge. I shall for simplicity's sake focus attention only on the duties of a judge and suppose that there are sanctions for neglect of them. The appointor by his act may be said to *'aggregate'*[33] the new judge to an existing recognized class who have certain distinctive duties, and he may also be said to *'invest'* the new judge with those duties. So this kind of power, considered as a power to include an individual in a recognized or established class, is called by Bentham 'a power of aggregation', or 'accensitive power',[34] and, considered as a power to invest individuals with rights or duties, as 'a power of investment'.[35] But—and this is our problem—Bentham insists that such powers are shares in the power of imperation and even calls them 'powers of imperation'.[36] Why does he say this in spite of the fact that the appointor does not issue any commands or prohibitions? Bentham's reason is as follows. The general law *de classibus* made by the legislator settling the rights, powers, duties of judges is in a sense indeterminate or incomplete in a very important respect, for though it tells us *what* judges are to do or not to do (their duties) it does not tell us which individuals have these duties. This we can learn only by reference to the declared choice made by the person given by the law power to appoint judges. Since this uncompleted aspect or gap in the general law is left to the appointor to complete when he eventually exercises

---

[33] *OLG* 82-3.   [34] Ibid. 82-4.   [35] Ibid. 83.
[36] Powers of aggregation are 'powers of imperation in particular terms' or 'powers of imperating de singulis' (*OLG* 91).

his power by signing the required document or complying with any other formality required, he completes *pro tanto* or fills in the gap left open in the general law. '[T]he legislator', says Bentham, 'sketch[es] out a sort of imperfect mandate which he leaves it to the subordinate power holder to fill up.'[37] Now so far as the legislator in such imperfect mandates imposes duties and sanctions on persons left to the appointor to identify, this is a direct exercise on the part of the legislator of the power of imperation though it is incomplete in the sense explained. Hence when the appointor completes or, in Bentham's language, 'fills up' the general law by identifying the individuals who are to have the duties and be liable to punishment, he participates in or shares in an exercise of the power of imperation by rendering it determinate. The appointor does not issue orders or threats himself but he does something which is recognized as bringing an individual (the new judge) within the scope of the legislator's existing orders and threats. These two activities, though different, are sufficiently closely related to make it possible to conceive of them as respectively direct and indirect forms of a single activity, viz. of securing that individuals are subjected to duties supported by sanctions, and so as direct and indirect variants of 'imperation'. But such terminology is dangerous since it obscures certain important distinctions, attention to which is necessary if we are to understand the ways in which the law creates such powers. But I shall defer consideration of these in order first to introduce some further features of Bentham's analysis which seem to throw light on some important legal phenomena.

IV POWERS OF ALIENATION AND CONTRACTS

It is to be noted that general provisions made by laws may be

[37] *OLG* 26. Bentham adds that '[t]his is one way among innumerable others in which . . . the complete power of imperation or de-imperation may be broken into shares' (ibid. n. h). In *Works* III 187, he says that a 'legal disposition' e.g. nomination to an office or the making of a gift or a contract 'may be considered under two aspects, either as serving to modify a general law, or as making by itself, under the authority of the sovereign, a particular law. In the first point of view, the sovereign is represented as making a general law, and leaving certain words blank, that they may be supplied by the individual to whom he grants the right to do so. In the second point of view, the individual makes the law, and causes it to be sanctioned by the public force.'

incomplete in many quite different ways besides merely leaving open the identity of the individuals who are to belong to the class with which the law is concerned. Laws may obviously leave open for others to settle such matters as the particular place or time, or other circumstances under which acts of a certain sort are to be done or, to take one of Bentham's examples, the law may leave open for variation by some subordinate authority the amount of precious metal to be contained by coins constituting legal tender. Bentham includes all these under powers of aggregation with suitable sub-heads such as *'in personam'*, *'in actum'*, *'in locum'*,[38] etc. I shall not enter into these complexities, but in order to illustrate the power of Bentham's analysis I shall consider his treatment of powers to alienate property or, as he calls it, 'conveyance', and of contractual powers or, as he calls it, 'powers to make covenants'.

In considering powers of alienation of property a sophisticated element in Bentham's general imperative theory of law to which I have only indirectly referred must now be taken into account. Bentham does not consider that the sovereign makes law only when he commands. Commands (and prohibitions, which are of course merely commands *not* to do certain actions) are no doubt for Bentham the fundamental and most important type of law. They are, as he says, 'coercive laws', but he also admits what he terms 'discoercive' or 'deobligative'[39] laws which the lawgiver issues when it undoes a command or revokes wholly or in part some existing coercive law. Such discoercive laws grant permission to do some act previously prohibited or to abstain from doing some act previously commanded to be done. This means that we must extend the idea of powers of imperation to include powers of 'deimperation', and this is, in fact, a phrase Bentham frequently uses to describe laws granting permissions. Further it is clear that the power of deimperation as much as that of imperation may be shared and conferred upon sub-

[38] *OLG* 83 ff.
[39] *PML* Concluding Note, paras. 3 and 15, in *CW* 302. At *OLG* 110 and 300, Bentham distinguishes permission to do something previously prohibited as a 'superventitious active permission' or 'repermission' from 'original' or 'inactive permission' of conduct not previously prohibited. In *OLG passim* Bentham uses the expression 'deobligative' for laws permitting acts forbidden by other laws.

ordinate power holders. If you have a power of deimperation
you are enabled by the law to change the legal position of
persons by exempting them to a greater or lesser extent from
some existing law, thus relieving them of the duties which it
imposes. So corresponding to the powers of aggregation and
investment which are, as we have seen, shares in the power of
imperation there will be powers of disaggregation and divestment which are shares in the power of deimperation.

The relevance of all this to the analysis of powers of alienation of property is as follows. Bentham thought, with good
justification, that in the last resort the legal institution of
property rested on laws prohibiting persons generally from
interfering with things or land, but this prohibition does not
extend to the person whom certain facts or events specified
by the law constitute the owner of the property. The facts or
events which secure for a given person this position and thus
bring him within the exception to the general prohibition
against interference constitute, as we say, his *title*.[40] Such
title-constituting or 'investitive' events will, in a system which
allows for the alienation of property, include the acts of previous owners signifying in more or less formal ways their intention to transfer the property to a new owner. A conveyance is therefore in many respects analogous to the
appointment of the new judge which we have already discussed. The old owner, we might say, appoints the transferee
to the 'office' of owner of the property. The differences are
of course great. Not only does the transferor substitute the
new owner for himself, but a large part of what he does requires for its explanation the idea of deimperation or permission rather than imperation. For the execution of the
conveyance takes the new owner out of the scope of the
general prohibition on interference with the property to
which he was previously subject; it lifts the duty not to interfere from him and grants him permission to do things previously prohibited to him. It thus gives him a power of contrectation over the property which consists, as we have seen,
essentially of a liberty denied to others to handle the property.
But of course this is only one of the effects of a transfer of

[40] *OLG* 180-1; 201-2; *PML* Chap. XVII, Concluding Note X, in *CW* 303. In
Works III 186-90 Bentham uses the terminology of 'dispositive' or 'collative' and
'ablative' events to explain the notion of title.

property. It also subjects the old owner to the duty not to interfere with the property from which, as owner, he was formerly exempt, and it confers rights on the new owner in the minimal sense that he is legally protected by or is a beneficiary of the general duty not to interfere. Even this is of course far from a full account of the complex operation of a conveyance or transfer of property in a modern system of law. But it is, I hope, enough to show at least in principle how powers of alienation yield to Bentham's analysis as a share in the powers of imperation and deimperation.

Bentham's explanation of contractual powers brings out some further points. The general law underlying the institution of contract is the law imposing a duty on persons to do those acts which they agree to do (by whatever form of agreement the law stipulates) and to pay damages if they do not do what they so agree to do.[41] Such a general law is 'incomplete' in a more radical way than the law underlying the institution of property, for it not only leaves the identity of the persons who are to do certain acts for determination by reference to the voluntary transactions of individuals; it also leaves open the determination of what acts are to be done, though of course this open area may be restricted in a greater or lesser degree by the law's insertion of compulsory clauses into contracts, or by its refusal to recognize the validity of certain types of agreement. But notwithstanding this great difference a contracting party, though he does not issue commands either to himself or to others, may be said to share in the exercise of the power of imperation, because by entering into the contract he brings himself and specific conduct on his part within the scope of the highly unspecific duty created by the general law which requires him to do what he agrees to do. He thus imposes a legal duty or obligation on himself to do an act the identity of which was left

---

[41] In *PML*, Chap. XVI, para. 35, in *CW* 228 n. g3, and *OLG*, 27 n. i, the fundamental law by which covenants are adopted is said to be the law prohibiting the wrongful withholding of services. A promise or covenant is for Bentham an 'expression of will' (*OLG* 24, n. g, and 65, n. k) but not a command or countermand and so not a 'mandate' (*OLG* 16). Yet it is 'converted into a mandate' by the Sovereign's adoption (*OLG* 25 and 79 n. c). '[T]he expression of will . . . may, without any alteration . . . in the import of it, be translated into the form and language of a mandate: of a mandate issuing from the mouth of the lawgiver himself' (*OLG* 27).

open by the general law for contracting parties to settle. His act is an 'investitive' act imposing obligations on himself and conferring corresponding rights on the other party. This it seems to me is a good account of contractual power which shows it to have the general character of a share in the power of imperation.

V POWER-CONFERRING LAWS

What sort of laws or legal provisions confer legal powers? In the case of powers of contrectation Bentham's answer is tolerably clear. According to Bentham the law confers powers of contrectation simply by permitting a man to do something which, if done by others or in other circumstances, would be a breach of legal duty or an offence. Though this is all that is required to create legal powers, or powers that are 'the work of the law', such powers may, as noticed above, be corroborated by further laws imposing duties on others not to obstruct or interfere with the exercise of such powers. Sometimes, when the law's permission is granted by an enactment subsequent to and partially repealing an earlier law imposing duties, it will be natural to regard the later law as a distinct 'discoercive', 'deobligative' or 'permissive' law and to regard the legal powers as conferred by it alone. In other cases, such as that of the owner's exclusive power to make use of his property, the owner's liberty to do what others are forbidden to do appears from the start as a condition limiting the scope of a single coercive law prohibiting what Bentham calls 'meddling' with property. In this and many similar cases the power may be said to be conferred not by a distinct discoercive or permissive law, but simply by that part of a coercive law which contains the limiting conditions. Very frequently in the exposition and formulation of rules of law we may have a choice: we may, as it were, consolidate an original coercive enactment and a later discoercive law making exceptions to it and treat them as a single law with different parts made at different times, or we may treat them as distinct laws. Conversely, we may have a choice between treating a single coercive enactment containing exceptions as a single law or as a coercive law together with a discoercive law introducing the exceptions.[42] Some of the considerations

[42] *OLG* 57.

which may incline us one way or the other are discussed by Bentham in *Of Laws in General*, much of which is devoted to the complex problem of the individuation of laws,[43] that is, the criteria for deciding what should be treated as merely part of a law and what as a single complete law. Fortunately these issues are not here relevant, but it is important to realize that there are these two alternative ways of representing the law which grants permission to some person or persons to do something generally forbidden.

Bentham's account of the way in which the law confers legal powers, other than those of contrectation, raises rather more fundamental issues, though it also makes use, and indeed an excessive use, of the same idea of a permission to do what is generally forbidden which enters into his analysis of powers of contrectation. His initial account of the way in which the law confers powers of 'imperation' and 'deimperation' is to be found in Chapter II of *Of Laws in General*, where it forms part of his explanation of two different ways in which 'mandates' may belong to the sovereign.[44] When the sovereign himself issues mandates they are said to belong to him by way of 'original conception'; when they are issued by a subordinate or by a past sovereign they belong to him by 'adoption'. Adoption has different forms and degrees which Bentham explains but these need not be noticed here. It is, however, central to Bentham's account of legal powers of imperation that what invests the subordinate with power to issue a mandate and so makes it a legal power is the fact that the sovereign 'allows' the mandate to be issued;[45] if he does not allow it, it is an illegal mandate and to issue it is an offence.[46] Such allowance by the sovereign consists either in permission given by him (explicitly or tacitly) to the subordinate to issue mandates or in the sovereign's command that those to whom the subordinate's mandates are directed

---

[43] Bentham considers that for some purposes the law should be represented as consisting only of obligative or coercive rules (*OLG* 233), and in one passage appears to deny that 'exceptive provisions' enacted at the same time as the law which they qualify could constitute an 'independent law' (see *OLG* 157). For a powerful criticism of Bentham's theory of individuation of laws and of his treatment of permissions, see J. Raz, *The Concept of a Legal System* (1970), especially 50–60, 70–7, and 170–5.

[44] *OLG* 21–7.   [45] Ibid. 22 and 27–8.

[46] Ibid. 19. See also *PML*, Chap. XVI, para. 54, in *CW* 263, n. r4, § ix.

must obey him. Bentham regards these alternative forms of
'allowing' as virtually equivalent, and he says that in both
cases alike in order to be effective the subordinate's mandates
will need to be supplemented in various ways, notably by
provisions of sanctions for disobedience.[47]

It is important to observe that in this first account, according to which powers of imperation are conferred by the
sovereign's 'allowing' mandates to be issued, Bentham includes not only a subordinate's powers to issue commands or
prohibitions, but also powers to make contracts and to alienate property, and he expressly claims that the validity of
covenants and conveyances is to be explained by reference
to the same idea of 'adoption',[48] consisting in the sovereign's
grant of permission to issue what would be otherwise an
illegal mandate or in the sovereign's command that the subordinate be obeyed. But the use of these ideas to explain
powers to enter into legal transactions such as contracts or
transfers of property is a mistake, and an important one,
from which Bentham perhaps never quite shook himself free.
The mistake springs from two connected faults. The first of
these is the failure to disentangle the very different ideas of
legal validity and invalidity on the one hand from legality
(or what is legally permitted) and illegality (or what is legally
prohibited) on the other. That this is a fault is evident from
some very familiar facts which show that though a person
who makes a valid contract or conveyance is usually permitted to do those acts or say or write those things which are
required to effect such transactions, their legal operation in
changing the parties' rights and duties does not spring from
that permission. In most legal systems even a thief is able in
certain circumstances to make a valid transfer of the stolen
property by the standard forms of sale, even though in doing
this he commits an offence. Conversely, if a person who has
no legal power to dispose of property or enter into a contract
purports to do these things by executing the standard forms,
the purported disposition or contract will be invalid or 'void'
though his acts may constitute neither a criminal nor a civil
offence, and so may be legally permitted.

Bentham's second fault is his failure to mark sufficiently

[47] *OLG* 27.
[48] Ibid. 23–7.

clearly and consistently an important distinction between two types of subordinate powers: on the one hand a power to issue legal commands and prohibitions, and on the other a power to enter into legally effective transactions which cannot be construed as commands or prohibitions, though their effect is to bring individuals within the scope of existing commands or prohibitions or exceptions to them.[49] The upshot of these two faults is that Bentham misrepresents as a mere legal permission to issue commands or prohibitions which it would be otherwise illegal to issue, something conceptually quite distinct from this and of great importance: namely the recognition by the law that certain acts of individuals in certain circumstances suffice to bring themselves or others within the scope of existing laws (or of exceptions to them) and so control their incidence.

So far I have assumed in Bentham's favour that, though his account of the creation of powers to enter into legally effective transactions such as a contract or conveyance is defective, his account is still an acceptable one of the creation of subordinate powers to issue commands and prohibitions or, as we should term them, subordinate powers of legislation. But in fact this account is acceptable only in very simple and comparatively unimportant cases where the courts would take no hand in enforcing the subordinate's orders or punishing those who disobeyed them, but would be concerned only with the question whether the subordinate's act in issuing or in enforcing orders was permitted by the law or was an offence because, e.g., it had exceeded permitted limits. A parent's power to give orders to a young child and to administer moderate punishment for disobedience may be of this kind, and in such cases the notions of 'has legal power to issue and enforce' and 'is legally permitted to issue and enforce' are indistinguishable. But where questions of the validity of the subordinate's orders arise, as they will when the orders which the subordinate has power to issue are enforceable by the courts, then the mere fact that the subordinate is permitted to issue the orders, even if it is true, is not in itself the important consideration. What is important

---

[49] Bentham seems to recognize this distinction in his reference (see n. 41 *supra*) to expressions of will which, though not themselves 'mandates', may be translated into mandates and become mandates when adopted by the sovereign.

is that the subordinate's act in issuing the orders is recognized by the law as a criterion distinguishing orders which the courts are to enforce, and so as a criterion of their validity. In such cases the orders issued by the subordinate have a double aspect: on the one hand, they are indeed orders addressed by the subordinate to others requiring them to do or not to do certain acts and in this respect are unlike legal transactions such as the making of contracts; on the other hand, the issuing of such orders by the subordinate is recognized by the law as bringing certain persons within the scope of existing laws requiring obedience to the subordinate, just as the making of a contract brings the parties within the scope of existing laws requiring performance of contracts from the parties to them.

What most needs to be stressed as a corrective to Bentham's account is that the fact that a person or body of persons is legally permitted, i.e. not prohibited by law, to issue orders is not equivalent to the recognition of the issue by such person or persons of such orders as a criterion of their validity or enforceability. Conversely, the fact that the issue of such orders is not permitted but is an offence must be distinguished from the invalidity of such orders even if these two features are commonly found together. Thus, even if members of a legislature were punishable (as usually they are not) for issuing orders which are *ultra vires* and void, the fact that in issuing such orders they have done what is not permitted, because legally prohibited, must be distinguishable from the fact that they have produced orders which are legally invalid. In such a case the would-be legislators have broken an existing law because what they have done is legally prohibited by it, but also they have failed to make a new law because what they have done is not recognized as a criterion of legal validity.

A better account of the way in which powers to effect legal transactions are conferred by law is at least implicit in Bentham's discussion of powers of aggregation and investitive powers, and it is an account which provides within the framework of his general imperative theory an analysis of the idea of legal recognition of the validity of a transaction which does not confuse it with the largely irrelevant idea of legal permission to do what is generally prohibited. Bentham's problem is the necessity of reconciling his general imperative theory of law with a realistic account of legal powers and the laws on which they rest. For his form of imperative theory recognizes only two types of laws: coercive laws imposing duties to act or to abstain from acting (commands and prohibitions), and discoercive laws permitting acts or abstentions previously forbidden. There is no further type of law, conferring powers as distinct from imposing or removing duties. To believe that there is would be inconsistent with the doctrine or dogma that laws are essentially commands or exemptions from commands.

Accordingly Bentham's solution to his problem is to treat legal powers as resting not on a type of law distinct from duty imposing laws but on certain parts of laws which impose duties. Thus, to revert to our well-worn example of the power to appoint judges, perhaps most lawyers would find acceptable the common view that here there are two relevant types of law, viz. (i) a general law settling the duties (and also rights etc.) of judges, and (ii) a law conferring power on some person, e.g., the Lord Chancellor, to appoint judges. Bentham rejects this view and holds that the provisions conferring the power to appoint are limitations or conditions forming part of the general law, and these determine who is to be included among judges and hence who is subject to the duties which the law imposes on them. This can be made apparent if we simply rephrase the general law in such terms as 'If the Lord Chancellor nominates a person as a judge then any person so nominated shall . . .' or 'All persons nominated by the Lord Chancellor as judges shall . . .' Similarly (though in more complicated ways) powers of alienation of property rest merely on certain qualifications, limitations or exceptions contained in general laws imposing duties not to interfere with property and these are in effect a catalogue of the conditions under which a man is said to have a title to property.

For Bentham the view that there are separate laws which confer powers is an illusion, and he plainly thinks it is fostered by the important fact that lawyers can and indeed constantly need to consider separately, in abstraction from the rest, those parts of duty-imposing laws which provide for legal powers. For all sorts of purposes, and not only when some exercise of a power is contemplated, lawyers need to have available detailed and comprehensive formulations or 'expositions', as Bentham terms it, of those events and circumstances which provide powers because they condition or limit the operation of coercive duty-imposing laws.[50] In relation to the law of property we have such an 'exposition' when the various kinds of 'investitive' events constituting a title (including those events which constitute voluntary transfers) are collected and explained in the general part of a civil code or in treatises or books on property and conveyancing.[51] But we must not mistake them for a special class of laws: what look like separate laws of a non-imperative kind are in fact only expositions of parts of imperative laws and legal powers to control the incidence of laws rest on such parts of laws. This is Bentham's doctrine and, though I disagree with it, it contains much that is illuminating.

Because it throws light on the structure of a legal system Bentham stresses the fact that many different duty-imposing laws will be found to share many common conditions providing for powers. The conditions which constitute a title to property, on which powers of alienation rest, are common to whole groups of laws creating offences against property. Other sets of conditions, for example those conferring powers of arrest will (through the medium of discoercive laws) be common conditions limiting the scope of duties imposed by many laws creating offences against the person.[52] In a striking image Bentham compares such groups of laws sharing common conditions to a cluster of pyramids with a common base.[53] '[M]any laws, any two laws almost, will have a vast portion of their substance in common: they will be like contiguous triangles, like the diagrams of pyramids represented as standing upon the same basis: but the matter of each will be separately describable: as in pyramids so represented the parts of each are separately assignable.'[54]

VI POWERS OF IMPERATION AND NORMATIVE POWERS

There remains the question whether what is valuable in Bentham's analysis of powers can be detached from his general

---

[50] *OLG* Chap. XVI, *passim.*   [51] *OLG* 179–82; 201–2.
[52] *OLG* 200–1.
[53] See also *PML*, Concluding Note, para. 12, in *CW* 304.
[54] *OLG* 23 n.

theory of law, which insists that laws are commands or prohibitions or permissions issued or adopted by the Sovereign.
I think it can, and this is best seen if it is appreciated how
Bentham's analysis of powers makes contact with certain
important themes of modern linguistic philosophy.[55] When
an act which constitutes the exercise of a power is the saying
or writing of certain words, as it will usually be in the case
of the appointment of a judge or a transfer of property or the
making of a contract, then whatever meaning such words
may have independently of the law they also, because of the
law, have a special dimension of meaning or a special 'force',
since the law provides that their utterance shall effect legal
changes. They are, as conveyancers call them, 'operative'
words. 'I hereby appoint X to be one of His Majesty's Judges'
or 'A hereby conveys unto B etc., etc.' are not, or not merely,
statements giving information about or self-descriptions of
the appointor or transferor; they are formulae the use of
which by the appropriate person on the appropriate occasions has certain legal consequences. But these are legal
normative effects or consequences, not *natural* effects. The
point is not that the use of such words *causes* later acts or
events to be done or to happen, but rather that if certain
acts are later done or not done they will because of the prior
use of such words be legally speaking 'in order' or 'out of
order', right or wrong, a performance of a duty or a breach
of it. Now what is true in the legal case is also true of many
non-legal cases where there is no background of imperative
laws to explain how it is that the use of words can have
normative effects and so constitute an exercise of informal
non-legal powers. When we promise to do something or when
a baby is given a name at a christening ceremony, the words
used to make the promise or give the name ('I hereby promise . . .' or 'I hereby name this child . . .') have the normative effect that a later failure to do the promised act is evaluated as 'wrong' or calling the baby by some other name is
'incorrect,' and various forms of censure or criticism are

---

[55] See J.L. Austin, *How to Do Things with Words* (1962), *passim* for his
account of 'performative' utterances and speech acts. See also the discussion of
the distinction between the meaning and the 'illocutionary force' of utterances in
Cohen, 'Do Illocutionary Forces Exist?' *Phil. Q.* (1964) and Strawson, 'Intention
and Convention in Speech Acts', *Phil. Rev.* 73 (1964) 439.

rendered 'in order', or appropriate. These informal non-legal
cases which parallel legal powers—and there are hosts of them
of varying degrees of informality and stringency—suggest that
powers to change normative situations need not rest on a
Sovereign's commands or on commands at all. Where they do
rest on commands, that will be a special case. For social rules
which are not commands may, like Bentham's general laws or
'imperfect mandates', have gaps left open for others to fill
up. There is no command (unless all social rules are to be
attributed to Divine Command) that we must do what we
promise to do or that a child is to be called by the name
assigned to it by a certain person at a certain type of ceremony. There are, however, as a background to these operations certain accepted rules or procedures, more or less
precise, under which if certain things are said or done this
changes the normative situation. Hence anyone who thinks
the notion of an accepted rule rather than a Sovereign's
commands is central to the analysis of a legal system could
still use the substance of Bentham's analysis of legal powers.
Moreover there is at least one legal phenomenon which the
shift to rules could explain but for which Bentham's imperative theory of law cannot provide a place. For since all
legal powers according to Bentham are conferred by the
Sovereign's legislation, express or tacit, the Sovereign's own
powers to make law are not legal powers. The supreme legislator's powers cannot be conferred by law. All we can say of
them according to Bentham[56] is that their *cause* is the general
habit of obedience which is a constituent of Sovereignty. But
in many legal systems the supreme legislator's powers *are*
conferred by law and indeed limited by law and, as I have
tried to demonstrate elsewhere, for the explanation of this
feature of law the notion of a rule, not that of a command,
is required.

There remains for discussion the question whether the
mere substitution of conditional rules imposing duties for
conditional commands imposing duties would be enough.
The full investigation of this cannot be attempted here but
my own view is that, on any reasonable criterion of what

[56] *OLG* 18 n. b; 137 n. h (139). See, for criticism of Bentham's theory of the
sovereign's legislative power, Chap. IX *infra*.

constitutes separate laws as distinct from 'parts of a law', legal provisions which are intended to guide those who exercise powers to bring about changes in the legal situation of themselves or others and which supply criteria for the assessment of the validity of such changes should rank as separate laws[57] and not merely as parts of laws imposing duties. Legal provisions of this kind guide those who exercise powers in ways strikingly different from the way in which rules imposing duties guide behaviour: they are more like *instructions* how to bring about certain results than mandatory impositions of duty.[58] Hence power-conferring rules are distinct from duty-imposing rules in their normative function though they are, of course, also intimately connected with them. To represent them as fragments of duty-imposing rules is to obscure their distinct normative character.

[57] See the discussion of criteria of individuation for laws in J. Raz, *supra* n. 43, esp. 140–7, and his application of these criteria in his article 'Legal Principles and the Limits of Law', *Yale Law Journal* 81 (1972) 823 for the wider philosophical issues see J. Raz and D. N. MacCormick, 'Voluntary Obligation and Normative Powers', *Proceedings of the Aristotelian Society*, Suppl. Vol. xlvi (1972) 79 ff.

[58] For the distinctions between the way in which laws conferring powers guide those who exercise powers and the way in which laws imposing duties guide the conduct of those subject to them, see H. L. A. Hart, *The Concept of Law*, 27–8, 31–3, and J. Raz, op. cit. (*supra*, n. 43) 161, 162–4. See also MacCormick, op. cit. p. 196, n. 5 *supra*.

IX

SOVEREIGNTY AND LEGALLY LIMITED GOVERNMENT

I GOVERNMENT BY LAW

For Bentham, government by law, or 'public dominanion' as he sometimes termed it, comprises the exercise of two interdependent sorts of power over persons.[1] The first is power over their 'active' faculties or will, and consists of the ability to induce men to act in certain ways by holding out the prospect of punishment or more rarely, reward, and so presenting them with 'coercive' or 'alluring' motives for obedience. This is the power of 'imperation', but this power in its usual coercive form is dependent on power of a simpler sort in the exercise of which men are assimilated to things, since it is power over their 'passive' faculties. This is the power of 'contrectation', i.e. to inflict on them the threatened punishment for disobedience. These twin powers over persons, when possessed by the Sovereign in a state or his subordinates, are the legislative powers required for government by law. There is however a vital difference, which Bentham emphasizes, between the powers of the Sovereign and those of his subordinates. The subordinates' powers are conferred by law—that is, by permissions and commands given by the Sovereign. But the Sovereign's powers are not conferred by law: 'of the power of all subordinate power-holders the ultimate efficient cause is the command or allowance of the Sovereign: of the power of the Sovereign himself the constituent cause is the submission or obedience of the people.'[2] It is of course in terms of 'submission or obedience of the people' that the Sovereign, whose expressions of will are law, is himself defined, for the Sovereign is 'that person or assemblage of persons to whose will a whole political

---

[1] *OLG* 18, n. b 137, n. h. For Bentham's complex theory of powers see Chap. VIII *supra*.

[2] *OLG* 16; 18 n. v. n. n (69); 137 n. h (139).

community are (no matter on what account) supposed to be in a disposition to pay obedience and that in preference to the will of any other person.'[3]

Bentham's account of legislative power agrees with that of earlier political theorists, such as Hobbes and Locke, in conceiving of such power and so of a political society as itself a human artefact, but he differs from them with regard to the nature of the artefact and in so doing brought into political and legal theory a new and uncompromisingly positivist strain of thought. It is of course true that Hobbes's theory of law as the command of a Sovereign resembled Bentham's in many respects,[4] but it differed from his in holding that the command of the Sovereign only constituted law because it was given to subjects already under a prior obligation arising from their contract with each other to obey him.[5] But ever since 'the scales fell from [his] eyes' on reading Hume's criticism of the theory of a social contract,[6] Bentham rejected it as a misleading fiction together with the whole notion of a prior obligation of obedience to the legislator which it was supposed to generate. For Bentham the Sovereign's legislative powers were conferred neither by law nor by contract nor by any normative right or duty-generating transaction or social relationship, and he dismissed talk of the Sovereign's *right* to legislate as yet another misleading confusion. Instead the Sovereign's legislative powers came into being as a result of a social situation for the description of which no normative terms were required. This social situation was 'the disposition of the people, no matter what the motive, to submission and obedience.'

Accordingly the Sovereign's legislative power for Bentham, like the legal obligation which its exercise creates, is in part natural and in part a man-made artefact. For on Bentham's view of legal obligation[7] to be under such an obligation to do a certain act is to have a reason for doing it which is in part natural and in part artificial. It is natural since all men seek to avoid pain or, as Bentham insisted in the sonorous opening

---

[3] *OLG* 18.
[4] *Leviathan*, Chap. XXVI.
[5] Ibid.
[6] *Fragment* Chap. I, para. 36, n. v in *CW* 439 (440).
[7] See Chap. VI *supra*.

sentence of *An Introduction to the Principles of Morals and Legislation*,[8] pain is one of the two sovereign masters—the other is of course pleasure—under the governance of which nature has placed mankind. But the reason for action thus provided is also in part artificial because the connection established in this case between action and pain or likely suffering in the event of disobedience is the work not of nature but of the legislator's will whose choice determines whether suffering shall be the likely consequence of conduct. If a man is required under pain of imprisonment to wear clothes while walking in the street and does so to avoid the punishment, the suffering the avoidance of which constitutes a reason for doing so is connected artificially to his action by the legislator's choice and is not dependent on the causal properties of his action. On the other hand if he wears clothes simply to keep out the unpleasant cold, his reason for doing so is connected to his action in virtue of its causal properties naturally and without the intervention of any human will. Of course in both cases the action taken is a 'means' to a desired outcome, that is something done in the expectation that it will have the consequence of avoiding suffering. But in the first case the action is such a 'means' only because the legislator has chosen that it should be and the legislator might attach similar suffering to any kind of action which he chooses irrespective of its character; whereas in the second case it is a 'means' in virtue of the natural properties of the action itself. Similarly the Sovereign's legislative power is in part natural and in part artificial. It is natural just in so far as it consists of an ability to control the flow and direction of that current of natural motivation which is the fear of pain or suffering; it is artificial because this ability arises not from the natural strength of the legislator but specifically as a result of the establishment in a society of certain human attitudes of submission and obedience.

II SOVEREIGNTY

It is one of the ironies of the history of jurisprudence that Bentham in developing his account of the Sovereign's legislative

---

[8] *PML* Chap. I, para. 1 in *CW* 11.

powers came to adopt views at variance with the doctrines both of Blackstone, the target of his fiercest criticism, and John Austin, his chief disciple among jurists. Both Blackstone and Austin held it a necessary truth that in every legal system there must be a Sovereign or supreme legislator whose legislative powers were not limited by law. Blackstone indeed presented his form of this doctrine in words which scarcely distinguished between legal limitations and practical restraints or obstacles. 'There is and must be in every state a supreme irresistible absolute and uncontrolled authority in which the *summa jura imperii* or the rights of sovereignty reside.'[9] Austin made a clear distinction between legal limits on the Sovereign's power and mere practical or moral restraints and found the former 'inconceivable'. 'Sovereign power is incapable of legal limitation.' 'Supreme power limited by positive law is a flat contradiction in terms.'[10] Austin and Blackstone thought that British constitutional arrangements plainly exemplified this general doctrine. But while Blackstone[11] like Bentham[12] took the conventional view that sovereignty in Great Britain was vested in the tripartite body of King, Lords, and Commons, Austin located it in the King, Lords, and *electorate*, holding the Commons to be mere agents to whom the electorate had delegated their share of the sovereignty. Bentham accepted that the sovereignty of the King in Parliament in Great Britain was subject to no legal limitations but from his earliest writings onwards felt misgivings about the general doctrine, though his doubts and the qualifications which he sought to introduce into the doctrine are never fully developed and are sometimes obscure. He was not in the least tempted to believe that a satisfactory theory of law must be modelled on the pattern of British institutions, for he was well aware of the historical counter-examples to the general doctrine, particularly those presented

---

[9] *Commentaries on the Laws of England* I 49. See for Dr Johnson's similar views Chap. III *supra*.

[10] *The Province of Jurisprudence Determined* and *The Use of the Study of Jurisprudence* Lecture VI, ed. Hart (1958), 254.

[11] *Commentaries* I 50, 91, 147.

[12] *OLG* 5. Austin's account (op. cit. n. 10 *supra* pp. 228–31) of the electorate's share of the sovereign power resembles Bentham's later description in terms of sovereignty of the 'constitutive power' of the people for which see his *Constitutional Code, Works* IX 96 ff. and 117 ff., and p. 228 *infra*.

by federal unions of states, and he castigated Blackstone for overlooking these in his dogmatic assertion of the necessity of absolute sovereignty vested in a single body in every state.[13] Moreover Bentham had followed with interest and indeed taken a minor part in the disputes about the legal omnipotence of the British Parliament which led up to the Declaration of Independence and the war with America, and he knew that at least an intelligible, even if mistaken, case had been presented on behalf of the American colonists to show that the legislative powers were limited as a matter of constitutional law and did not include the power to tax the unrepresented colonists.[14] Bentham did indeed consistently hold the view that to fetter the supreme legislator by laws limiting its competence was never wise and indeed was 'mischievous and absurd' and he dedicated a section of his *Book of Fallacies*[15] entitled 'Fallacy of Irrevocable Laws' to the topic. All laws he thought should have only 'a defeasible perpetuity' and be repealable by the legislature.[16] But legal limitations on a supreme legislature were not for Bentham, as they were for Austin, inconceivable.

Bentham's difficulties in accommodating the possibility of legal limitations on supreme legislative power sprang from the conception that the legislative powers of the sovereign are not conferred by law. This conception in its turn was the consequence of his identification of all law with the expression, explicit or tacit, of the Sovereign's will. There is here an important contrast between the legislative power of the Sovereign and those of his subordinates: since the latter were conferred by laws they could obviously be, and normally were, limited by those laws in various ways to specific spheres of conduct or to specific geographical areas or to both of these. Hence to a subordinate's attempts at legislation an important group of legal terms involved in the idea of limited legislative powers are applicable: such attempts might be *intra vires* and so legally valid, or *ultra vires* and so legally invalid. But Bentham seems curiously reluctant to use

---

[13] *Fragment* Chap. IV, para. 34 in *CW* 488.
[14] For Bentham's part in the dispute see Chap. III *supra*.
[15] The *Book of Fallacies*, *Works* II 402 ff.
[16] Loc. cit.

these terms or synonyms for them such as 'legally effective'
or 'void'[17] even of subordinate legislation and he frequently
fails to disentangle the idea of legal validity and invalidity
from the idea of legality and illegality or what is legally permitted and legally prohibited.[18] It is as if Bentham was so
preoccupied by his discovery, as he thought it, of the exclusively imperative or permissive character of all law that
legality and illegality, legally permitted and legally prohibited had come to appear as the only legal dimensions in
which law-making operations needed to be assessed. It was
the same preoccupation which made the phenomenon of
legally limited government so intractable for him.

It is important in considering Bentham's attempt to solve
this problem not to interpret his doctrine of sovereignty as
if it were virtually identical with Austin's more familiar
doctrine and I shall devote some pages to distinguishing
between them.

Austin esteemed Bentham's doctrines on sovereignty very
highly. Indeed, in defending Hobbes's account of the legally
illimitable nature of 'sovereign power' Austin says, 'I know
of no other writer excepting our great contemporary, Jeremy
Bentham, who has uttered so many truths at once new and
important concerning the necessary structure of supreme
political government'.[19] It is true that at one point Austin
criticized Bentham for making, as Austin thought, a careless
mistake in 'forgetting to notice'[20] that among the defining
characteristics of a sovereign there was an essential negative
characteristic that the sovereign (as well as being habitually
obeyed by the bulk of the community) 'must not be habitually obedient to any other certain individual or body'. I
discuss this criticism later, but here I wish to draw attention
to the fact that Austin either did not know, or for some inexplicable reason, thought it unnecessary to mention, that
Bentham's doctrine of sovereignty differed from his own in

---

[17] Bentham discusses the meaning of 'void' applied to laws in *Fragment*
Chap. IV, para. 31 in *CW* 487 and uses 'invalid' of contracts in *Principles of the
Civil Code*, *Works* I 331. 'Nullity' and 'validity' are among the terms with the
exposition of which Bentham held 'universal jurisprudence' to be concerned:
see *PML* Preface in *CW* 6 and n. c thereto.

[18] See Chap. VIII *supra.*

[19] Op. cit. n. 10 *supra*, 279.

[20] Op. cit. 212.

certain far more important respects. For, apart from the negative characteristic already mentioned, two other attributes which Austin regarded as essential attributes of sovereignty were not so regarded by Bentham.

Austin agreed with Bentham in regarding all positive law as the command, express or tacit, of a sovereign, but insisted both that the sovereign power to create law by issuing commands was 'incapable of legal limitation' and that in any political society the sovereign is *one* individual or *one* body of individuals. The meaning of these two stipulations can best be grasped by considering the possibilities they exclude. The first stipulation excludes the possibility that there may be some law which the sovereign could not legally make: if he is sovereign he cannot lack legal competence to make any conceivable law; his making of it cannot be an illegal act; and it cannot be void or invalid. The second stipulation is more complicated than appears at first sight, for it excludes two different possibilities: (i) that there might in any given political society be more than one sovereign person or bodies each with legally unlimited sovereign power, and also (ii) that the sovereign power might be divided or distributed among separate independent persons or bodies, each separately competent to legislate in relation to different spheres of conduct or different sectors of the population or territory, and each within that sphere not subject to any legal limitation. So Austin's two stipulations taken together exclude the following three things: (i) legal limitation of sovereign power; (ii) division of sovereign power; and (iii) plurality of sovereigns each having full sovereign power.

Of the three things which I have distinguished as excluded by Austin's definition of sovereign power, the first two, legal illimitability and indivisibility, are of course the most important; for it is Austin's insistence on these two attributes of sovereign power which made it impossible for him to give an undistorted account of those legal systems where a rigid constitution imposes restrictions on the legislative power of its supreme legislature, or divides legislative power between a central federal legislature and a legislature of constituent states or provinces. In such cases there is no legally unlimited or undivided sovereignty to be found, and many of Austin's critics, including myself, have been concerned to show that

Austin never succeeded in squaring his doctrine of illimitable and undivided sovereignty with the legal phenomena presented by the constitution of the United States and other 'rigid' constitutions.[21] But the third possibility noted above and excluded by Austin's doctrine, that there might be more than one sovereign in a single political society each vested with unlimited legislative power has scarcely been discussed in the literature. No doubt this is because the idea of a constitution providing for two or more omnicompetent or sovereign legislatures seems too absurd to entertain, unlike the legal limitations and divisions of supreme legislative power which are prominent features of many modern constitutions. But a plurality of sovereigns is not logically impossible. Hume, in one of the most perceptive of his essays entitled *Of Some Remarkable Customs*, drew attention to the fact that in the Roman Republic two independent legislative bodies (the *comitia centuriata* and the *comitia tributa*) each possessed full and absolute authority

to establish two distinct legislatures, each of which possesses full and absolute authority within itself, and stands in no need of the other's assistance in order to give validity to its acts; this may appear beforehand altogether impracticable as long as men are actuated by the passions of ambition, emulation and avarice, which have hitherto been their chief governing principles . . . but there is no need for searching long in order to prove the reality of the foregoing supposition; for this was actually the case with the Roman Republic.

Bentham may have noted this passage in Hume's essay. For on one of the occasions when he expressed himself doubtful about the necessity of there being one absolute sovereign in each political society, he cited, among other examples, the Roman Commonwealth as a counter-example.

III LEGALLY LIMITED GOVERNMENT

Two main solutions of the problem which Bentham found in the phenomenon of legally limited government can be distinguished in this work. In the first of these Bentham treats the notion of the sovereign's limited legislative power as the correlate of a limited habit of obedience, and pays no specific attention to the attitude of the courts or to what they think,

---

[21] For my criticisms see my *Concept of Law*, 72-6, 242-3.

do and say, though this is, in my opinion, crucial for any plausible account of the structure of a constitutional legal system. In his second approach to the problem Bentham does pay attention to the courts, but as I shall argue, it is the wrong sort of attention, since here he identifies a legal limitation on the Sovereign's legislative powers with a legal obligation, and his failure to disentangle the notions of illegality and invalidity is most apparent.

(a) Limited government as the correlate of limited habits of obedience

Bentham's views on the possibilities of limitation and division of the supreme legislative power have to be collected from passages and often from footnotes of his *Fragment of Government, An Introduction to the Principles of Morals and Legislation*, and *Of Laws in General*. I do not include any discussion here of Bentham's account of popular sovereignty which he gives in his *Constitutional Code*[22] and to which Professor Burns has drawn attention in a valuable article.[23] In the *Constitutional Code* Bentham uses the expression 'Sovereignty' to mean 'the supreme constitutive authority' residing in a democracy in the electors and consisting in their power to 'locate' and 'dislocate' (appoint and remove) the members of the supreme legislature in whom is vested 'the supreme operative power'. My reason for not discussing this later sense of sovereignty is that to do so would be to move away from Bentham's problems concerning limited government to another topic. For sovereignty as 'supreme constitutive authority' does not form part of any general theory of the nature of law since, as Bentham points out in his *Constitutional Code* there are states, e.g. a hereditary monarchy, in which there is no supreme constitutive power.[24] The concept of popular sovereignty as developed in the *Constitutional Code* is therefore not only a quite different concept from that which enters into Bentham's discussion of the possibility of limited sovereignty but involves a quite different theory of law. This is so because the constitution which confers on the electors the 'supreme constitutive

---

[22] *Works* IX 76 ff. and 117 ff.
[23] Bentham on Sovereignty: An Exploration in *Bentham on Legal Theory* op. cit. *supra* p. 114 n. 31.   [24] *Works* IX 97.

authority' is, according to Bentham, law though it does not derive its status as law from any sovereign or any command but from the fact that it is 'generally acknowledged to be in force'.[25]

Bentham first approached the topic of sovereignty in Chapter I of the *Fragment* in the course of an attempt to disperse what he calls 'the mist' which Blackstone's ambiguously worded discussion of the origins of government had caused to settle on the notions of 'government', 'society', and 'state of nature'. To clear the air, Bentham puts forward firm definitions of these terms and defines political society as follows: 'When a number of persons (whom we may style subjects) are supposed to be in the habit of paying obedience to a person or assemblage of persons of a known and certain description (whom we may call governor or governors) such persons altogether (subjects and governors) are said to be in a state of political society.'[26] In the following paragraph and an elaborate footnote to it he explains further, among many other terms, 'authority', 'superior', and 'habit of obedience'. It is important to observe, as Austin did, that in this passage Bentham does not say that the governor must satisfy the negative condition of not habitually obeying any other determinate individual or body. But this is not, as Austin thought, a mistake on Bentham's part, for in this passage Bentham is not concerned, as Austin later was, to tell us either what constitutes a single independent political society or the supreme or sovereign power within it. Instead Bentham is here concerned to state the general characteristics of political union, i.e. what it is for men to be in a state of political society as distinct from a state of nature. This is elucidated by reference to the notion of habitual obedience to a governor or superior and it is immaterial for Bentham's purpose at this

---

[25] Op. cit. 9. Professor Burns thinks that some early anticipation of Bentham's later conception of popular sovereignty may be seen in the discussion of 'Offences against the Sovereignty' in *PML* Chap. XVI, para. 54, n. r 4 S IX in *CW* 260 (263), where Bentham refers to an 'investitive power' or 'right of investiture' to designate the possessors of sovereign power. But there is no suggestion in *PML* that such investitive powers or rights are derived otherwise than from laws enacted by the legislature as the electors' rights in England are. Bentham's latest view was that in England there was no constitution in the sense of the *Constitutional Code* and so no constitutional law (*Works* IX 9).

[26] *Fragment* Chap. I, para. 10 in *CW* 428.

stage whether the governor is subordinate or supreme. He is not, therefore, in this passage concerned with the characteristics of sovereignty or supreme power.

In Chapter IV of the *Fragment*, however, 'the supreme governor', 'the supreme power', and the 'authority of the supreme body' are certainly the subjects of discussion, and here Bentham faces the question whether the supreme power may be limited, or as he puts it have 'assignable bounds'. On this question Bentham appears at first sight to adopt firmly the general doctrine that with one exception 'the authority of the supreme body cannot. . .be said to have any assignable, any certain bounds.' But although this exception is made tolerably clear the general doctrine is not; for Bentham seems to oscillate between thinking it impossible (apart from this exception) and thinking it merely dangerous or inexpedient to limit the supreme legislature.

The exception which Bentham allows is the case where the supreme governor's authority is limited by what Bentham terms 'an express convention'.[27] This is the case where one independent state submits on terms to the government of another, or where a number of independent states by agreement unite in a federal union and set up a federal legislature with limited authority over the constituent states or 'composite state'. It is here that Bentham reproves Blackstone for his acceptance of the general doctrine unqualified by this important exception: it is wrong, Bentham held, to say, as Blackstone did, that in 'all forms of government there must be an authority which is absolute'. This, Bentham claims, would be saying that there is no such thing as government in the German Empire; nor in the Dutch provinces; nor in the Swiss Cantons; nor was of old in the Achaean League'.[28] Bentham repeats this point a little more tentatively in the *Introduction* to the *Principles of Morals and Legislation*. There, he tells us, that he would be afraid to have said that there must necessarily be an absolute power in the government of every society. 'In the United Provinces, in the Helvetic, or even in the Germanic body, where is that one assembly in which an absolute power over the whole resides? Where was there in the Roman Commonwealth? I would not

[27] Op. cit. Chap. IV, para. 26 in *CW* 485.
[28] Op. cit. Chap. IV, paras. 23, 26, 34–6 in *CW* 484, 485, 488–90.

undertake for certain to find an answer to all these questions.'[29]

Bentham says tantalizingly little about the juridical status of the express convention which may limit the supreme legislature. He does not tell us whether it or the limitations it imposes are to be thought of as legal, but he does give some account of his reasons for allowing this form of limitation and not others. And his explanation shows that in his view the importance of an express convention in limiting the authority of a supreme legislature was derivative from what he takes to be the fundamental fact of the subjects' limited habitual obedience. The express convention itself seems to be important in Bentham's view only as a 'signal' showing the extent of the subjects' disposition to obey; it marked off those laws which the subjects were prepared to obey from those which they were not. Bentham, unlike Austin, always insisted that the habit or disposition to obey might be present with regard to one sort of act and absent with regard to another, and limited sovereignty is simply the correlative of a limited habit and disposition to obedience. 'For a body then which is in other respects supreme to be conceived as being with respect to certain sort of acts, limited, all that is necessary is that this sort of act be in its description distinguishable from every other.'[30]

This explanation of limited sovereignty is simple even if it is, as I shall later attempt to show, an inadequate one. What complicates the story is Bentham's apparent yet not consistently maintained refusal to accept any other mode of limitation except 'express convention' between formerly independent states. He insists, indeed, that except where there is an express convention, it is an abuse of language to speak of an act of supreme legislature as 'void' or exceeding its authority, or to speak of a law which that legislature cannot make.[30] Yet it is also plain that Bentham contemplated the possibility that legal limitation on supreme legislative

---

[29] *PML* Chap. XVI, para. 17, n. x in *CW* 200. In the case of 'the Roman Commonwealth' the reference is presumably to the plurality of sovereigns noted by Hume (*supra*, p. 227). As Professor Burns has observed (loc. cit., p. 228, n. 23) this is the first mention by Bentham of limitations not attributable to 'express convention' between formerly independent states.

[30] *Fragment* Chap. IV, para. 35 in *CW* 489. In the *Pannomial Fragments, Works* III 219, Bentham says the disposition to obey may have either 'habit' or 'con-

power might be secured by something like a system of judicial review. He allows that some meaning could be given to the otherwise meaningless statement that a law enacted by a supreme legislature was void if it were the case that the judges exercised a controlling power over the acts of the legislature and he envisated that the Courts would exercise this controlling power by ignoring the 'void' law when they came to decide in particular cases who was and who was not to be punished.[31] This 'mode of opposition' to the legislature 'passes' he says 'under the appellation of a *legal* one'[32] and Bentham apparently thought of it not as impossible but as generally dangerous, 'Give to the Judges a power of annulling [a parliament's] acts and you transfer a portion of the supreme power from an assembly which the people will have had *some* share at least in choosing to a set of men in the choice of whom they have not the least imaginable share.'[33]

In spite of his general disapproval of the idea of limiting supreme legislative power by judicial control, Bentham's denies that this would be tantamount to transferring supreme authority from the legislature to the Courts, since it would give the latter only a repealing power or 'negative part' in legislation and one exercised only on certain specific grounds or reasons given. In general he thought such powers 'too great indeed for judges',[34] but also concedes characteristically in a footnote that such arrangements might be in the public interest as likely to stimulate 'a public and authorised debate' on the propriety of the law.[35]

Bentham does not further explore this sketch of judicial review, but in *Of Laws in General* he returned (mainly in enormous footnotes)[36] to the idea of limited obedience and its 'innumerable modifications'. 'The people may be disposed to obey the commands of one man against all the

---

vention' for its cause 'a convention arises from the will of any one moment which the will of any other moment may revoke; habit is the result of a system of conduct of which the commencement is lost in the abyss of time.'

[31] *Fragment* Chap. IV, para. 31 in *CW* 489.

[32] Op. cit. Chap. IV, para. 30 in *CW* 487.

[33] Op. cit. Chap. IV, para. 32 in *CW* 488.

[34] Op. cit. Chap. IV, para. 33 in *CW* 488; cf. *Constitutional Code, Works* IX 121.

[35] *Fragment* Chap. IV, para. 33, n. l in *CW* 488.

[36] *OLG* 18, n. b.

world in relation to one sort of act, and those of another in relation to another sort of act, else what are we to think of the constitutional laws of the Germanic body.'[37] This would be a case for divided sovereignty. But Bentham also adds '[The people] may be disposed to obey a man if he *commands* a given sort of act; they may be disposed not to obey if he *forbids* it and *vice versa*', and cites as examples 'the Jews who would have done everything else for Antiochus but they would not eat his pork.' 'The exiled Protestants would have done anything else for Lewis but they would not go to mass'.[38] These are cases where the supreme power was limited but not divided.

Bentham then asks, referring to the points at which obedience is withheld, 'Why might not this (in point of practicality I mean) be settled by law as well as by an inward determination which bids defiance to the law?'[39] But again this is a suggestion tantalizingly left undeveloped since we are given no explanation of what could count for Bentham, given his imperative theory of law, as 'settled by law' or how the description of it as 'settled by law' could be reconciled with the general theory that law consists exclusively of the commands, prohibitions, or permissions of the sovereign or his subordinates. Nor, as Joseph Raz has demonstrated in his *Concept of a Legal System*,[40] has Bentham any account to give to what, when sovereignty is divided, entitles us to say of the person or sets of person who are sovereign in relation to different issues that the laws which they make belong to a single legal system, or why, as Bentham states, they may be considered as composing one sovereign although they never act together and their respective legislative powers are not derived from any law defining their scope.

If temporarily, we leave aside all these latter difficulties, Bentham's first effort to accommodate within this theory the notion of a legally limited supreme legislature can be shown in many different ways to be inadequate. The simplest way is this. Let us suppose that under a constitution some liberty, say religious liberty, is specifically protected by the provision that the legislator shall have no power to

[37] *OLG* 19.   [38] Ibid.   [39] Ibid.   [40] Oxford (1970), 10.

legislate on matters of religion and the Courts are recognized as having powers of review. Suppose that for some time no attempt is made to pass such legislation but a mood of religious enthusiasm sweeps the country and the legislator now enters for the first time this new field of conduct and enacts legislation requiring attendance at places of worship under penalty and that this is received with enthusiasm and regularly obeyed. Suppose the enthusiasts realize that the enactments are outside the scope of the legislator's powers and that they are legally free to disobey, but obey purely out of personal inclination, and it is clear that this is likely to continue. It may be that no cases come before the Courts to test the validity of the legislation; yet if such a case does arise, the fact that the legislation has been and is likely to be obeyed would not prevent the Courts holding that, because of the restrictive prohibitions of the constitution, this legislation is invalid and has created no legal obligation to attend places of worship and no legal obligation on the Courts to punish those who fail to attend.

This simple example is enough to show that limited obedience by the *population* is not a necessary condition of legal limitations on government: and legally limited powers to legislate are compatible with general obedience to commands outside the limits. The validity or invalidity of legislation is not to be identified with its effectiveness or ineffectiveness in securing obedience nor are these different properties of legislation always concomitant. Plainly both the giving of obedience and the withholding of it by a population are susceptible of different interpretations and their legal status is ambiguous until the attitude of the Courts is known. The obedience may or may not be required under a constitution but since it may be forthcoming in either case it cannot itself show that a legislator's powers are not legally limited. Similarly the withholding of obedience may or may not be permitted by law and it cannot by itself show the legislator's legal powers to be legally limited. These are quite elementary truths concerning the nature of legally limited government but they are not accommodated in Bentham's analysis.

However, let us suppose that Bentham under the pressure of this argument would agree that until the attitude of the Courts is known the significance of popular obedience .or withholding of obedience cannot be known. His theory might then shift away from regarding the relevant limited obedience to the Sovereign to be that solely of the general population and instead would treat as the determining feature the scope of the habitual obedience of the Courts when required by the legislator to punish those who disobeyed his commands or prohibitions. Perhaps indeed this is what Bentham meant by his undeveloped suggestion that limited obedience might be 'settled by law';[41] and it is in any case clear that he recognized that legislative power, as a combination of the powers of imperation and of contrectation, presupposed the readiness of the Courts to punish acts of disobedience. Bentham then might claim consistently with the main features of his general theory that we could construct a satisfactory notion of limited legislative powers which is not open to the objections which I have just made, for he might argue consistently with his own theory of legal obligation that if the courts are not ready to punish one who disobeys a legislator's command, then the subject is not likely to suffer for disobedience. So, given his account of legal obligation in terms of likely suffering, the commander would in these circumstances have failed by his command to create an obligation. This he might argue is all that we need to make applicable the distinction between legally valid or legally invalid legislation and hence of legally limited government. So the legal status of obedience or withholding of obedience by the subjects which was ambiguous when the Courts' attitude was not considered can now be determined by reference to the attitude of the Courts.

This reconstruction of Bentham's attempt to explain limited legislative powers as the correlate of limited obedience is certainly superior to the unreconstructed theory, since it recognizes that a reference to the attitudes of the Courts must figure in any plausible explanation of the limits. None the less it too fails, because the characterization of the relevant attitude of the Courts in terms of 'habit of obedience' is inadequate and indeed misleading. To see this, some scrutiny of Bentham's use of these terms is necessary. In the course of his various discussions of the obedience which is a constituent or effective cause of the Sovereign's power

---

[41] *OLG* 18, n. b.

Bentham's terminology changes. In his first references to such obedience he uses the expression 'habit of obedience' and defines a habit as 'an assemblage of acts' (or 'voluntary forbearances')[42] and later finds some difficulty in explaining how a habit so defined could influence or give birth to further conduct.[43] Perhaps for this reason he shifted to the phrase 'habit of obedience and disposition to obey' and explained that 'habit' referred to past acts and 'disposition' to future ones. Eventually he settled for the phrase 'disposition to obey' alone.[44] I do not myself think these changes are significant or reflect any change in Bentham's conception of what was required by way of obedience and disobedience to constitute limited legislative powers. Apart from the case of express convention I think he held it to be a necessary condition of the existence of such limits that there should antecedently have been what Bentham calls an assemblage of acts or forbearances: that is prior acts of disobedience to a specific class of legislative commands or prohibitions repeated over considerable periods of time. On this view the 'disposition' like a 'habit' must have been manifested by repeated acts of disobedience. However, this interpretation (which we may call the 'habit' interpretation) is certainly open to doubt and since the alternative 'disposition' interpretation, is more plausible, since according to it a settled intention not to obey a certain class of legislative commands, if they should be given, is enough to constitute a disposition not to obey even before such commands are issued and so before any opportunity arises for the manifestation of the disposition, I shall consider the merits of the theory on both interpretations.

[42] *Fragment* Chap. I, para. 12 and n. o in *CW* 429.

[43] *PML* Chaps. VII, para. 19 with n. 1 in *CW* 78; X, para. 38 and n. z thereto in *CW* 118-19, where the difficulty is mentioned that a habit being a fictitious entity, not really distinct from the acts by which it is formed, cannot be the cause of anything. This 'enigma' Bentham thought solved by reference to the 'principle of association' attributed to Hartley.

[44] *Fragment* Chap. IV, para. 35 in *CW* 489. There is a sophisticated account of 'human dispositions in general' in *PML* Chap. XI. See para. 1 thereof in *CW* 125, where a disposition is identified as a 'fictitious entity' to express what is supposed to be permanent in a man's frame of mind when he is influenced by a motive to engage in an act which as it appears to him was of such or such a tendency. No such reference to motive appears to be involved in Bentham's use of the phrase 'disposition to obedience'.

First, the 'habit' interpretation. To be acceptable a theory of the nature of limited legislative power must leave open as a logical possibility that the Courts could hold even on a first attempt by a legislature to make laws in relation to a given field of conduct, outside the limits, that such legislation was beyond its powers *ultra vires* and so void, and could explain or justify on that ground their refusal to punish those who disobeyed the purported legislation. But on the 'habit' interpretation of the theory this is logically impossible: only after a series of refusals by the Courts to punish acts of disobedience could the legislator's power be said to be legally limited and until the series has amounted to an established habit the Courts could not on this theory explain or justify their refusal to punish on the grounds that the legislative powers were legally limited or on any legal ground.

Because it reveals so well the inadequacy of the underlying ideas it is worth making the attempt, not withstanding the objections made so far, to force the idea of constitutionally limited legislative power into the conceptual mould of limited habits of obedience or disobedience, interpreted to include repeated judicial acts of obedience to the legislature's command to punish the citizens' disobedience. To give the theory any chance of explaining the situation in which the first attempt is made by a legislator to legislate on matters outside the scope of its constitutionally limited powers, we would have to describe the past obedience by the Courts to the legislator's commands, which is to manifest their habits of obedience, not in simple unqualified terms as acts of obedience to his commands but as 'acts of obedience to his commands other than those relating to religion' on which he has not yet attempted to legislate. But why should *this* description of the Courts' past acts of obedience be chosen out of the many alternative descriptions which would be available, and would fit the Courts' past course of conduct? These available descriptions range from (a) acts of obedience to any command of the legislature; (b) acts of obedience to any command issued in a certain form or manner; (c) acts of obedience to any command not relating to some class of entity or issue about which the legislator has not yet in fact attempted to legislate, though it would be within his powers to do so; and (d) acts of obedience to any

command on any issue save those excluded by the constitution such as religion. Plainly the only reason for selecting
(d) as the appropriate description of the regularities of past
judicial conduct is the knowledge that the past conduct is
merely a subordinate aspect of the fact that the courts act
under the guidance of the constitution accepted as the
standard of correct judicial behaviour and providing authoritative legal reasons for refusing to enforce legislative commands on the matter of religion. Just as the regularities of the
chess player's movement of the chess pieces are manifestations
of a settled intention to follow certain rules in moving the
pieces, and the hypothesis that they are, makes his past
moves intelligible and his future moves predictable, so the
acceptance by the Courts of a constitution as providing
authoritative reasons for their enforcement of some legislative commands and refusal to enforce others is the fundamental fact required to explain legally limited government.

So much for the 'habit' interpretation and Bentham's
explanation of limited legislative power. Criticism of the
'disposition' interpretation follows a similar course. It is of
course true that if the Courts operating under a written
constitution recognize that the legislator's powers are legally
limited they will be 'disposed' to refuse to punish in certain
cases where the legislator requires them to punish and it will
make perfectly good sense to say that they are already so
disposed on the occasion of the first attempt by the legislator
to legislate outside the limits and indeed even before any
attempt is made. But this disposition is a derivative consequence of a fact which escapes Bentham's form of analysis,
namely the fact that the Courts recognize the provisions of
a constitution as a standard of correct adjudication and so
as providing a reason for withholding obedience to certain
classes of legislative commands or prohibitions and a reason
for yielding it to others. Bentham's theory of limited legislative power as the correlate of limited obedience inverts the
order of primary and derivative. The Courts are disposed to
disobey because they recognize that the legislator's powers
are limited, but according to Bentham the powers are limited
because the Courts are disposed to disobey. It is of course
true that 'habit' in the sense of an established practice of
some sort does come into the explanation of this phenomenon,

but it is not a habit of disobedience but an established practice of regarding the constitution which limits the legislature's powers as setting the standards of correct adjudication and providing reasons for punishing or refusing to punish disobedience in particular cases.

Long before the Courts are actually called upon to adjudicate on an actual first attempt by the legislature to make laws beyond the scope of its powers it can be clear that such a judicial practice of so regarding the Constitution is firmly established. The direct evidence that it is established is the manner in which in deciding past cases Courts have explained and justified their decisions by reference to the constitution as setting the standards of correct judicial decision even though these past cases did not themselves involve that part of the constitution limiting the legislative powers. Indirect evidence may be of many different kinds including general declarations and statements of intention by the Courts to abide by the constitution in deciding cases. The crucial point that such evidence establishes is that the Courts recognize the provisions of the constitution as constituting authoritative reasons for judicial decision and action. Such reasons are of a distinct kind and though Bentham would not recognize them as reasons of any kind they are in my view indispensable elements in many important legal and other normative phenomena besides legally limited legislative powers with which we are presently concerned.

(b) Limited Government and Laws *in principem*

I turn now to Bentham's alternative account of legally limited legislative power as the correlate not of limited obedience but of a binding obligation[45] not to issue certain laws.

In this his second very condensed and at times obscure approach to the problem Bentham pays explicit attention to the part played by the Courts but at a crucial point he fails to disentangle the distinction between legal validity and invalidity from the distinction between the legally permitted and the legally prohibited or illegal. Bentham was led to develop this second explanation because he acknowledged that if an adequate account is to be given of the varieties of constitutional arrangements which may exist, his theory

[45] *OLG* 64–9.

must recognize a special class of laws which bind the supreme legislator. He calls these 'Laws of a transcendent class' and explains that they are laws *in principem*, that is, laws against the Sovereign as distinct from ordinary laws *in populum* or laws against the people. These laws Bentham acknowledges may prohibit the Sovereign from legislating on certain topics and Bentham thinks of them as arising by the self-limitation by the Sovereign of his own powers, which limitation may be recommended to and adopted by his successors. Such laws are therefore of the nature of royal 'concessions' or *pacta regalia* made by the Sovereign by a kind of covenant with his people to govern within certain limits thus constituting 'privileges'. Throughout Bentham characteristically views the problem as if it were the question: how can a Sovereign be *bound* by any such concessions and how can his successors be *bound*? In answering this we can almost see Bentham groping his way. At first he says that such concessions are merely promises to keep legislation within certain limits and not laws: so though we may call the law issued in breach of such promises unconstitutional, we cannot call it illegal. Later he concedes that they are laws but not supported as ordinary laws are by full legal sanctions but only by the 'auxiliary' sanctions of popular opinion or religion and the risk that there may be of a withdrawal of general obedience if the laws in the prohibited field are issued either by the Sovereign who made the promise or by his successor to whom he recommends observance of the limits. Finally Bentham concedes that in certain imaginable circumstances such laws *in principem* may be supported by legal sanctions administered by the Courts. This would be the case if the Courts when the Sovereign was brought before them accused of a breach of his promise were able to punish him for breach and so enforce the promise. In such a case Bentham seems to conceive that strictly the Sovereignty would be lodged in the legislator and the Courts jointly, though in a looser popular usage the legislator would still be described as Sovereign.[46]

---

[46] Op. cit. 68–9. This conception resembles Austin's identification of the sovereign, e.g. in the United States, not with the ordinary legislature which may be subject to legal limitations but with an 'extraordinary legislature' by which such legal limitations are created. See op. cit. (n. 10 *supra*) 222–3 and 245–51.

Now so far as this second approach rests on the notion of limited obedience to the Courts it is open to objections which I have already made. But I wish to stress a quite different objection. The problem is not as conceived by Bentham of distinguishing between legislative commands which the Sovereign is bound not to issue and those that he may issue, but between those of his commands that are valid and those that are not. For this distinction Bentham allows here no such room. For the finding by a court that the Sovereign in issuing laws contrary to the laws *in principem* has done something prohibited and so illegal for which he may be accused and punished by a court, is not a finding that what he has done is invalid or legally void, and the second finding does not necessarily follow from the first. It is of course true that very often what is valid when done (be it the enactment of a law, or the making of a contract or a lease) is the result of an act which is legally permitted. It is also true that very often what is invalid when done may be the outcome of an illegal prohibited act like a bigamous marriage. But the two notions may, and quite often do, fall apart. In many countries it is illegal to sell stolen goods but the sale if made in a shop or market may be legally valid conferring rights on the purchaser and obligations on others. Similarly in some countries a polygamous marriage may be recognized as valid even though it is a punishable offence and so illegal to enter into. In failing to separate clearly these two distinctions, Bentham fails to identify what it is the Courts do when they hold that a legislator's powers are legally limited and that the legislation is *ultra vires* and so invalid. But no adequate account of legal limitation on supreme legislative power can be given without the introduction of that distinctive form of reason for action or decision which is involved in the Courts' recognition of a constitution, which I have already mentioned and shall further discuss in Chapter X.

Bentham perhaps caught a glimpse of the need to bring in this notion in his early discussion in *A Fragment of Government* of arrangements whereby judges might exercise a controlling power over the acts of the legislator. Though he disapproved of such arrangements as contrary to utility he conceded that they made sense of the notion that some purported acts of the legislature might be spoken of as 'void'.[47] Certainly, had he explored the implications of the view advanced much later in his *Constitutional Code* of the idea (inconsistent as it was with his imperative theory of law) that a constitution was 'a really existing constitutional branch of law'[48] if it was generally acknowledged to be in force, he could not have failed to see the inadequacy of the notions of obedience and disobedience to explain what it was that such an acknowledgement involves.

---

[47] *Fragment* Chap. IV, para. 32 in *CW* 488; cf. *Constitutional Code, Works* IX 119 and 121.

[48] Op. cit., *Works* IX 9.

X

COMMANDS AND AUTHORITATIVE
LEGAL REASONS

A pervasive theme of the later essays in this book is that the central concepts of Bentham's imperative theory of law, viz. command and permission, habits of obedience, legality and illegality, are inadequate in the sense that there are important features of law which cannot be successfully analysed in these terms and are distorted by Bentham's attempted analysis of them. These features include legal obligation and duty, legislative power, legally limited government, and the existence of a constitution conferring legislative power and legally limiting its scope, and also the notions of legal validity and invalidity as distinct from what is legally permitted and prohibited. I have argued that to understand these features of law there must be introduced the idea of an authoritative legal reason: that is a consideration (which in simple systems may include the giving of a command) which is recognized by at least the Courts of an effective legal system as constituting a reason for action of a special kind. This kind of reason I call 'content independent and peremptory' and I explain these terms below. In touching on this idea I have expressed the view much disputed by some contemporary writers, that while its introduction into the analysis of the features of law which I have mentioned would certainly involve discarding Bentham's imperative theory of law, it would still be possible to preserve a distinctive 'positivist' part of his theory which insists on a conceptual separation of law and morality. Accordingly in this concluding essay I attempt a threefold task. The first is to examine critically Bentham's account of what a command is and the curious theory of assertion, indeed of meaning, on which his analysis in part rests. The second part is to show that though Bentham's account of what a command is is in various ways defective, he does touch on certain elements embedded in the notion of command out of which the idea of an authoritative legal reason may be illuminatingly constructed. Thirdly and lastly I raise the question (but certainly do not dispose of it here) whether, as I think, it is possible to bring the notion of an authoritative legal reason into the analysis of the relevant legal phenomenon without surrendering the conceptual separation of law and morality.

I

Given the importance which Bentham attributes to the notion of a command, he is surprisingly cavalier about its analysis. He does indeed say important and interesting things. He presents, as explained in Chapter V, with great originality and clarity the elements of a logic of imperatives in his *Logic of the Will* exhibiting relationships of compatibility, incompatibility, and necessary connection between the four 'forms of imperation' which he calls command, prohibition, permission, and non-command,[1] and he also correctly identifies a command as a form of rational communication. But what he gives us by way of analysis is open to certain criticisms partly along lines made familiar by contemporary philosophers[2] in their discussion of 'speech acts' and their analysis of meaning. The main criticism which I shall make, though it is consistent with and indeed supported by this modern analysis of meaning, was first suggested to me by Hobbes who said some simple but illuminating things about commands and the similarity and differences between commands and covenants as sources of obligation or as obligation-creating acts. But I do not think I should have seen the full importance of Hobbes's remarks on these topics had I not had the benefit of the work of Joseph Raz[3] on what he terms 'exclusionary reasons' which resembles in many respects the notion which I have taken from Hobbes.

Bentham, in his first simple account of the connection

---

[1] *OLG* Chap. X; cf. Chap. V *supra*.

[2] For this modern analysis, which is both wider and far more complex than appears from the simple use of a part of it which I make here to elucidate the notion of a command, see the seminal work of H.P. Grice in 'Meaning' in *Philosophical Review* 66 (1967) and a critique of Grice's theory in Schiffer, *Meaning* (OUP 1972).

[3] See his *Practical Reason and Norms* (London 1975); *The Authority of the Law* (OUP 1979).

between laws and commands given in his first considerable work *A Fragment on Government*,[4] tells us that statutes passed by legislatures are commands and that commands are the expression of a will of a superior concerning the conduct of others. He does not define here the term 'superior' but seems to treat it as a synonym for 'governors' defined as the person or assembly of persons to whom a number of persons are supposed to be in the habit of paying obedience.[5]

Bentham distinguishes explicit commands (which he calls 'parole expressions of will') where the expression of will is made by words, from what he calls 'fictitious' or 'quasi-commands' where the commander's will is expressed by acts other than speech acts and of these he cites acts of punishment as an example.[6] For Bentham the common law was comprised of such quasi-commands, and his thought was that the judge expresses his will that an act be done by punishing the non-performance of such an act and the sovereign adopts the judge's will as his own by allowing judges thus to punish those who disobey.

In the more elaborate definition of law with which *Of Laws in General*[7] opens Bentham introduces the wider notion of the 'volition' conceived or adopted by the sovereign; this comprises the four aspects of the will distinguished as command, prohibition, and the two forms of permission (non-prohibition and non-command). He then distinguishes the following different constituents of law:

(i) a volition which is conceived by the sovereign or if conceived by someone else is adopted by the sovereign concerning the conduct to be observed by other persons who either are or are supposed to be subject to a sovereign's power.

(ii) words or other signs which are declarative of the volition conceived or adopted by the sovereign.

To this Bentham adds that the legislator must rely upon

---

[4] *Fragment* Chap. I, para. 12, n. o in *CW* 429.

[5] Op. cit. Chap. I, para. 10 in *CW* 428, but see *Comment* (Alternative Draft for Chap. I) in *CW* 275, where Bentham says: 'When I speak of a superior being making laws for me I mean only that he can make my happiness less or greater than it is.' Cf. Austin, op. cit. 24: 'Superiority signifies might, the power of affecting others with evil or pain and of forcing them through fear of that evil to fashion their conduct to one's wishes.'

[6] *Fragment* Chap. I, para. 12, n. o in *CW* 429.

[7] *OLG* 1.

certain motives if the law which he makes is to produce the effects in terms of obedience at which he aims, and he frequently describes the sovereign as trusting both to what he calls the auxiliary sanction (popular opinion or divine displeasure) and the specifically legal sanctions which will be provided by the legislator himself.[8] The position is complicated because although to modern ears the word 'sanction' suggests punishment, Bentham admits, as a class of possible laws declarative of the sovereign's volition, those which he calls 'praemiary' where the subject is not punished for disobedience but rewarded for obedience. Secondly, Bentham makes use as I have already explained in Chapters V and VI *supra* when he expounds his logic of the will, of a technical or, as he terms it, 'confined' sense of the word 'command' which merely describes the 'decided' aspect of legislator's will without regard to the motive or sanction relied upon for the accomplishment of that will.

I shall for the moment leave aside Bentham's account of sanctions and their part in motivating obedience and also what he has to say about the two forms of permission, and shall consider in the case of command the two elements of the legislator's volition and the declaration of that volition which enters into his analysis.

Bentham gives no explicit account of a volition; he refers to it sometimes as an 'internal state of the will'[9] and contrasts it with belief which is 'a state of the understanding',[10] will and understanding being both 'states of mind'.[11] In the case of the 'decided' aspects of the will (commands and prohibitions) as distinct from the 'undecided' aspects (the two forms of permission) he frequently uses as synonyms for volition the expressions 'wish' or 'inclination of the mind' or 'will towards an act'.[12] Nearly all the examples of the use of these varying expressions suggest that Bentham's meaning may be best rendered by the word 'wish', that is a wish that an act be done by another person.

So much, then, for the psychological component of

---

[8] *PML*, Chap. III para. 12, in *CW* 37: Chap. XIV, para. 26 in *CW* 172: *OLG* 70, 245, 248.

[9] *OLG*, Chap. X, para. 8 in *CW* 97.

[10] *PML*, Chap. XVII, para. 29, n. b 2 in *CW* 299.

[11] Ibid.   [12] *OLG* 93, 94, 298.

commands which Bentham calls 'volition'. On this account it is a necessary condition of an utterance constituting a command that the utterer wishes the person to whom the command is directed to do the act commanded. Of course in the case of most commands this necessary condition is satisfied since commands are normally given only when the speaker wishes his hearer to do the act commanded and indeed are normally given to bring this about. But there are a variety of exceptions to this which would have to be taken into account in any full analysis of the notion of a command. Thus, to take a fictional but perhaps not unrealistic example from army life, a sadistic sergeant-major, finding an incompetent and absent-minded recruit whom he delighted in punishing, gave him command after command hoping, as was often the case, that the recruit would forget or fumble over what he was told to do and would thus provide the sergeant with the opportunity which he sought for inflicting punishment. Such cases of what might be called insincere commands include also not only commands given to the counter-suggestible to procure contrary behaviour to that commanded, but more impressive examples of commands given simply to test obedience, as in the case of God giving Abraham a command to sacrifice his son. Of course in such cases it is not true that the commander intended the subject to do the actions commanded (though it is true that he intended the subject to believe that he so intended): yet there seems little doubt that we must speak of him as giving a command or order. Such insincere commands where the speaker does not in fact intend the person to do as he commands him are parasitic on 'normal' commands where the speaker does so intend. For the speaker makes an insincere or deviant use of a distinctive conventional linguistic device such as the grammatical imperative mood which is used to give 'normal' commands. Bentham does not notice this case but on his descriptive analysis of commands explained below, the difference between a sincere and an insincere command would simply be the difference between a true and a false first-person descriptive statement.

I turn now to the second element in Bentham's account of command: the words or other signs which constitute a 'declaration', as he terms it, of the commander's volition.

Bentham gives no explicit definition of a declaration[13] but he seems consistently to have thought of commands and prohibitions as assertions or statements of the fact that the speaker has the relevant volition. So command at least includes a statement that the speaker wishes an action to be done, and the form of permission which Bentham calls non-command is a negative statement asserting that it is not the case that the speaker wishes the action to be done. So, too, *mutatis mutandis*, for prohibition and non-prohibition, which last Bentham calls permission.

Though Bentham has much to say of interest on the difference between the indicative or, as he actually calls it, the assertive style of discourse and the imperative and the way in which the former may 'mask' the latter[14] he did not succeed in identifying the radical difference of function in communication which they standardly perform. A command for Bentham was a kind of assertion differing from others only because it was specifically an assertion about the speaker's volition concerning the conduct of others. He did not recognize it as a form of non-assertive discourse. That this is so is not only suggested by his calling the words used in giving a command a 'declaration' of volition, but is made clear by two other observations which he makes. First he quite generally held that to express anything in speech, whether it be the expression of one's will or one's belief, is to assert[15] something about one's will or belief. Secondly, he considered that the ordinary imperative forms of language used for giving commands are essentially elliptical and when expressed at full length would display the fact that they were assertions about the speaker's will. Thus he says the imperative form 'Kill that robber' is an elliptical way of saying 'My will is that you kill the robber'[16] and a law expressed as 'Export no corn' is an elliptical form for the assertion 'It is my pleasure that you do not export any corn'.[17]

If this doctrine, that commands and prohibitions because

---

[13] He uses as synonyms 'manifestation' in *PML*, Chap. XVI, para. 25, n. 2, in *CW* 206, and more frequently 'expression', e.g. *OLG* 94, 99, 298.

[14] *OLG* 106, 178-9, 302, 303.

[15] *PML* Chap. XVII, para. 29, n. b 2 in *CW* 299-300.

[16] *PML* loc. cit.

[17] *OLG* 154.

they are expressions of will are assertions seems a gross error, it is I think to be remembered that Bentham was not alone in failing to grasp the distinction between what is said or meant by the use of a sentence, whether imperative or indicative, and the state or attitude of mind or will which the utterance of a sentence may express and which accordingly may be implied though not stated by the use of the sentence. When I say 'Shut the door' I imply though I do not state that I wish it to be shut, just as when I say 'The cat is on the mat' I imply though I do not state that I believe this to be the case. Philosophers are no doubt now quite familiar with these distinctions which enable them for any proposition 'p', not mentioning the speaker's belief, to explain the oddity of saying 'p but I do not believe that p' without maintaining that we have here a contradiction or that p means or entails that I believe p. The same is true of course of the relationship between 'Shut the door' and 'I do not want you to shut the door'.

But Bentham, like Hume who seems not to have distinguished between reporting and expressing a 'sentiment', lacked these modern tools for making this kind of distinction, and his doctrine that commands are assertions about the speaker's will was grotesquely paralleled by the doctrine which appears in his early writings that ordinary statements of fact in the indicative mood, like 'The cat is on the mat', are elliptical ways of asserting that the speaker has a certain belief. Bentham even says that the simplest form of proposition is complex. To quote again his own example,[18] 'if I say "Eurybiades struck Themistocles" all I assert and can assert is "It is my opinion that Eurybiades struck Themistocles" '.

I have sketched in the Introduction the paradoxes which would result if this view were taken and its refutation. Together with the doctrine that the ordinary forms of imperative and indicative sentences are elliptical it is plainly mistaken, and the differences between commands and statements must be sought elsewhere than in a difference between two kinds of statements, one asserting that the speaker believes something, and the other asserting that he wishes something to be done.

[18] *Essay on Logic, Works* VIII 321.

More interesting perhaps is the fact mentioned in Chapter V that Bentham's logic of the will as he calls his account of the compatibilities and incompatibilities between commands, prohibitions, and permissions seems to reflect a conception of these as statements about the will of the commander and not as forms of non-assertive discourse. Thus he speaks for example, of a prohibition and a permission as being contradictories so that it will always be the case of any action that it is either prohibited or permitted but not both. This could be maintained as an obvious truth if sentences expressing prohibitions and permissions are assimilated to indicatives, and a prohibition identified with the statement that the speaker wishes an action not to be done and a permission to act with a statement that it is not the case that the speaker wishes the act not to be done. So too all the other relationships which Bentham identifies (contraries, contradictories, etc.) could rest on the ordinary formal logic of propositions combined with the assumption that as a matter of the meaning of the verb 'to wish' it is impossible both to wish that an act be done and that it not be done by the same person at the same time. If we abandon this propositional account of commanding and this assumption concerning the meaning of the verb 'to wish', something which Bentham does not give us but which I have attempted to supply in Chapter V is required to show that commands, prohibitions, and permissions are related to each other in ways sufficiently analogous to the relationships of contrariety and contradiction between statements which have truth values to justify the use of these terms in their case.

However, it may be that something more creditable to Bentham may be said about his account of a command as an assertion. It may I think be taken as a mistaken or clumsy way of putting a point of quite central importance of which contemporary philosophical analysis of meaning has stressed: namely, that a command is a form of human communication and that the way in which its utterance is intended to get the hearer to whom it is addressed to act is very different from the way in which one who says 'Boo' intends his utterance to get a person to jump, and yet it is also very different from the way in which one who says 'Your house is on fire' may intend thereby to get his hearer to go home.

In some sense it is true that one who commands intends his hearer to take what he says as the expression of the speaker's wish that he should do some action and the question is in what sense is this true? Bentham saw that commands as expressions of will belong to a large class of utterances which also include invitations, exhortations, requests, and certain forms of giving advice. He also said correctly that common language has no word for this broad class[19] for which contemporary philosophers sometimes use the general classificatory term 'imperatives'. Bentham also saw that in utterances of this kind the speaker says what he does in order to get his hearer to do an act for certain reasons: their use therefore is a form of communication between rational beings. These utterances have also in common the feature that they make use of a special linguistic device, namely the imperative mood, to discharge the function of communication which they have, though this also may be discharged by other linguistic forms.

Now Bentham's insistence that a command is an assertion elliptically expressed that the speaker wishes the hearer to do an act may be regarded, perhaps somewhat charitably, as a way of putting the point that in such cases the speaker not only speaks with the intention of getting his hearer to act but also intends that the hearer shall recognize that this is the speaker's intention and that this recognition should function as at least part of the hearer's reason for acting. It is this latter feature which differentiates saying 'Please jump' in order to get a person to jump from saying 'Boo' with the same purpose, though this of course is only to give one necessary condition of an utterance being an imperative. What constitute sufficient conditions is still a matter of complex debate between philosophers who broadly accept what may be called the recognition-of-intention analysis of imperative meaning. Bentham was therefore right in thinking that it is part of commanding and the other imperative speech acts which characteristically make use of the imperative mood that the speaker intends his hearer in some way to recognize his wish that he should do the act. Where he went wrong was in not seeing or at any rate in not making clear

[19] *OLG* 14, n. 1; 298, n. a (299).

two things. First that strictly what the commander intends his hearer to recognize is not that he, the commander, merely wishes the act to be done but more specifically that his intention in speaking is to get the hearer to do it through the latter's recognition that the commander has spoken with that intention. In other words, the commander intends his hearer to recognize the giving of a command as a step intentionally taken towards furthering the commander's intention to get his hearer to act. Secondly, the use of the imperative mood is not as Bentham said an elliptical form of assertion: it is not a way of stating that the speaker wishes something to be done, for, when the imperative mood is used, though the speaker mentions the content of his wish or intention, he does not state that he has that wish or intention. So the way in which the commander intends his hearer to recognize that he intends him to do the act is not, via a belief that something said by the commander is true but by way of an inference from the fact that he has said it irrespective of any question of truth or falsity of anything said. If a man says to another 'Leave the room' he intends the hearer to infer the speaker's intention much as he might infer it from his starting to push the hearer towards the door. In both cases the hearer is intended to infer it because what the speaker does by words mentioning the content of the speaker's wish in one case and by the act of pushing him in the other case is recognized as something which people do when they wish others to leave the room and as a step towards securing this. In one case the means used is a conventional linguistic means; in the other it is a natural means.

What I have said up to this point is far from a complete analysis of commands or other imperative speech acts. I have displayed only certain necessary conditions of an utterance constituting a command and I have carried the analysis only so far as is required to focus attention on the fact that where a command is sincere the commander intends the expression of his intention to function as at least part of the hearer's reasons for doing the act in question. But in fact there is something quite distinctive in the case of a command in the way in which the expression of intention is intended to constitute a reason for action, and I shall turn now to Hobbes, who was I think the first to notice this distinctive feature, for he said something, though all too briefly, which illuminates the point.

Hobbes, like Bentham, thought that all laws were commands of a Sovereign but, unlike Bentham, thought the commands were laws only if given to those who were under a prior obligation to obey, and his account of this prior obligation was that it arose from the subject's covenant or contract to obey the commander. So on Hobbes's view the Sovereign in giving his commands which are law is exercising a right arising from the subject's contract. Bentham, however, would have none of this prior obligation to obey nor of the social contract alleged to generate it nor of the idea that in making laws the Sovereign was exercising a right or normative power, so, as shown in Chapter IX, he defined the Sovereign in flatly descriptive non-normative terms as one who is habitually obeyed by his subjects and himself habitually obeys no one. But Hobbes in discussing the general notion of a command and in differentiating it from the mere giving of advice or counsel in imperative form says something not said by Bentham. Hobbes in Chapter XXV of his *Leviathan* says 'Command is when a man saith do this or do not do this yet without expecting any other reason than the will of him that saith it.'[20] By this Hobbes meant that the commander characteristically intends his hearer to take the commander's will instead of his own as a guide to action and so to take it in place of any deliberation or reasoning of his own: the expression of a commander's will that an act be done is intended to preclude or cut off any independent deliberation by the hearer of the merits pro and con of doing the act. The commander's expression of will therefore is not intended to function within the hearer's deliberations as a reason for doing the act, not even as the strongest or dominant reason, for that would presuppose that independent deliberation was to go on, whereas the commander intends to cut off or exclude it. This I think is precisely what is meant by speaking of a command as 'requiring' action and calling a command a 'peremptory' form of address. Indeed the word 'peremptory' in fact just means cutting off deliberation, debate, or argument and the word with this meaning came into the English language from Roman law, where it

[20] *Leviathan*, Chap. XXV.

was used to denote certain procedural steps which if taken precluded or ousted further argument. If we remember this we can call the reasons which the commander intends his hearer to have for action 'peremptory' reasons.

Of course the commander may not succeed in getting his hearer to accept the intended peremptory reason as such: the hearer may refuse or have no disposition at all to take the commander's will as a substitute for his own independent deliberation, and it is typical of commanding, therefore, to provide for this failure of the primary peremptory intention by adding further reasons for acting in the form of threats to do something unpleasant to the hearer in the event of disobedience. Now these further reasons are indeed intended to function within the hearer's deliberation as dominant reasons or reasons strong enough to overcome any contrary inclinations. But these secondary reasons are in a sense a *pis aller*: they are secondary provisions for a breakdown in case the primary intended peremptory reasons are not accepted as such. It is, however, important to observe that the concentration on the threats of sanctions which commonly attend the giving of a command obscures the most important feature differentiating commanding from most of the other speech acts which may be performed by use of the imperative mood.

So much then for the peremptory character of the reasons for action involved in the notion of a command. I turn now to pick out a second important feature of the reasons intended to be operative when a command is given. I shall call this feature the 'content-independent' character of such reasons. This is a term which I used many years ago[21] in seeking to differentiate the notion of obligation from the general notion of what morally 'ought' to be done. Content-independence of commands lies in the fact that a commander may issue many different commands to the same or to different people and the actions commanded may have nothing in common, yet in the case of all of them the commander intends his expressions of intention to be taken as a reason for doing them. It is therefore intended to function as a reason independently of the nature or character of the actions to be done. In this of course it differs strikingly from the standard paradigmatic cases of reasons for action

[21] See my essay on 'Legal and Moral Obligation' in *Essays on Moral Philosophy*, ed. Melden (Seattle 1958).

where between the reason and the action there is a connection of content: there the reason may be some valued or desired consequence to which the action is a means, (my reason for shutting the window was to keep out the cold) or it may be some circumstance given which the action functions as a means to such a desired consequence (my reason for shutting the window was that I felt cold).

It is I think true that reasons with these two characteristics, which I have called peremptory or deliberation-excluding and content-independent are to be found involved in many interpersonal normative transactions besides commands. They are for example both involved in promising: for the giving of a promise is intended to be a reason not merely for the promisor doing the action when the time comes but for excluding normal free deliberation about the merits of doing it. This is I think what is meant by speaking of the promisor as committed in advance to doing the action and any full account of the way in which a promise creates an obligation must I think include the giving of a promise as such a peremptory or deliberation-excluding reason for action. Since we may promise to do very many different sorts of actions in no way related to each other, the giving of a promise regarded as a reason for doing the action promised has also the feature of content-independence. This is true even though the range of possible actions which one may validly promise to do is not unlimited and does not include grossly immoral actions or those intended to be harmful to the promisee.

II

The relevance of the two features of command which I have stressed, namely the peremptory and content-independent character of the reasons for action to legislation and law-making events is the following. It is of course true, as I have said, that a commander's primary peremptory intention may not be realized; the person commanded may not accept the command as a peremptory reason and either may not obey the command at all or if he obeys the command he may obey only out of fear of punishment after full deliberation of the pros and cons. On the other hand, the command may be taken just as the commander intended it to be taken: the

command may be accepted as such a peremptory reason so
that the hearer obeys without deliberation on the merits
from his point of view of what he is commanded to do. More
than this, it may be that the commander, before he issues his
command, has ample reason for believing that those to whom
he addresses his command are generally disposed to recognize
in his words (perhaps whatever he commands or perhaps only
his commands within some limited field of conduct) as
a peremptory reason for doing what is commanded. Such a
standing recognition (which may be motivated by any of a
variety of ultimate reasons) of a commander's words as
generally constituting a content-independent peremptory
reason for acting is a distinctive *normative* attitude not a
mere 'habit' of obedience, and in my view this is the nucleus
of a whole group of related normative phenomena, including
not only the general notion of authority, legislation or law-
making but many other cases where by words or deeds we are
unable to bring into existence or to vary or to distinguish
obligations of one sort or another.

If we consider as a model a commander, placed in the
setting of a social group where the normative attitude to his
commands which I have described is widely shared, that is
where there is a general acceptance of the commander's
expression of will as a peremptory reason for action or
decision, there is room for four kinds of variation. First the
commands may be addressed either to individuals and refer
to single actions or may be addressed as general commands to
classes of person and referring to action types. Secondly
those who are disposed to recognize the commander's words
as constituting such reasons for action may have very diverse
ultimate reasons for being so disposed, though I do not exclude as absurd the possibility that some may have no reason
for this attitude beyond a wish to please or a simple satisfaction
they find in identifying their wills with that of the commander.
Some may have a moral reason, or the well- or ill-founded
belief that the commands to be issued would be likely to be
in the best interests of all or would co-ordinate the actions of
different persons in a generally beneficial way or would be
just or fair. Others still may adopt this attitude as part of the
tradition in which they have been reared or simply because
they wish to do what others do. Others still may adopt this

attitude out of fear on the footing that the alternative of calculating each time afresh when the question of obedience comes up the chance of being punished for disobedience is too dangerous, or they may adopt this attitude in the hope of getting rewards.

Thirdly, the commander's words may be taken not only as a peremptory guide to action by those who are themselves commanded to act, but may be taken by them and others also as a standard of evaluation of the conduct of others as correct or incorrect right or wrong (though not necessarily morally right or wrong) and as rendering unobjectionable and permissible what would normally be resented, that is demands for conformity, or various forms of coercive pressure on others to conform, whether or not those others themselves recognize the commands as peremptory reasons for their own actions.

Fourthly, the normative attitude in question recognizing the commander's words as such reasons may be widely spread throughout the group: all or nearly all may share it though for different ulterior reasons. On the other hand it may be narrowly confined and at its narrowest may be shared only by a well organized or powerful minority able to coerce by threats the majority into acquiescence. Or the majority may conform to the commands given not because they look upon them as reasons for action but simply because the contents of those commands happens to coincide generally with what they are already disposed to do for moral or prudential reasons independently of the giving of the command.

This model of a normative command situation may be regarded as an embryonic form of a society in which a developed legal system is in force. It is merely embryonic because a feature of crucial importance in the development of a system is missing from it and the addition to the model of this feature would transform it in many ways. This missing feature is the existence of effective law-applying and law-enforcing agencies, that is of courts effectively directing the enforcement in particular cases of the commander's commands and applying them in the settlement of disputes. Where courts with these functions exist the normative attitude consisting in the recognition of the commands as content-independent peremptory reasons for action and as standards for the assessment of conduct as right or wrong is itself institutionalized as defining public standards of correct adjudication, and a duty to conform to these standards is attached to the office of judge and assumed by individual judges when they take up that office. I shall discuss later one important way in which this institutionalization of the recognition of a commander's words as peremptory reasons for action transforms the simple embryonic model; but here I wish to stress that even in this embryonic, pre-legal social situation there are present some of the essential elements which constitute practical authority: and show what it is for a person or persons to have authority as distinct from coercive power over others. For to have such authority is to have one's expression of intention as to the actions of others accepted as peremptory content independent reasons for action. But this same embryonic model also indicates how some of the features of a developed legal system which Bentham's analysis in terms of commands and habits of obedience distorts, are to be understood. Among these features are the idea that a legislator, even a supreme legislator, exercises a legal authority or legal power and not merely a coercive power, the idea that this legal power may be legally limited and not merely ineffective in respect of certain areas of conduct, and thirdly the idea that what a legislator attempts to do by way of legislating may be assessed as valid or invalid and not merely as permitted or prohibited or as successful or unsuccessful in causing men to behave in certain ways.

Thus the general recognition in a society of the commander's words as peremptory reasons for action is equivalent to the existence of a social rule. Regarded in one way as providing a general guide and standard of evaluation for the conduct of the commander's subjects, this rule might be formulated as the rule that the commander is to be obeyed and so would appear as a rule imposing obligations on the subject. Regarded in another way as conferring authority on the commander and providing him with a guide to the scope or manner of exercise it would be formulated as the rule that the commander may by issuing commands create obligations for his subjects and would be regarded as a rule conferring legal powers upon him. The legal limitation of a commander's power to legislate would simply be a reflection of the fact that the sphere of conduct in relation to which his words are recognized as constituting peremptory reasons for action is limited. Thirdly, in this setting of a general recognition of the commander's words as peremptory reasons for action his words are more than commands which may or may not secure obedience or have other natural consequences; for in this setting the issue of a particular command within the scope of the commander's powers will have certain normative consequences, in addition to whatever natural consequences it has. That is, it will make certain actions right and obligatory, and others wrong, a violation of obligation and an offence. If on the other hand the command issued is not within the scope of the commander's powers it will fail to have such normative consequences whatever natural consequences it has, and success or failure in this respect will be shown by the assessment of the commander's words as valid or invalid.

However, as I have said, this model of a command situation is a merely embryonic version of a law-making situation and if it is to approximate to law-making in a developed legal system it must be amplified, but also modified, in a number of different ways, not all of which I can discuss here. However, the first and most important step would be to generalize the notion of a content-independent peremptory reason for action and to free it from any necessary or specific connection with the notion of a command which would then fall into place as one particular variant of the general idea. Indeed in the history of legal theory it has often been pointed out that, except in very simple societies, a simple command is an inappropriate model for legislation since, except in those societies, a definite law-making procedure must be complied with if the legislator's words or deeds are to make law, and if this procedure is complied with then a law is made. For this reason the enactment of a law is very unlike a simple command or expression by an individual of his wishes or intentions as to other persons' conduct, and the habit of speaking of the Sovereign as if he were a single individual is unfortunate just because it may encourage too close an assimilation of law-making to the giving of a command and conceal the need and importance of a recognized procedure compliance with which is required for the making of the law. Given such a procedure which may include the voting and counting of votes, the reading of a bill, the issue of certificates, etc., law is created by compliance with it and the analogy of a simple command or order expressing the will of an individual is misleading. Perhaps indeed instead of words like 'imperative' or 'prescriptive' which are commonly used to characterize the act of legislation it would be better to use the technical word employed by conveyancing lawyers, namely, 'operative' or the word introduced by J. L. Austin, 'performative'.[22] These do not carry with them any specific connections with a command but would stress illuminatingly the similarity between law-making and other rule or convention governed practices whereby new reasons or guides to action are created. I mean here to refer not only to the things that lawyers are accustomed to call legal transactions altering legal rights and duties such as wills, leases, contracts, and the like, but also to non-legal transactions like the taking of a vow or the giving of a promise where individuals create obligations for themselves and their words are recognized as content-independent peremptory reasons for their own action.

What is crucial for legislation is that certain things said or done by certain persons which can be construed as guiding actions should be recognized by the Courts as constituting just such peremptory reasons for actions, and so as law-making events. This generalization of the idea of content-independent peremptory reasons beyond the particular case of commands allows room for something of great importance which Bentham's imperative theory focused on the idea of a command fails to accommodate. This is the feature that in most legal systems there are radically different sources of law or ultimate criteria of legal validity recognized by the Courts, which are neither forms of legislative actions or derived from such an action, even if in some systems they may be subordinate to the latter in the sense that in case of conflict the requirements of legislative enactment may prevail over the requirements of law identified by reference to other sources. Thus the fact of customary practices of various sorts (local, commercial) may be recognized by the Courts (though no

[22] Austin, *How to Do Things with Words* (2nd edn. OUP 1975).

doubt subject to various limiting conditions as to lengths of time, reasonableness, etc.) as itself a peremptory content-independent reason for action falling within the scope of the customary practices and so as rendering them legally obligatory. Similarly, in a system where there is a strict theory of precedent the judge's decision in a particular case or a sufficient line of cases may be recognized as a fact constituting a peremptory reason for deciding similar cases in the same way and so though not itself a command, as creating a general legal rule.

This recognition of content-independent reasons as sources of law, though not derived from statute even if subordinate to statute, eliminates the need for the elaborate and unsuccessful explanation found in Bentham of the status of such sources of law as due to 'tacit' forms of legislative commands. What such sources of law all have in common is not that they are commands but they are recognized as different forms of content-independent peremptory reasons.

More important, it is clear that the notion of a content-independent peremptory reason for action or something closely analogous to it enter into the *general* notion of authority, that is not only authority over persons in matters of conduct, but also authority on scientific or other theoretical matters and so in one sense authority in matters of belief rather than conduct. For where some great scientist for example is regarded as an authority on some subject, say, astrophysics, then within that sphere his saying what he says—'Aristotle has said it'—is accepted as constituting a reason for believing what he says without an independent assessment of the arguments pro and con, that is without the theoretical deliberation within which the merits or strengths of reasons for believing what he says are considered and assessed. So though the statement of an authority on some subject is not regarded as creating an obligation to believe, the reason for belief constituted by a scientific authority's statement is in a sense peremptory since it is accepted as a reason for belief without independent investigation or assessment of the truth of what is stated. It is also content-independent since its status as a reason is not dependent on the meaning of what is asserted so long as it falls within the area of his special expertise.

III

I now want to use this last case of authority on theoretical matters to enter a *caveat* against a possible misinterpretation of what I have been saying. I certainly think that a shift from the notion of a command to the notion of a content-independent peremptory reason for action is needed to overcome the deficiencies of Bentham's account of law and law-making and generally to explain the 'normativity' of law. But I do not by any means think that, if we make this shift, we shall also have finally settled the issue concerning the relationship of law and morals raised by the denial that there is any conceptual or necessary connection between them. The point may be illustrated by reference to the concept of authority on theoretical matters in the following way. To be an authority on some subject matter a man must in fact have some superior knowledge, intelligence, or wisdom which makes it reasonable to believe that what he says on that subject is more likely to be true than the results reached by others through their independent investigations, so that it is reasonable for them to accept the authoritative statement without such independent investigation or evaluation of his reasoning. Hence a characterization of the person as being an authority on a certain subject entails that he has the requisite expertise and is not only a matter of how his statements are in fact regarded. Moreover, even to *regard* a person as a scientific authority however mistakenly is to believe that he really has the superior knowledge or qualifications which would make it reasonable to believe the statements he makes within the areas of his competence without independent investigation of them. So the idea that the authority is a suitably qualified expert and hence the reasonableness of treating his statements in this way enters into the ideas both of *being* such an authority and of being *regarded* (rightly or wrongly) as such an authority. The statement 'X is a scientific authority' commits the speaker to the belief that X is qualified in the appropriate way, whereas 'X is regarded as a scientific authority' only commits the speaker to the belief that some other persons believe that X is so qualified.

Now against the whole style of positivist jurisprudence, which like Bentham's and my own work denies that there is any conceptual or necessary connection between law and morality, and so (as I have explained in Chapter V) attributes to expressions like legal right and legal duty meanings which are not laden with any such connection, it has been urged that there is in fact a strong parallel between being a theoretical authority and having practical, e.g. legislative authority over people which shows the positivist view to be mistaken. The parallel suggested is that just as in the case of a scientist, if he is to rank as an authority on his subject, there must be good reason for accepting his pronouncements as sufficient reason for believing what they state without independent investigation, so in the case of a legislative authority there must be good reason for accepting its enactments as peremptory reasons for action or, at least, it must be believed by some that there are such good reasons. In the case of the theoretical authority the good reasons are provided by his superior expertise and this is prior to the notion of theoretical authority which cannot be explained without reference to it; in the case of legislative authority as in any form of practical authority over people the good reasons must be moral reasons for accepting its enactment of laws as content-independent peremptory reasons for action. So the moral legitimacy of the legislature is prior to its authority over people which cannot be explained without reference to it. The moral legitimacy of a legislator may of course arise in many different ways: for example it may arise from the fact that the composition of the legislature, e.g. in a parliamentary democracy, conforms to morally acceptable principles of government; or it may arise from the fact that whatever the composition of the legislature or its defects, it secures order and co-ordination necessary for a tolerable social life and without it there would be greater evils than any which the government itself perpetrates.

The question whether there is in fact this suggested parallel between theoretical and legislature authority raises issues similar to those raised by the questions discussed in Chapter VI as to whether there is an essential moral component in the idea of legal obligation, so that statements of legal obligation (at least if they are 'committed' statements in the sense of commitment explained there) are a form of moral judgement. It will be recalled that in Chapter VI, I distinguished two forms of the theory opposed to the positivist doctrine that legal and moral obligation are not conceptually connected. The first extreme form of this theory claims that a legal obligation actually is a species of moral obligation, while the second moderate form of the theory claims only that for legal obligations to exist there need only be the belief, true or false, that what is legally required is morally obligatory, and that only committed statements of legal obligation carried with them the implication of such a belief. There is a similar possibility (allowed for in my initial description of the suggested parallel) of an extreme and moderate form of the theory that there is a parallel between theoretical and legislative authority. On the extreme view, for a legislative authority to exist there actually must be good objective moral reasons for accepting its enactments as peremptory reasons for action, while on the moderate view there need be only the belief that there are such moral reasons or even, as in Raz's version, only the pretence or show of such belief or readiness to avow it.[23] I will not here discuss the extreme form of this theory since as I have attempted in Chapter V to demonstrate in the case of Dworkin's account of the conceptual connection between legal and moral rights and obligations, it is clearly incapable of explaining what must be admitted, as Dworkin says, viz. that what is legally right is not always morally right, and there can be morally iniquitous legal systems where the clearly settled law none the less creates legal rights and obligations.

The moderate view, however, that for legislative authority to exist, there need only be belief in its moral legitimacy and in the limiting case such belief may be confined to the Courts and officials of the legal system presents a more formidable case for one form of conceptual connection between law and morality. Its main thrust, so far as my exposition in this chapter of the idea of a legal authoritative reason is concerned, is that it was a mistake on my part when speaking of the Courts as 'accepting' a legislative command as an authoritative legal reason, not to have included as a constituent of such acceptance belief in the moral legitimacy of the legislature or at least a disposition to avow such a belief. I think

[23] *The Authorities of the Law* 28.

the strongest argument supporting this criticism is the one which insists that the notion of the acceptance of some consideration as an authoritative legal reason cannot stand alone. How can an artefact of the human will such as a command, or compliance with a legislative procedure, either in itself be or be believed to be a reason for action? Surely, the critic may urge, such products of the human will could only be such a reason if there were some non-artificial ulterior reason for taking the former as guides to action, and the only kind of ulterior reason which could satisfactorily explain what courts do and say involves their belief in the moral legitimacy of the legislature.

This argument, in my opinion, goes too far and fails at the last step. I agree that it would be extraordinary if judges could give no answer to the question why in their operations as judges they are disposed to accept enactments by the legislature as determining the standards of correct judicial behaviour and so as constituting reasons for applying and enforcing particular enactments. But if all that is required is that judges should have some comprehensible motives for behaving as they do in this respect, this can be easily satisfied by motives which have nothing to do with the belief in the moral legitimacy of the authority whose enactments they identify and apply as law. Thus individual judges may explain or justify their acceptance of the legislator's enactments by saying that they simply wish to continue in an established practice or that they had sworn on taking office to continue it or that they had tacitly agreed to do so by accepting the office of judge. All this would be compatible with judges either having no belief at all concerning the moral legitimacy of the legislature or even with their believing that it had none. Raz, who has given more careful thought than any other writer to this matter, characterizes judicial acceptance of the legislator's authority for such personal reasons as these as a 'weak'[24] form of acceptance, and insists that what is required is either a 'strong' form of acceptance which involves their belief that there are moral reasons for conforming to and enforcing the enactment of the legislature or at least involve the pretence of such belief.

[24] Op. cit. 155, n. 13.

I have already considered in Chapter VI what I take to be
the main argument for this view. In relation to the present
issue it consists of two points. The first is that when judges
accept the authority of a legislature this characteristically is
manifested, in the course of applying and enforcing its laws,
by their statements that the subjects to whom the laws are
applied have a legal obligation or duty to do what such laws
require. Secondly since this requirement may be to act in
ways which are contrary to the subject's personal interests,
desires, or inclinations, such statements of legal duty must be
a form of moral judgement. Such a judgement will be sincere
if the judge believes in the moral legitimacy of the legislature; insincere or 'pretence', if he does not.

In Chapter VI, I rejected this argument and I do so here in
its more general application to an account of legislative
authority, because its factual implications seem to me open
to question. Of course many judges, when they speak of the
subject's legal duties, may believe, as many ordinary citizens
may do, in the moral legitimacy of the legislature, and may
hold that there are moral reasons for complying with its
enactments as such, independently of their specific content.
But I do not agree that it must be the case that judges either
believe this or pretend to do so, and I see no compelling
reason for accepting an interpretation of 'duty' or 'obligation' that leads to this result. Surely, as far as the facts are
concerned, there is a third possibility; that at least where the
law is clearly settled and determinate, judges, in speaking of
the subject's legal duty, may mean to speak in a technically
confined way. They speak as judges, from within a legal
institution which they are committed as judges to maintain,
in order to draw attention to what by way of action is 'owed'
by the subject, that is, may legally be demanded or exacted
from him. Judges may combine with this, moral judgment
and exhortation especially when they approve of the content
of specific laws, but this is not a necessary implication of
their statements of the subject's legal duty.

Of course if it were the case, as a cognitive account of duty
would hold it to be, that the statement that the subject has a
legal duty to act in a way contrary to his interests and
inclinations entails the statement that there exist reasons
which are 'external' or objective, in the sense that they exist

independently of his subjective motivation, it would be difficult to deny that legal duty is a form of moral duty. At least this would be so if it is assumed that ordinary non-legal moral judgements of duty are also statements of such objective reasons for action. For in that case, to hold that legal and moral duties were conceptually independent would involve the extravagant hypothesis that there were two independent 'worlds' or sets of objective reasons, one legal and the other moral.

Until the alternative interpretation which I have offered of judicial statements of the subject's legal duty is shown to be absurd or to distort the facts, I do not think it should be excluded. But I am vividly aware that to many it will seem paradoxical, or even a sign of confusion, that at the end of a chapter, a central theme of which is the great importance for the understanding of law of the idea of authoritative reasons for action, I should argue that judicial statements of the subject's legal duties need have nothing directly to do with the subject's reasons for action. I can also see that it may well be objected that if the judge's acceptance of the legislature's authority means only that he accepts its enactments as setting the standards of correct adjudication and law enforcement so as providing the judge with peremptory content-independent reasons, for their official action in applying and enforcing the law, this is to whittle down the notion of acceptance of the legislator's enactments as reasons for action to something very different from what I represented it to be when I first introduced it in the model of a simple society whose members accepted a commander's words as content-independent peremptory reasons for doing what he commands them to do.

I do not think I have at present a sufficient grasp of many complexities which I suspect surround this issue to do more than offer the following reply to this last objection. The charge of 'whittling down' is in a sense well taken; but it is something for which I expressly made provision when I said on p. 257 that the introduction into the simple society of specialized law-applying and law-enforcing agencies would mean the institutionalization of the recognition of the commander's authority as now defining public standards of official adjudication and this would transform the situation depicted in the model. Of course except in societies where only the Courts and officials accept the authority of the legislature, the rest by and large conforming to the law for other reasons, this institutionalized 'whittled down' form of acceptance will coexist with full-blooded acceptance by many others of enactment by the legislature as reasons for their conforming to what is enacted and for making upon others and accepting from others demands for conformity. But in neither case need there be, though there may often be, belief in the moral legitimacy of the legislature or the pretence of such belief.

I would however in conclusion stress the fact that whoever is right on this larger issue between the legal positivist and his critics, which needs much further discussion, this would not affect the point that the notion of a content-independent peremptory reason for action is required for the understanding of legal authority and law-making. So though it was a mistake and a large one on Bentham's part to attempt to explain legal authority and law-making in terms only of command and obedience to a commander, the mistake is none the less an illuminating one; for buried in the idea of command there are, as I have attempted to show, elements which are crucial to the understanding of law.

INDEX OF NAMES

INDEX OF SUBJECTS